AF535039

Praise for Paradigm Shift

Mark Teter makes a strong case for Linux becoming the lingua franca of twenty-first century computing. If he is right (and he probably is), you won't find a better guide to Linux literacy than *Paradigm Shift.* Teter has bundled the technical, historical and cultural ethos of Linux within a framework of good management practice and mature common sense. I recommend the book to anyone who sees Linux in their future and — maybe even more so — to those who don't.

Dr. Kevin Daly
CEO
Maxxess Systems

With the balance of power currently weighted in favor of proprietary software, *Paradigm Shift* explores the rationale, risks and ROI of a transition to Linux and open source applications as a means for businesses to regain control of their budget. Armed with this knowledge, Teter then provides a proven methodological framework for executing such a transition.

Brian S. Freed
Vice President, Equity Research
Morgan Keegan and Company

A practical roadmap for implementing a successful Linux-based computing environment. Teter completes the picture on how to replace proprietary software solutions with those based around open source — a key strategic initiative for any company competing in today's global business environment.

Jeff Specht
CEO
Bird's Eye Images

One stop shopping for everything your need to know about Linux and open source. *Paradigm Shift* covers the gamut of licensing issues, business risks, financial analysis and proper planning in plain English. For an issue of increasing importance to any business, you won't find a better work under one cover.

Linux Magazine

Many companies have overlooked the power of Linux and open source. *Paradigm Shift* is a wake-up call for organizations content with their current proprietary application environment. The book is a great starting point for those that are just beginning to investigate open source, and for those experienced organizations that are interested in performing a reality check on their current practices.

Randy Richey
VP Professional Services
Govplace

This book is perfect for the Executive or IT Manager wondering if Linux can make a difference in their organization.

Adam Ball
Information Technology Manager
SRC

At a time when there is a pressing need to dramatically reduce costs and improve the overall application computing environment, Teter's message and methodology is right on. This book is much more than a "must read." It is a "must do" plan for achieving a reliable and cost-effective Linux and open source computing platform.

Open Source Software Institute

Every few years a new IT fad comes along that promises to revolutionize computing. Some of the past ones include 4th generation languages, neural networks, and artificial intelligence. What's different about open source is that it isn't focused on a particular technology or application domain: as Mr. Teter indicates, it's about a fundamental shift away from proprietary IT towards a fully standardized, low cost, non-proprietary computing model. To help business technologists understand the revolution at hand, Mr. Teter has compiled an eminently readable, business-focused and level-headed overview of this revolution that is an excellent road-map for joining the drive towards the computing model of the future.

Luc Trudel
CIO
DigitalGlobe

Paradigm Shift

Seven Keys of Highly Successful Linux and Open Source Adoptions

Mark Teter

MEDIA RESOURCE TECHNOLOGY

Many of the designations used by manufactures and sellers to distinguish their products are claimed as trademarks. Where those designations appear in this book, and the publisher was aware of a trademark claim, the designations have been printed with initial capital letters or in all capitals.

The author and publisher have taken care in the preparation of this book but make no expressed or implied warranty of any kind and assume no responsibility for errors or omissions. The information contained herein represents the author's initial commentary and analysis and has been obtained from sources believed to be reliable. No liability is assumed for incidental or consequential damages in connection with or arising out of the use of the information or programs contained herein.

Library of Congress Cataloging-in-Publishing Data

Teter, Mark.

Paradigm Shift: Seven Keys of Highly Successful Linux and Open Source Adoptions/Mark R. Teter

p. cm.

ISBN 0-9773437-054995 (pbk.)

1. Linux and open source computing. 2. Information technology management. 3. Migrating to Linux. 4. History of Linux and open source. 5. IT optimization. I. Title

T174.5.T764 2006
600.4'038—dc21
2006001466

Cover design by Besoushko Design

The publisher offers discounts on this book when ordered in quantity for bulk purchases or special sales, which may include electronic versions and/or custom cover and content particular to your business, training goals, marketing focus and branding interests.

For more information, contact:
Advanced Systems Group, Inc.
Marketing Department
12405 N Grant Street
Thornton, CO 80241
(800) 894-3619

Published by
Phantom Books
Divsion of Media Resource Technology

Contents

Forward xiii
Preface xv

Part I
Linux — A Very Different Animal 1

Chapter 1 A Brave New World 3
Chapter 2 A Historical Perspective 23
Chapter 3 Free and Open Source Software 47
Chapter 4 The Complexity of Open Source 67
Chapter 5 Linux and Linux Distributions 75
Chapter 6 The Consistent Approach 95

Part II
Linux and Open Source Adoption 103

Key #1 Defining the Business-Level Objectives 105
Chapter 7 Laying the Foundation 107

Key #2 Surveying the Application Landscape 117
Chapter 8 The Application Landscape 119
Chapter 9 Today's E-mail Dilemma 137
Chapter 10 Desktop Linux 147

Key #3 Designing the Infrastructure Blueprint 175
Chapter 11 Infrastructure Optimization 177
Chapter 12 The Push Toward Commodity Technology 197
Chapter 13 Scaling Linux Environments 209

Key #4 Finding the Right Project 227
Chapter 14 Taking Costs Out (or TCO) 229

Key #5 Ensuring Project Success 247
Chapter 15 Integrating Linux and Open Source 249

Key #6 Performing the Great Escape 263
Chapter 16 The Great Escape 265
Chapter 17 Automating the Process 277

Key #7 Practicing Continuous Process Improvement 283
Chapter 18 Continuous Process Improvement 285
Chapter 19 Looking Ahead 297

Appendix A Application Matrix..301
Appendix B Integrating Windows Applications 303
Appendix C Storage Networks for Linux......................................307
Appendix D Financial Lingua Franca 313
Appendix E Maintaining Golden Images......................................317
Appendix F Management Solutions 321
Acroynms...325
Index 329

Forward

Linux, coupled with the open source model, is increasingly viewed by its adopters as a platform of innovation. It is about improving your application processing environment. It's all about getting more performance. And it's definitely about lowering your cost of computing.

In his book, *The Google Legacy*, IT consultant Stephen Arnold claims Google can put more horsepower under its hood more cheaply than competitors, thanks to its use of commodity servers and a customized version of Linux. "The net of these advantages is that Google does not have a search system; Google has a supercomputer that delivers applications."

The lure of Linux and open source software is that it is "free" in the sense that anyone can use it, modify it, create derived works from it, and redistribute it – and there are no license fees. You have access to a worldwide development community that improves, adapts and fixes the software, often much faster than in the proprietary vendor world. You are not beholden to a vendor for fixes and enhancements; there is no vendor product lock-in.

In 2000, Eric Raymond famously characterized this new form of development in his "cathedral and bazaar" paper. Proprietary development was like a cathedral: massive, closed, slow and even reverent. Open source development was like a bazaar: flexible, open to new ideas and approaches, faster and very independent.

At the same time, open source software is not a silver bullet; it is not inherently good just because it is open source. Open source software is not appropriate for every situation; it will not displace proprietary software overnight. There is plenty of good proprietary software on the market, which can and should be deployed.

Thankfully, there is *Paradigm Shift: Seven Keys of Highly Successful Linux and Open Source Adoptions*. This book is the executive guide for helping your organization adopt Linux and the open source model. It is for IT management that wants to learn the best way to move toward a commodity-based Linux and open source infrastructure. By studying technology's current realities and anticipating its future shape, this book provides organizations with the necessary balance between tactical decision-making and strategic planning.

And the time has never been better for a book like this. Every organization wants to customize their business applications, and *Paradigm Shift* is by far the best resource that I know of to help take on the complex challenge of embracing an open source initiative within a production, commercial computing environment.

Paradigm Shift is a unique and practical guide for IT professionals, business executives, end-users and business owners on how best to deploy and manage a Linux and open source computing environment according to a disciplined methodology that will minimize organizational risks and failures. It is the only resource I have seen that is organized around a methodology. In fact, the methodology advanced is a framework that can be applied to many software and hardware re-deployments.

This book will survey the reach and capabilities on Linux in today's corporate network. It will detail the many types of business and networking applications where Linux already offers best-in-class solutions. It will also list deficits, enumerate barriers to enterprise adoption, and provide a guide to important emerging technologies that are helping make Linux and open source the computing platform of choice.

It provides the clearest, best organized, and most useful means of addressing the considerable challenges posed by the open source movement. These are not sentiments that can be applied to many books, but *Paradigm Shift* is no ordinary book. Not matter your position at your organization, or the current stage of your Linux and open source initiative, the following chapters provide practical steps for achieving a successful migration away from proprietary computing environments.

Chad Sherman
Chief Technology Officer
Department of Information Technology
Central Intelligence Agency

Preface

Linux and Open Source Background

Linux is perhaps the most well-known software in the modern open source movement.

By using the inherent power of open source software development, Linux has quickly evolved into one of the most popular operating systems now available. In fact, the Linux operating system is one of the few software-based technologies today that continues to experience record growth rates.

Open source extends from the lowest reaches of Linux at the operating system level to databases, application servers, development tools, business and desktop applications. It is important to note that open source software is not just for Linux-based systems, but represents a broad collection of software available for almost any operating environment. However, open source software and Linux are an extremely potent combination.

The lure is that Linux and open source are "free" in the sense that anyone can use it, modify it, create derived works from it, and redistribute it — and there are no license fees.

You have access to a worldwide development community that improves, adapts and fixes the software, often much faster than in the proprietary vendor world. You are not beholden to a vendor for fixes and enhancements; there is no vendor product lock-in.

As a testament to this powerful, collaborative environment, the open source Apache Web server, running on Linux, serves more Web sites than any other, including Microsoft's IIS and Sun's Java System Web Server. In fact, the growth rate for Linux server deployments has now surpassed Microsoft operating system (OS) shipments. So while Windows is currently the leader in server OS shipments worldwide, Linux is seriously challenging its coveted position.

To put Linux in perspective within the industry, it's best to look at what Microsoft is doing. Microsoft is trying to perfect the best "closed" system.

This is not because of its use of standards (or lack of them) nor about its development processes or program interfaces. Microsoft's platform, known as Vista, is fashioned to be a self-consistent, interlocking system. That is, its real value comes from its complete integration with other Microsoft products.

Linux and open source, on the other hand, is trying to perfect the best open system, maximizing the value of innovation. It's not how they are built or distributed, but the way that it integrates new ideas. In fact, it's inherently messier (less Cathedral and more Bazaar in the words of Eric S. Raymond in his O'Reilly published book *The Cathedral & the Bazaar*), but more robust, more future-proof and more adaptive to your requirements.

Since Linux is based on open source, it is truly an open system. Linux provides a reliable, scalable platform with the high-end attributes of traditional Unix and Windows systems, yet it differs from them in several key areas. Unlike Unix and Windows, Linux development occurs via a worldwide programming effort that provides it with improved reliability, scalability and performance features. And because Linux is open source, it runs on virtually any hardware platform providing a much more flexible and cost effective deployment strategy over the hardware and software compatibility requirements necessary for Unix and Windows.

Linux and open source have developed a loyal following among many different businesses, government institutions and universities, as well as top computer manufacturers such as Dell, Hewlett-Packard, IBM and Sun Microsystems. In addition to large software suppliers like BEA, Novell, Oracle and SAP, there are a growing number of companies offering open source business applications and solutions.

The net effect from working on Linux-based projects has allowed many organizations to adopt best-of-breed open source processes into their development methodology. In fact, companies have discovered that by leveraging Linux and open source software, they have become so competitive that they were able to outperform off-shore projects in terms of development speed, quality and price.

With thousands of successfully installed and implemented Linux systems around the world, it is easy to see why Linux in particular and open source software in general are gaining in popularity. Linus Torvalds' Linux has evolved into a flexible, highly-portable, industry-leading operating system kernel, which — when combined with the open source components such as Samba, MySQL, and other open source licensed programs — offers superior reliability, adaptability and cost effectiveness to both Unix and Windows operating systems.

However, with all of the evidence to the contrary, the use of Linux remains extremely controversial. And considering that annual sales of Microsoft's Windows operating system alone exceed USD $10 billion, it seems fairly obvious that substantial economic interests influence the debate for potential alternatives.

Who Is This Book For?

One thing IT professionals believe about open source software: It provides more opportunity for innovation than commercial or proprietary software. Most organizations contend that open source spurs more opportunities for technical innovation with a significant majority endorsing it because it encourages business innovation.

Linux and open source also present specific challenges. When and how should your organization adopt Linux? How many distributions and platforms should your company support? How will you perform software support? How will you package and deploy software? How will you manage and secure Linux?

Paradigm Shift is devoted to IT executives, technology decision-makers and project managers who could benefit from a crash course on Linux and open source adoption. Written for those in charge of planning and implementing strategies and infrastructure projects, the Seven Keys presented in this book provide practical information and recommendations in non-technical terms to enable readers to quickly understand the principles behind Linux-based computing as well as mitigate the challenges it presents.

This book provides a pragmatic approach for determining if migrating to Linux is best for your organization. If after going through the first four Keys you determine that your organization would greatly benefit from Linux and open source, this book provides you with the necessary information and processes to ensure project success. The last three Keys provide a primer on getting your project on track, putting the necessary processes in place and rolling out your new application computing environment.

Paradigm Shift answers the questions surrounding Linux as a legitimate business and technical computing platform. After reading this book, you'll be well positioned to make a balanced assessment of the impact of Linux and open source for your organization. By studying technology's current realities and anticipating its future shape, *Paradigm Shift* provides organizations with the necessary balance between tactical decision making and strategic planning.

How Is This Book Organized?

Paradigm Shift is a two-part book. Part I provides a historical look at the technological, cultural and economic reasons that led to the need for Linux and open source strategies. After reading Part I, you will completely understand the context and framework that has made Linux and open source computing so popular.

Part II provides the Seven Keys. The Seven Keys are the fundamental elements to ensuring success with Linux and open source computing. Part II discusses the processes behind migrating to a Linux-based computing environment, providing a reliable aid for commercial Linux and open source deployments. It is organized according to the steps you would follow in conducting the proper analysis and justification, building the proper project management support and performing the migration to the new computing environment.

One final point is that this book is written from a vendor-neutral perspective; it does not contain recommendations to any particular vendor or vendor solution but presents the reader with the most salient, non-bias information relating to this subject matter. The focus is on conducting best practices for Linux and open source adoption. Due to the rapid changes in this industry, it is difficult to predict which companies will lead as the market evolves. The concepts outlined in *Paradigm Shift* serve as a guide in choosing the appropriate products and services to support your organization today and in the future.

PART I

Linux — A Very Different Animal

Over the past few years, the Linux operating system has become a real and viable operating system alternative, opening the door to a new era of business computing. In fact, widespread Linux adoption during the next five years will result in major changes to today's information technology landscape.

However, open source is not new. The open source movement has been a part of computer science programs dating back to the 1960s. In fact, it has been most associated with Unix systems — not Linux. Hence, what is so compelling about Linux and open source?

The answer lies with the nature of these two animals. Open access and collaboration are at the very core of Linux and the open source movement. Open source is a philosophy of idea generation and development. The open and collaborative nature of open source fuels innovation. By tapping a worldwide development community that knows no corporate boundaries, and sharing that expertise, Linux and open source breeds innovation, be it for corrections, enhancements or new functionality.

Linux and open source places the scarce resource of software into everybody's hands, the way the Gutenberg press placed the scarce resource of texts into everybody's hands. The open, collaborative approach levels the playing field, enabling anyone and everyone to contribute and participate. And this is exactly why your organization needs to put Linux and open source software at the center of your business strategy. In combination, Linux and open source software decrease the time to market for your key products and services.

Chapter 1

A Brave New World

There are no great people in this world, only great challenges which ordinary people rise to meet.
— William Frederick Halsey, Jr.

Linux and open source offers organizations many benefits over traditional operating system environments — advantages they have wanted and needed for a long time. This flexible operating environment not only allows your organization to deploy its applications on virtually any hardware platform but provides you a way to easily redeploy those applications on other hardware platforms as workload requirements change.

Linux is an operating system that crosses the chasm of all electronic machines from cell phones, game consoles, PDAs and technical workstations to high-end symmetrical multiprocessing (SMP) systems and massive application grid arrays. It provides operating system support across a broad spectrum of devices, from lightweight embedded and mobile devices to enterprise-class 64-bit multiprocessor server environments. It delivers the power and scalability for a high-end server as well the functionality and support for a desktop.

Open source provides a rich set of utilities, applications, graphical user interfaces, file and printing services, corporate database services, application clusters and high-performance compute grids. There are viable open source databases, Web and application servers, middleware and management solutions. Because Linux is demonstrating such momentum in the OS market, open source is showing equally great traction with the remainder of the software stack. Linux and open source software are ready for mainstream business.

The Swiss Army Knife

Open source software, combined with Linux, radically reduces the cost of computing. In fact, its low cost for deployment, better price per performance and lack of dependence on any single vendor are the most frequently cited reasons for organizations adopting Linux and open source solutions. The savings can be substantial in terms of hardware costs alone, since organizations can deploy Linux across a wide range of inexpensive com-

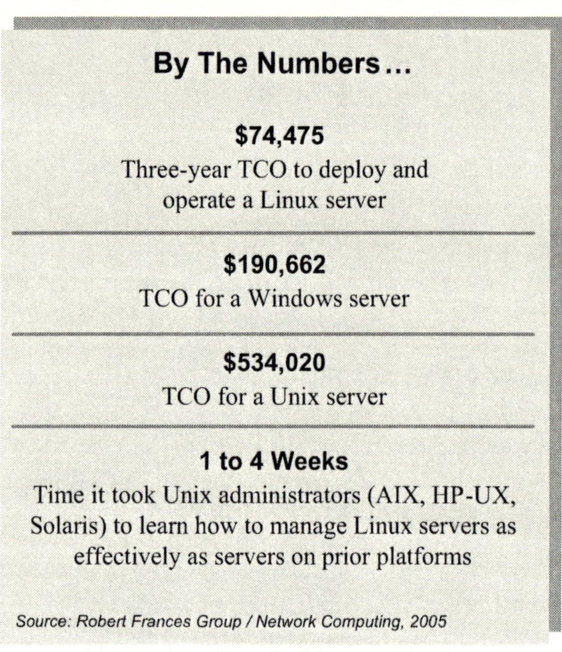

Figure 1-1. *Finanical Perspective.*

modity hardware. As a result, the cost for implementation and maintenance is much less than the total cost of ownership associated with proprietary Unix systems, as shown in Figure 1–1.

Linux in particular shares an important characteristic that TCP, HTML, XML, Java and all other major Internet and computing technologies have — that is, it works everywhere. It is the only operating environment that works across every chip architecture and on every commercial computing platform. It truly is a Swiss Army Knife operating system.

Relative to rival, proprietary solutions, Linux and open source alternatives represent a practical upgrade path for existing and new computing solutions. Combined with growing support from a wide variety of independent software vendors (ISVs), they both can make a significant bottom-line impact to your organization. Figure 1–2 summarizes why organizations choose Linux as their long-term platform strategy and the sidebar **Open Source Success Stories** highlights how companies are succeeding with it.

Linux Advantages

- Lower cost of ownership
- 100% POSIX compliant operating system
- Single, stable and modular kernel
- Key ingredient for utility & grid computing
- World's largest development environment
- Lack of dependence on any single vendor
- Excellent price per performance ratio

Figure 1-2. *Major Advantages.*

The Road to Ubiquity

In 1991, Linus Torvalds (first name pronounced /lee'nus/) was introduced to the Minix operating system, written by Professor Andrew Tanenbaum. Dr. Tanenbaum wrote Minix as an open source example to accompany a book he wrote about operating systems. Torvalds used the Minux source as a reference and eventually created his own OS derivative that now is known as Linux.

From that modest beginning, Linux has experienced exponential growth becoming one of the fastest maturing operating systems in history. In four years, Linux has advanced to the same level that it took Unix 10 years to achieve. According to International Data Corporation (IDC), the worldwide Linux business is expected to grow 25.9 percent annually, doubling from USD $20 billion in 2005 to more than USD $40 billion in 2008. This represents a revenue increase of more than four times the overall industry average for all platforms through the same time period.

With the release of the 2.6 Linux kernel, Linux has made inroads on virtually every major hardware platform in the IT and electronics industry. Linux provides an end-to-end operating environment within the confines of a PDA, MP3 player, cell phone or desktop computer — or can provide a complete operating system for enterprise multiprocessor servers. In fact,

Linux is the number two embedded operating system, behind Wind River's VxWorks.

Fundamentally, Linux in combination with open source software provide a considerably different platform than any other enterprise computing environment. First and foremost, Linux is open source. And since it is open source, a development community of more than a half million developers is participating in building and extending the Linux operating environment.

There is complete transparency into the entire development process, allowing companies to get what they need when they need it. That is exactly why an open source algorithm was chosen for the AES (Advanced Encryption Standard) in 2002 to replace the aging DES (Data Encryption Standard). The algorithm was selected after a three-year global competition led by the U.S. National Institute of Standards and Technology.

From this large community of developers, more than 10,000 stable open source software products provide companies with source code. This inevitably encourages code reuse and weakens the not-invented-here syndrome that often plagues organizations with poor application delivery and quality. This development process is faster and smoother because your developers can use available, tested components rather than having to create and test components from scratch. Source code availability results in quicker problem solving, provides a better feature-enhancement process, and promotes collaborative learning amongst your team. No other operating environment has such a large collective group of developers and gradients of accessibility.

Second, Linux and open source is built from the combined effort of many industry development groups. This effort is making the hardware platform readily substitutable, decreasing the dependency on proprietary systems. And since developers are not constrained by proprietary protocols, which often require using one vendor's products, your organization instead can follow a best-of-breed strategy leveraging industry-based practices and standards.

This allows your organization to use a "mix and match" approach rather than the "all or nothing" approach that often comes with solely replying on commercial vendors' solutions. This even means your organization can leverage various open source components in combination with commercial applications. For instance, many organizations have successfully used their Oracle database environment in combination with open source components such as Tomcat (application server), Jetspeed (portal framework), Apache (Web server), Struts (application development framework) and Lucene (search engine). The result is a highly cost-effective, customizable Web portal platform.

Third, Linux source code is freely available. Since Linux as well as most open source software is licensed under the GPL (General Public License), developers who modify and distribute their applications commercially must ensure that the modified (read enhanced) source code is made publicly available.

This ability to freely copy open source software and deploy as much as is needed within an enterprise means the historical licensing problem of counting the number users or processors goes away, along with the required audit licensing costs involved. This also ensures that solutions are built according to real application requirements, and not designed around goals of trying to minimize the number of costly software licenses.

With the ability to deploy as many application and database servers as is required across the enterprise freely because of a lack of per system license fees, the solution can be designed and built to real infrastructure requirements. The solution can grow more organically to meet the needs of the enterprise at marginal additional costs.

The GPL licensing model also helps spur innovation since developers can experiment with components they would never even try if they had to purchase them. In fact, this allows your organization to try and experiment with leading edge software solutions. If the new technology is not suitable, the only sunk cost is your time.

This method of experimenting with open source software in your computing environment gives your organization potentially more buying power with its commercial suppliers and vendors. The threat of substituting open source software alternatives helps keep the cost of proprietary solutions much more competitive.

Fourth, Linux is the enabling technology for the next generation of data center hardware. Linux is becoming the de facto operating system for blade computing, grids and clustering technology, providing the foundation for a new set of virtualized computing capabilities. As the foundation for virtualized computing resources, grid computing, along with Linux and open source, represents the next frontier for computing infrastructures.

Not to mention 64-bit computing has allowed Linux to compete head-to-head with the traditional proprietary Unix servers provided by the large system vendors. Consequently it is no surprise that the TOP500 organization (http://www.top500.org) which publishes a list of the most powerful com-

Why Are Microsoft Users Migrating to Linux?

People turn to Linux for many reasons (see Figure 1-5), but one of the most prevalent is the chance to move away from a proprietary environment toward an open one. Linux, which uses open source solutions built from industry standards, provides just that opportunity. But how is this different from using a Microsoft deployment strategy?

System architectures based on Microsoft products are subject to vendor lock-in dependencies. For example, Microsoft application software can only be installed and used on Microsoft operating systems. This applies to all Microsoft server applications such as MS SQL Server and MS Exchange, as well as most other Microsoft desktop applications.

The popular MS Great Plains business application requires MS Windows Server, MS ISS (for portal functionality), MS Active Directory, a Microsoft Desktop (for client access) and MS SQL Server. If you choose to use a Microsoft application, you have little choice but to turn to Microsoft for all your upgrades, service packs, security patches and client licenses.

Such dependencies among Microsoft's operating systems and applications characterize the increasing integration and vendor lock-in with this platform. Essentially, a Microsoft strategy makes for a very homogeneous (read not best-of-breed) and expensive computing environment. With Linux, there is a choice-not only of hardware but of OS distribution, applications and technical support.

puters in the world, has recorded multiple Linux-based systems in their top 10.

Lastly, Linux and open source is strategic. System vendors such as Dell, Hewlett-Packard, IBM and Sun Microsystems have announced formal support for the Linux operating environment as well as for many open source software initiatives. Most have even gone so far as to promise to migrate all of their proprietary OS functionality to the Linux platform and the open source community.

Inflection Points for Linux

- Migration to 64-bit business applications
- Requirement for better application scaling
- Need for server consolidation using commodity-based hardware
- Requirement for better system management
- Deployment of industry-accepted standards
- Power and thermal challenges in datacenters

Figure 1-3. *Inflection Points.*

Developed and Supported By Standards

A lot of effort has been put into standardizing Linux. Organizations like the Free Standards Group, FreeDesktop.org and Open Source Development Labs (OSDL) are continuously working on many different projects in support of Linux and open source. These projects use and extend existing standards like POSIX, the Single UNIX Specification, XML, DOM, CORBA and many more.

In particular, Linux is developed and supported by:

- **Consumer Electronics Linux Forum:** This industry consortium includes Matsushita, Sony, Hitachi, NEC and other consumer electronics companies that want to collaborate on making Linux more appealing for the embedded consumer electronics market. Through a joint development, CE Linux Forum is working on areas such as improved boot times, real-time programming and audio and visual graphics. For more information, visit http://www.celinuxforum.org.

- **Filesystem Hierarchy Standard (FHS):** This standard consists of a set guidelines and requirements for file and directory management and structures. The guidelines are intended to support interoperability of applications, system administration tools, development tools and scripts as well as greater uniformity of documentation for these systems. For more information, visit http://www.pathname.com/fhs.

- **Freedesktop.org:** As an informal collaboration, freedesktop.org provides improved interoperability and usability for the Linux desktop environment. For more information, visit http://www.freedesktop.org.

- **Free Standards Group (FSG):** The Free Standards Group is a nonprofit organization dedicated to accelerating the use of free and open source

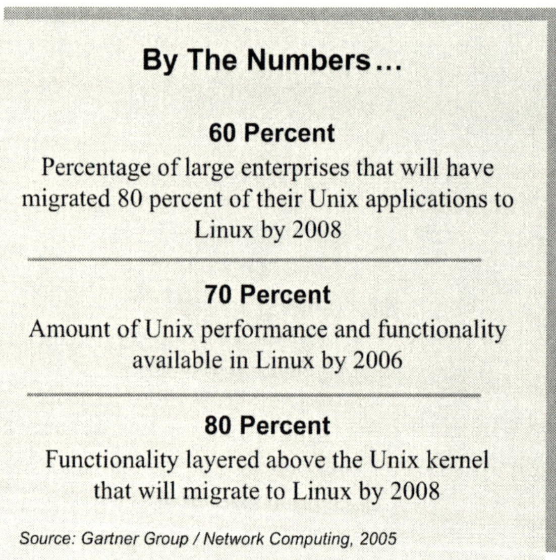

Figure 1-4. *Deployment Trends.*

software by developing and promoting standards. Free Standards Group projects include the Linux Standard Base and OpenI18N (Internationalization Initiative). For more information, visit http://www.freestandards.org.

- **GNOME Foundation:** While this organization does include an industry advisory board, the foundation is mostly a governing body for the GNOME project. The GNOME Foundation works to further the goal of the GNOME project by creating a computing platform for use by the general public. For more information, visit http://www.gnome.org.

- **LI18NUX Project:** Part of the Free Standards Group, the LI18NUX Project (Linux Internationalization Initiative) is an internationalization guide for platform and application developers, allowing Linux and Linux-based programs to reach greater language localization capabilities. For more information, visit http://www.openi18n.org.

- **Linux Standard Base (LSB):** A working group of the Free Standards Group, LSB is an effort to create a standard to which all Linux distributions adhere, allowing software developers to build applications that will install and run on any LSB-compliant distribution. For more information, visit http://www.linuxbase.org.

- **OpenForum Europe (OFE):** Set up by the not-for-profit IT Forum Foundation, OFE is accelerating, broadening and strengthening the use of open source, including Linux, within the European business and government communities. For more information, visit http://www.openforumeurope.org.

- **OpenPrinting:** OpenPrinting is a workgroup of the Free Standards Group whose goal is to develop and promote a set of standards for a scalable print environment within Linux, addressing the needs for desktop and enterprise-level management, security, scalability and network accessibility. For more information, visit http://www.openprinting.org or http://members.freestandards.org/openprinting.

- **Open Source Development Lab (OSDL):** OSDL is a joint effort of a number of industry leaders, including Computer Associates, Hewlett-Packard, IBM, Intel, NEC and Sun Microsystems, focused on improving Linux as an enterprise-grade operating system. OSDL provides working groups and specifications for Carrier Grade, Data Center and Desktop Linux and has recruited Torvalds as its first fellow, allowing him to dedicate his full-time efforts to the development of the Linux kernel. For more information, visit http://www.osdl.org.

- **The Embedded Linux Consortium (ELC):** The ELC is a nonprofit trade association whose goal is the advancement, promotion and standardization of Linux throughout the embedded, applied and appliance computing markets. For more information, visit http://www.embedded-linux.org.

Looking Ahead

Chandler

Today's personal information managers (PIMs) force users to adapt to technology.

Frustrated by this inability of PIMs to adapt to his way of organizing his work, Mitch Kapor, the original creator of Lotus-123, turned to the open source development process, invested millions of his own money and created the Open Source Applications Foundation (http://www.osafoundation.org), where a team of two dozen developers are creating Chandler, a next-generation PIM.

The major emphasis in Chandler is collaboration — the ability to share information using flexible policies. With Chandler, all data is organized into a single central repository. User notifications are handled using the Jabber peer-to-peer instant messaging platform rather than through central servers.

With Chandler, end-users will be able to organize diverse kinds of information for their own convenience — not the computer's convenience. Chandler will have the ability to not only associate and interconnect items but also to gather and collect related items in a single place creating a context-sensitive view of many types of data — mixing and matching e-mail, mailing lists, instant messages, appointments, contacts, tasks, free-form notes, blogs, Web pages, documents, spreadsheets, slide shows, bookmarks, photos or MP3s, either stored on the end-user's local PC or on other systems.

The Dashboard

Nat Friedman, founder of Ximian (now part of Novell) believes the future of the Linux desktop lies in collaboration. Recently, he launched a Desktop Integration Bounty Hunt (http://www.gnome.org/bounties) for the GNOME project, offering bounties (read money) for making more than 50 enhancements to GNOME aimed at improving the collaboration experience in the desktop environment.

Nat also coordinates the GNOME dashboard, a project that aims to bring relevant information to users, rather than requiring them to dig around for it. While you read e-mail, browse the Web, write a document or chat with your friends on IM, the dashboard does its best to proactively find objects that are relevant to your current activity.

The dashboard is not just a single piece of software you can install. It requires some modifications to front-end applications such as the Web browser, PIM software and chat software to allow them to send "clue packets" to the dashboard.

Volunteers in the GNOME project are now retrofitting GNOME applications to support the dashboard concept. Microsoft is working on a similar concept (for Vista), which it calls "implicit query."

Linux-Based Internet Tablet

Nokia has introduced its first device in the new Internet tablet category. The Nokia 770 Internet tablet is a dedicated device optimized for Internet browsing and e-mail communications in a pocketsize format. The Internet tablet features a high-resolution wide screen display with zoom and on-screen keyboard — ideal for viewing online content over Wi-Fi — and can connect to the Internet using Bluetooth wireless technology. It includes an Internet radio, RSS news reader, image viewer and media players.

The device runs the Linux-based Nokia Internet Tablet software, which includes widely deployed desktop Linux and open source technologies. The Maemo development platform (http://www.maemo.org) will provide open source developers with the tools and opportunities to collaborate with Nokia on future devices and OS releases in the Internet tablet category.

Taking Advantage of Technology Breakthroughs

Businesses and technology organizations today are turning to Linux and open source solutions for the broad range of available software and broad implementation of open standards. Because of its low deployment cost and, perhaps most importantly, the thriving community of users and developers who continue to provide the rapid cycle of innovations and enhancements, Linux and open source are a perfect combination to help stretch your IT budget. With Linux providing the OS support, open source software alternatives are delivering the applications, databases and tools.

Reasons to Switch

- Incompatibility between MS Office versions
- License management is expensive & time-consuming
- MS Office is not based on open standards
- Employees ignorant of "time saving" capabilities
- Most of MS Office 2003 productivity boosters readily available
- Must adhere to Microsoft's update time lines (and not according to business plans)
- Cannot cut unnecessary components (all or nothing proposition)
- Will not have continual accessibility of old document versions

Figure 1-5. *Microsoft Vulnerabilities.*

But why is Linux one of the fastest growing operating system in the industry? How is Linux building so much momentum? Obviously, Linux benefits from its open source development effort as well as its adherence to open standards, but Linux is also taking advantage of some major trends that are occurring in the industry.

Among these technological shifts are multi-core, multithreaded CPUs and 64-bit computing technology. Both are helping Linux increase its viability in today's IT environment. If anything, the big news of the immediate present and the foreseeable future it's multi-core, multithreaded CPU designs. Chip designers are now putting a "cluster" of processor cores each capable of processing multiple threads concurrently on each microchip — multiprocessing in uni-processor packaging (commonly known as SMT or simultaneous multithreading).

This chip design and fabrication breakthrough is not only providing better overall performance characteristics, it is also greatly reducing the amount of energy required to perform the same amount of processing compared to the traditional CPU design. Pound for pound, there is less watts needed per

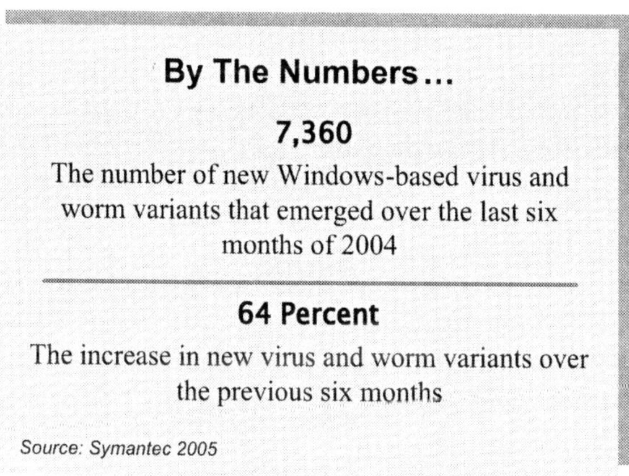

Figure 1-6. *Security Vulnerabilities.*

CPU cycle since these new chip designs are capable of handling multiple processes concurrently.

In conjunction, 64-bit operating environments has radically changed the course of computing, especially to the advantage for Linux-based systems. Once only available through expensive, SMP-based Unix servers, 64-bit servers are widely available being built from commodity-based hardware. And with Linux becoming the preferred OS for non-SMP systems, 64-bit architectures are helping expand its deployment turning the traditional economics of IT computing upside down. Eight- and 16-way SMP servers now have a 50 percent to 80 percent cost disadvantage compared to the equivalent four-node two-way or four-node four-way Linux configurations.

Figure 1–3 highlights these common inflection points for Linux adoption.

To Infinity and Beyond

Clearly, the use of Linux is on the rise. Supply-side data from IDC shows the Linux server market is the most rapidly growing segment of the entire worldwide server market. As a relative measure of economic impact, IDC forecasts that the Linux server market will grow from today's USD $2 billion to nearly USD $7 billion by 2007. Few operating systems have experienced such explosive growth. As illustrated in Figure 1–4, Linux increasingly is becoming the *de facto* server environment.

However, Linux is not only seeing growth within the server OS market but is achieving record growth rates on desktops. As shown in Figure 1–5, there are many reasons why companies are looking at Linux outside the server environment. IDC reports that the installed base of Linux desktops will reach more than 27.8 million units by 2006. It is easy to see why this growth is occurring based on the security vulnerabilities being reported on Microsoft Windows, as indicated in Figure 1–6.

It's also worth noting that the open source nature of this operating system makes counting Linux adoption an inexact science at best. Linux is easily available from any number of Web sites, allowing users to burn and redistribute their own CDs and install it on thousands of machines across an enterprise from a single purchased copy, making IDC's prediction an even more conservative estimate.

The adoption of Linux has been a rapid and changing process. Although its open source origins guaranteed a vastly different development history, the deployment and adoption of Linux have, in many respects, paralleled that of Windows nearly a decade and a half ago and Unix a decade before that.

The Open Source Advantage

All organizations today should have a plan for Linux and open source. Linux and open source software represent a strategic opportunity for your organization to build a path to a highly cost-effective, highly adaptive application computing infrastructure. In combination, they provide a powerful mechanism for your organizations to replace and update your proprietary, and most very likely, your extremely expensive applications, databases, management tools, server infrastructure and desktop environments with a less costly and more reliable alternative.

Linux and open source computing have achieved a critical mass, assuring the world and business community that it will be continually improved upon, taught in schools and sold in supported distributions for the future ahead.

Open Source Success Stories

Acxiom Corporation

Acxiom's corporate strategy is to use technology to create a competitive advantage for its clients. Its Customer Information Infrastructure (CII) is the latest and by far the most comprehensive of such initiatives. Going against conventional wisdom, CII processing is based on a data and workflow grid rather than a commercial relational database . Each node is a Linux-compatible server. The grid consists of more than 4,000 rack-mounted Linux nodes organized into "pods." The pods can be dedicated to specific clients or projects or used as a common resource.

Cendant Corporation

Cendant Corporation's Travel Distribution Services (TDS) Division is one of the world's largest and most geographically diverse collections of travel brands and distribution businesses. TDS has saved nearly USD $100 million since 2001 by leveraging Apache and Tomcat to concentrate on the wide-scale reuse of its assets — its software programs and Linux-compatible computer hardware.

CNET Networks

CNET Networks was forced to build a system that could handle massive content replication that delivered fast, accurate results — and it had to be accomplished on a very tight budget. The result was ATOMICS (Apache TO MySQL In CNET Search). It is entirely from open source components leveraging standard interface specifications.

Continental Airlines

Continental hosts JBoss and Zope application servers, MySQL database and Plone for its Web-based applications. Plone is a content management system built on Zope. These open source programs provide Continental with a system for managing its Web portal content.

Cox Communication

Cox Communications is the fourth largest cable-television provider in the United States, serving approximately 6.3 million customers. As a Fortune 500 company, Cox has built communications networks and delivered quality cable television programs since 1962.

To maintain optimum performance and customer-service levels, Cox has developed a huge data warehousing application. At the heart of this business-critical system is a 2-billion row MySQL database.

Craigslist

craigslist was founded in 1995 as a down-to-earth community site where people could address everyday needs such as finding a job or a place to live, and as a result, it has revolutionized the ease with which people can create an online community to facilitate the exchange of ideas, goods and services. According to Alexa Traffic Rankings, craigslist is now one of the Top100 most trafficked Web sites in the world. The infrastructure supporting this Web site comprises entirely on the open source LAMP (Linux, Apache, MySQL, Perl).

E-Trade Financial Corporation

E-Trade has saved billions of dollars converting to Linux and open source. The company uses Linux for its customer-facing Web applications and plans by 2006 to move off all proprietary Web middleware to a common Web services transaction-messaging infrastructure. E-Trade prides itself on using technology to innovate in the financial services market, and open source and Linux are critical to its mantra.

Fidelity Investments

Fidelity has leveraged the open source Struts platform to build its own enhanced Web application framework. Known as Struts Plus, this open source platform provides the development framework for Fidelity's Java Web applications.

Google

Google views its ability to innovate as critical key to its long-term success against rivals such as Yahoo and Microsoft. This quest for innovation is also behind the company's embrace of open source technologies. Originally Google was planning on deploying commercial database solutions such as Oracle or Sybase for Google's back-end infrastructure, but engineers convinced the company that MySQL was actually better suited to the company's needs.

Nielsen Media Research

Nielsen runs Red Hat Linux on Linux-compatible systems. A critical business application used to analyze TV ratings is developed under the JBoss application server. Using this open source application server, Nielsen has standardized the way it performs Java, HTML and JavaBeans processing.

Sabre Holdings Corporation

In 2000, Sabre Holdings initiated a USD $100 million project to move its air travel shopping and pricing services off the mainframe environment. Now it runs more than 200 MySQL database servers along with JBoss, Tomcat and Ace Orb.

The Weather Channel

Weather.com, the online counterpart of The Weather Channel Interactive Inc.'s 24-hour TV channel, has traditionally relied on proprietary commercial software to serve up millions of Web pages of maps, forecasts and hour-by-hour weather data every day.

Today, the Atlanta-based Web site serves more than 50 million pages, but it runs almost entirely on open source software and commodity hardware. And since the move to the new architecture, it has slashed IT costs by one-third and increased Web site processing capacity by 30 percent.

U.S. Census Bureau

Most Americans are aware that every ten years, the United States Census Bureau conducts a massive survey of the 105 million U.S. households to collect updated national demographic information. What many people don't know is the U.S. Census Bureau Web development team relies on open source software such as Perl, Apache, Linux and PHP to develop and publish these Web sites.

Yahoo Inc.

Three of Yahoo's primary open source technologies are the Apache Web server and MySQL. It extensively uses PHP to automate core Web processing. The Yahoo Finance Web site, which is aggregated from over 100 sources worldwide, as well as its stock charts, insider trading, SEC filings, conference calls, and earnings reports, are built using open source technologies.

Chapter 2

A Historical Perspective

Every good work of software starts by scratching a developer's personal itch.

—Eric Raymond, Founder of Open Source Initiative

In 1969, AT&T Bell Labs began working on an operating system. Based around the prior works of MULTICS developed out of MIT, AT&T released their development and named it Unix. And in 1976, Unix was being taught in every college and university around the world.

At the time, AT&T liberally licensed Unix. In fact, AT&T gave it away to universities and colleges to take advantage of any developments computer science departments might make to it. They permitted free academic access to the Unix source code while charging USD $20,000 (in 1976 dollars) for commercial or government use.

Since many universities were connected to each other through the ARPAnet, the precursor to the Internet, developers and academic programmers could share their improvements by participating in a world-wide peer-to-peer environment. The era of collaborative programming had arrived.

During this time, an academic variant of Unix became extremely popular. Known as the Berkeley Systems Distribution (BSD), this variant of Unix was receiving major enhancements to the OS including new features such as virtual memory and IP networking as well as many other programming utilities. Unfortunately, lawsuits eventually ensued between AT&T, the Regents of the University of California and other parties over access to and distribution of the Unix source code.

As a result, an opportunity was created for the commercialization of Unix. And in 1984 it officially became a proprietary, commercial offering (derived from licensed AT&T Unix and BSD code) from vendors such as DEC, Hewlett-Packard, IBM and Sun Microsystems.

Resursive Acronyms

The liberal code-sharing days that allowed developers to take advantage of each other's code improvements had quickly come to an end. However, such constraints on intellectual property rights to software code provided strong motivation for one researcher from the Massachusetts Institute of Technology (MIT) to write another operating environment.

Richard Stallman, a researcher at the Artificial Intelligence Laboratories of MIT, wanted to continue the tradition of open source and code sharing. He also wanted to write an operating environment that would be portable, but could be licensed in such a way that it would not be constrained by any intellectual property claims.

The new operating system was named GNU after a recursive acronym standing for "GNU's Not Unix." GNU was purposely licensed under a General Public License (GPL) intended to guarantee the freedom to share and freely modify the software (this will be discussed in more detail in Chapter 3). As a result, GNU became the first truly "free" software. Stallman is the president of the Free Software Foundation (FSF), the principal organizational sponsor for the GNU Project.

The GNU development effort began with the creation of software tools, compilers and utilities in source code form that could be compiled and executed on any platform. By 1990, developers and programmers around the world had contributed a nearly complete GNU operating environment, with the exception of a fully finished OS kernel.

A kernel is the core operating software module running on a computer. It is the first thing that loads into hardware memory and is responsible for memory, process, task, I/O and disk management. Since the only major software component missing from GNU was a kernel, the GNU Project decided to implement Hurd, a replacement for the now proprietary Unix kernel.

Hurd Begets Unix

Hurd is a collection of services that runs on the Mach microkernel (developed at Carnegie Mellon University and University of Utah), which implements file systems, network protocols, file access control and other features just like the Unix kernel. Unfortunately for Hurd, Mach was delayed. This postponed the final release of Hurd as a production-ready kernel.

During this time, the development and release of commercial Unix software was becoming popular. Vendors such as DEC, IBM, HP and Apollo began selling or licensing their respective versions of Unix.

With the complete withdrawal of AT&T source code from the academic environment and the BSD operating system mired in legal challenges, Andrew Tanenbaum, a computer science professor at Vrije University in the Netherlands, saw an opportunity. Tanenbaum needed the code for a Unix-like operating system that he could use as a teaching aid in his computer science courses. For that purpose, Tanenbaum developed a Unix-like OS and called it Minix.

Linus, Linux and Open Source

With the cornucopia of open source software now available in universities, corporations and government agencies, programmers were continually improving upon Unix and its supporting applications. It is at this point that Linus Torvalds, considered the father of Linux, decided to write an operating system he could run on his Intel 80386 PC.

Torvalds decided to use Minix as his prototype. He and colleague Lars Wirzenius eventually released their software (a Unix-like kernel), named it Linux and licensed it under the GPL.

Linux was a kernel without utilities and GNU was an operating environment lacking a finished kernel. The Linux code was combined with the GNU system to create GNU/Linux — or simply Linux, as it has come to be known. All of the unencumbered non-kernel BSD pieces contributed by the open source community were finally available in a complete, Unix-like operating environment.

In short order all of the components were combined with installation and maintenance tools and, by 1993, the first distribution of Linux was release by Slackware. In only a few years, a worldwide Linux community evolved, comprised of programmers, developers and users attracted by the reliability and flexibility of this free operating system. Slowly, the term "free software" has been replaced by "open source software" as the commercial adoption of Linux grew. It is made clear in the sidebar **What Is Free Software?** that these terms ultimately mean the same thing.

Linux Distributions

The Linux project is actually not an operating system, but the kernel of an operating system. Linux vendors such as Red Hat and Novell and other open source efforts like the Debian project focus on offering complete operating systems that include all the required hardware drivers, software utilities and development tools as well as a collection of necessary server and desktop applications. But it is because of the GNU software development efforts that Linux has been able to constantly evolve and improve itself.

Since the Linux source code is freely available, several companies have developed their own distributions of Linux. A distribution is a complete system, and the key component is the Linux kernel. Other utilities, services and various applications are included as well, depending on the distribution and its intended use.

To create a fully usable product, Linux distributions bundle the kernel, drivers, applications and all the other components necessary for a complete Linux package. Major Linux distributions include those packaged and supported by Asianux, Mandriva, MontaVista, Novell, Red Hat, Turbolinux, Ubunta and Yellow Dog.

Even though the development of Linux is mostly distributed and decentralized, Torvalds still exerts a great deal of authority and coordination among developers. However, he specifically focuses on developing the mainline or stable kernel, known as 2.6.x. In this fashion, Linux follows an open source model of development. It combines the innovation that comes from open source code, yet retains the vision of the original author through a delegation of authority.

Open Source Bandwagon

Few remember that open source software was the business model the computer industry adopted back in the 1960's. Nobody would buy a computer — a huge investment at that time — that was not immediately ready for use.

Today the open source movement is helping turn significant chunks of the application computing infrastructure into commodities by offering free alternatives to proprietary — and sometimes very expensive — business software. The promises of the open source movement have finally begun to materialize, and organizations that don't come to terms with the open source revolution will end up paying too much for IT.

The commoditization wrought by open source is happening fastest at the lowest level of the infrastructure — the level that most businesspeople never see — where network edge devices, security appliances, infrastructure servers and application middleware dwell.

Major enterprises are now running mission-critical services and functions on open source software with significant reductions in total cost of ownership. As outlined in Figure 2–1, the open source movement presents many compelling advantages for technology organizations.

Why Companies Are Using Open Source Software

- Ability to lower licensing costs, leverage commodity hardware and avoid cumbersome software licensing agreements
- Being part of community-based development efforts, it reduces dependency on individual technology providers and provides more flexibility in responding to changing business requirements
- Open source extends across the entire software stack and allows its development to be aligned to customer needs, not vendor release cycles
- Open source software is more aligned with open industry standards and providing application interoperability

Figure 2-1. *Why Use Open Source?*

This is not an accident: 58 percent of the open source community is made up of professional IT administrators and programmers (with 11 years of professional experience, on average) who use open source to fix problems they encounter in their jobs, according to a recent survey by Boston Consulting Group.

An Empowering Technology

Linux has contributed greatly to the adoption and success of open source software. Figure 2–2 shows the relative measure of how organizations are now deploying Linux.

To avoid getting stung, technology organizations should pursue open source software agenda for at least part of their software deployment efforts. Not only does open source force organizations to become familiar with the requirements of their application computing infrastructures but it offers

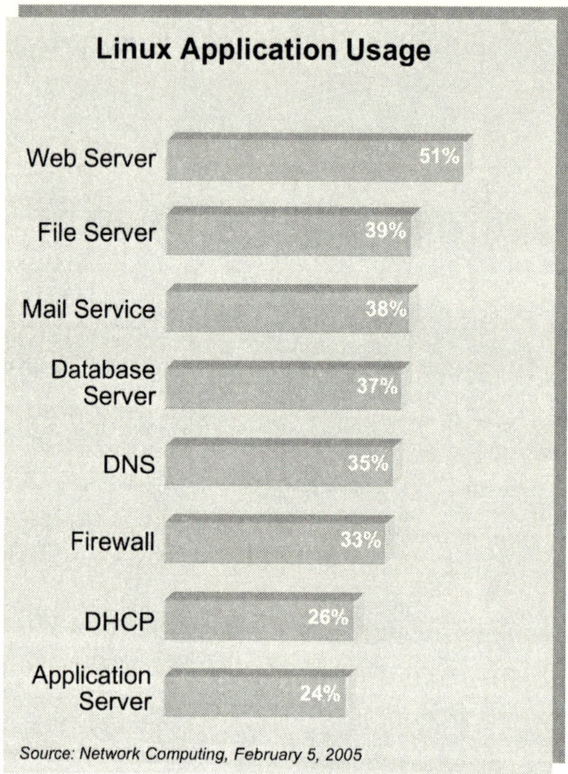

Figure 2-2. *Application Usage.*

them the opportunity to become more self-reliant through source code modification.

Open source empowers customers to implement projects in a way that is consistently mindful of enterprise goals rather than the goals of a proprietary software vendor. One of its strengths is its modularity, allowing users to tailor systems to meet specific needs. It also gives organizations free rein with their integration decisions. As shown in Figure 2–3, the pace of Linux and open source adoption will continue to accelerate as more organizations recognize these benefits.

The business model of open source reduces the cost of software development and maintenance by distributing it among many collaborators. The success of the open source model arises from copyright holders relaxing their control in exchange for more and better collaboration. Developers allow their software to be freely redistributed and modified, asking only for the same privileges in return.

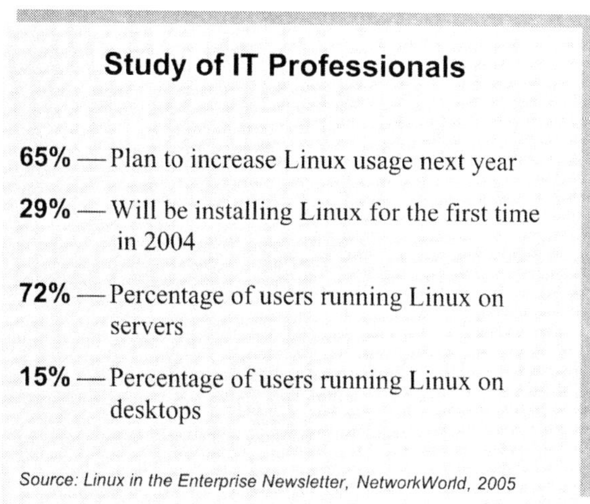

Figure 2-3. *IT Professionals Usage.*

Open source also is creating opportunities for the vendor community. In 2005, Sun Microsystems announced a major contribution to the open source community by making Solaris (http://www.opensolaris.org) as well as four of its Java technology innovations (http://www.java.net) freely available. Additionally, Project Looking Glass, Java 3D technology (the Java 3D API used by NASA for its command and control system for the Mars Rover mission), JDesktop Integration Components (JDIC) and JDesktop Network Components (JDNC) are also now available to the Java developer community Web site (http://www.javadesktop.org).

The aim of these open source projects, according to Sun, is to promote innovation, ease of development, integration and interactivity on the desktop and stimulate growth of the Java platform for all participants.

IBM also is participating in the open source movement with the recent release of the Eclipse source code. IBM rearranged its integrated development environment (IDE) software portfolio, with a value at USD $40 million. Since Eclipse allows developers to target Linux, Java or Windows, it potentially replaces Sun or Microsoft with a standard cross-development framework in which IBM can better integrate its proprietary Rational IDE software.

What Is Free Software?

Many people new to free software find themselves confused because the word "free" is not used the way they expect. To them free means "at no cost." However, an English dictionary lists almost 20 meanings for "free" and only one of them means "at no cost." The rest refer to liberty and lack of constraint. When we speak of free software, we mean freedom, not price.

Software that is free only in the sense that you don't need to pay to use it might not be free at all. You may be forbidden to pass it on, and you are almost certainly prevented from improving it. Consequently, software licensed at no cost is often a weapon in a marketing campaign to promote a related product or to drive a smaller competitor out of business. There is no guarantee that it will remain free.

For example, software placed in the public domain can be snapped up and put into non-commercial programs. Any improvements then made are lost to society. To stay free, software must be copyrighted and licensed.

To understand what kinds of things people are implying when they refer to software as "free," we must take a little detour into the world of software licenses. In most countries, software is automatically copyrighted. A license is the author's way of allowing use of his creation by others in ways that are acceptable to him. It is up to the author to include a license that declares the ways in which the software may be used. For a proper discussion of copyright, visit http://www.copyright.gov.

Of course, different circumstances call for different licenses. Software companies are looking to protect their assets so they release only compiled code and put many restrictions on the use of the software.

Authors of free software, on the other hand, generally are looking for some combination of the following:

- Not allowing use of their code in proprietary software. Since they are releasing their code for all to use, they don't want to see others steal it. Use of the code is seen as a trust: You may use it as long as you play by the same rules as the author.

- Protecting their identity as author of the code. People take great pride in their work and do not want someone else to come along and claim they wrote it.

- Distribution of source code. One of the problems with most commercial code is that you can't fix bugs or customize it since the source code is not available. Also, the company may decide to stop supporting the hardware you use. Many free licenses force the distribution of the source code. This protects users by allowing them to customize the software for their needs.

- Forcing any work that includes part of their work (called derived works) to use the same license.

One commonly misunderstood aspect of free software is that it can be sold for money. Even though the license allows for free redistribution, once a person gets a copy, he can redistribute it — and even charge for the distribution. While the idea of selling free software seems to go against the whole idea of free software, it is actually one of its strengths.

In practice, it costs essentially no money to make electronic copies of software. Supply and demand will keep the cost down. If it is convenient for a large piece of software to be distributed on some media, such as CDs, the vendor is free to charge what it wants. If the profit margin is too high, however, new vendors will enter the market and competition will drive the price down.

While free software is not totally free of constraints (only something in the public domain is), it gives users the flexibility to do what they need in order to get work done. At the same time, the constraints protect the rights of the author. Now that's freedom — and that's free software.

Source: http://www.debian.org/intro/free.

In the same vein, IBM has also adopted Apache for its Web server software, dropping the development of its own proprietary alternative. Apache continues to accelerate in popularity, with more than 50 percent of the Web server market today. This has allowed IBM to better position WebSphere applications with open source computing initiatives.

Safety in Numbers

There are many ripe opportunities where open source is readily available to provide a quick replacement for proprietary commercial applications. One common area is with commercial software that have either over-served the needs of the users, over-served the market for too long or is based on commonly accepted industry standards.

Areas of high commoditization often due to standards and maturity provide an excellent feeding ground for open source development. Good examples of this are with network management tools, Java application servers, HTTP servers, middleware, portals or content management systems. There are a plentitude of open source alternatives for these environments such as Apache, Coccon, JBoss, JOnAS, Geronimo, Tomcat, Python, PHP, Zope, just to name a few. These solutions can be easily tailored for your specific infrastructure requirements.

Another excellent opportunity for open source alternatives is in areas that have high collaboration between the user community and its developers. A classic example is with software development frameworks. Software development frameworks are an area where developers are very capable of collaborating with the projects. From Web development solutions (i.e. Struts, Spring MVC, WebWork, Tapestry), Java configuration management (i.e. Spring IoC, Hivemind, PicoContainer) to scripting language frameworks (i.e. Ruby and Python), open source solutions have been developed and perfected based on the personal needs of this specific user community.

In examining open source business models, it is apparent that IT organizations and vendors have much to gain. Businesses and agencies can freely use open source licensed software, allowing them to lower costs while delivering extremely reliable, enterprise-quality computing services. The critical point to understand is that open source is not the answer, but the means to the end. The key value of the open source community and the collective repository of its software is that it empowers organizations and the end-users who use its software.

The Open Sourcing Business

Commercially sold software is often based on open source. Well-known Web sites using open source software include Google and Yahoo. As Berkeley political scientist Steven Weber says, open source is about fostering creativity and challenging the status quo.

Here is a list of popular open source solutions and companies in the industry.

Operating Systems

Linux, FreeBSD, OpenBSD, NetBSD, OpenSolaris

Developed at the University of California, Berkeley, the BSD Unix OS variant provides the inner workings for network interconnect devices such as routers, virtual private networks (VPNs) and Domain Name System (DNS) servers. Another BSD-based open source project is Darwin, which is the base of Apple's Mac OS X. The OpenSolaris project is an open source operating system, a community development effort and a place for collaboration and conversation about Sun Microsystems' Solaris technology.

File Systems

Ext2, JFS, Lustre, Reiser, XFS

Linux brings to the market many open source file systems. These file systems are perhaps the fastest, most efficient and scalable alternatives in the industry. JFS and XFS have been donated to the open source community from IBM and SGI, respectively.

Internet

Apache, BIND, sendmail, Mozilla, OpenSSL

BIND is the distribution for all of the DNS root servers on the Internet. BIND and sendmail are so popular that no commercial competition has ever been successful in replacing them. Netcraft's June 2004 survey polled all of the Web sites it could find (totaling 51,635,284 sites) and discovered Apache accounted for more than 67 percent of the market. Microsoft had 21 percent and Sun less than 3 percent.

The OpenSSL Project is an open source effort providing a toolkit for implementing Secure Sockets Layer (SSL) and Transport Layer Security (TLS) protocols. It also provides a full-strength, general-purpose cryptography library.

Desktop

GNOME, KDE, OpenOffice, Java Desktop System, Zimbra, Thinkfree, Writely

GNOME and KDE are very powerful desktop environments. Both are part of the GNU Project, an effort to create a complete, free and easy-to-use desktop environment. OpenOffice, nearly equivalent to the MS Office suite of applications, uses open standards such as an XML-based file format. The Java Desktop System (JDS) is an open source desktop environment from Sun Microsystems.

Open source-based Zimbra Inc. challenges IBM and Microsoft in the collaboration software space with its Zimbra Collaboration Suite. Zimbra, Thinkfree and Writely are part of a growing number of companies that are betting on AJAX (Asynchronous JavaScript And XML). Using AJAX, developers can marry the graphical user interface of desktop computers with the benefits of the Web, creating an interactive user interface that's comparable to what's available with today's desktop applications.

Databases

MySQL, PostgreSQL, EnterpriseDB

MySQL is a key component of LAMP (Linux, Apache, MySQL, PHP/Perl/Python). PostgreSQL began at University of California, Berkeley. Both offer superior performance and rich database server functionality. EnterpriseDB was founded in 2004 to bring the benefits of open source databases to enterprise customers. EDB is built on top of PostgreSQL.

Middleware / Content Management

JBoss, JOnAS, Geronimo, Tomcat, Zope, Cocoon, Plone, Mambo, Drupal

Middleware encompasses a variety of applications including application servers, content management systems, intranets, portals and custom applications. JBoss is an open source J2EE-based application server implemented in Java. The Jakarta Project offers a diverse set of open source Java solutions and is a part of The Apache Software Foundation (ASF), which encourages development under an open software license. There are many other development projects under way at ASF. Among those is Tomcat, which is the most widely used JSP/Servlet Web application container and the reference implementation for the J2EE 1.4 JSP/Servlet specification.

Management Tools

Heartbeat, rsync, ClusterSSH, YUM, Cfengine, Nagios, OpenNMS, Beowulf Clusters

Heartbeat, rsync, ClusterSSH, YUM and CFengine represent a small sample of open source system management tools available to provide automated functions and controls. Nagios and OpenNMS are open source host, service and network monitoring programs. These solutions provide an effective framework that can easily be tailored to address most network and system management concerns. Beowulf Clusters provide a very scalable, high-performance clustering solution based on commodity hardware running Linux.

Programming Tools and Frameworks

Ant, Arch, Perl, PHP, Python, Ruby, Tcl/Tk, GNU Compiler Collection, JUnit, CruiseControl, Make, Autoconf, Automake, Eclipse IDE, Mono, Struts, Spring MVC, WebWork, Tapestry, Hibernate, Castor, iBatis, Spring IoC, Hivemind, PicoContainer

Apache Ant is a Java-based development tool. GNU Arch is a revision control system — similar in purpose to tools such as CVS, SCCS and Subversion — that is used to keep track of the changes made to a source tree and to help programmers combine and otherwise manipulate changes made by multiple people or at different times.

The Perl, PHP, Python, Ruby and Tcl/Tk programming languages are among the most popular engines on the Web. GCC, Make, Autoconf and Automake are the most powerful and extensible sets of compilers and development tools in the world. Almost all open source projects use them as their core development tool environment.

The Eclipse Integrated Development Environment (IDE) is the most widely used integrated development framework, with a series of tools that enable programmers to develop, deploy, test and debug Java-based applications. Mono is an open source development platform based on the .NET framework that allows developers to build Linux and cross-platform applications with improved developer productivity.

JUnit and CruiseControl provide a technological cornerstone for software testing. JUnit is for writing tests for small units of code, and CruiseControl builds and runs tests. This is critical in a distributed development environment, where testing needs to be fully automated.

Business Applications

Alfresco, GroundWork, Gluecode, SugarCRM, GreenPlum, WebGUI, OpenCms, Eclipse BI and Reporting, JasperReports, Pentaho, Compiere, Asterisk, JasperSoft

This is only a small sample of the ever-growing list of open source companies providing business application solutions for business intelligence, content management, enterprise resource management, software-based PBX, customer resource management and more. In fact, there is an open source equivalent to just about every type of commercial software available on the market.

Open Source Initiatives at Commercial Companies

Below is a very abbreviated list of companies that have active open source initiatives as part of their software or hardware development efforts.

ActiveState. ActiveState leads the industry in providing professional tools for Perl, Python and Tcl/tk developers.

Agitar. Agitar delivers tools for software quality testing, including automated test creation and management for Java application development.

Apple. Apple released the core layers of Mac OS X Server as an open source BSD operating system called Darwin. Apple was the first mainstream computer company to build its future around open source, and is partnering with the Apache Group, FreeBSD, NetBSD and other open source developers to work on evolving the Mac OS X platform. Apple has expanded its involvement by open sourcing the QuickTime Streaming Server and the OpenPlay network gaming toolkit.

Assembla. Assembla helps vendors grow with open source inspired strategies for new product initiatives. Assembla assists software vendors with developing differentiated product and technology strategies leveraging the competitive advantage afforded by open source software and development methods.

Covalent. Covalent Technologies develops commercial software enhancements and full commercial support packages for the Apache Web server platform. Covalent maintains its role as a founding member of the Apache Project and actively participates in the research, development and administrative efforts of the Apache Software Foundation.

Digium. Digium, the creater of Asterisk, has created an entire line of hardware that supports the full range of voice and data protocols that Asterisk supports. Digium hardware has been proven and tested in a wide range of installations worldwide providing a complete telecommunications platform.

Funambol. Funambol provides software infrastructure that allows developers to synchronize, provision and manage mobile devices. Funambol's mobile application server provides synchronization and management protocols for the wireless market.

HP. HP supports and bundles Linux on its complete line of servers. HP also offers integrated support options for commercial customers who want support running open source software.

IBM. IBM has chosen the open source Apache Web server to support and bundle with its WebSphere product line. IBM has since released Secure Mailer in open source and launched the AlphaWorks site to disseminate IBM technology in an open source form. Since that time, IBM's commitment to open source has grown substantially, from contributing a new journaled file system to Linux kernel development. The company has also made Linux the primary operating system on most of its server product lines.

JBoss. JBoss Inc. pioneered the Professional Open Source model, which combines the best of open source and proprietary software. JBoss provides royalty-free software and supports an active open source development community, but also provides a pay-for-support business model for companies that want traditional software support services. JBoss AS is widely recognized for supporting Java standards and was the first open source application server to achieve J2EE certification.

LogicBlaze. LogicBlaze Inc. is a leading provider of business integration solutions based on open source technologies. LogicBlaze combines open source development with professional services offerings.

MySQL. MySQL AB develops and markets a family of high-performance, affordable database servers and tools. With millions of installations world-

Rating System to Evaluate Open Source Software

Open source software has opened up many new doors for technology organizations in addressing their application needs. However, in order to embrace open source, companies often have get involved in the time-consuming process of testing and evaluating the software. This arduous process of validating open source solutions to ensure that they perform reliably and offer the functionality they claim has actually slowed the adoption rate of open source.

Commercial Linux companies now recognize that open source applications won't be broadly adopted until they're supported, certified and tested. Traditionally, hardware and software vendors take care of compatibility testing for their commercial software, but in the open source community, you've been essentially on your own.

To address the problem, SpikeSource Inc. and SourceLabs Inc. offer a Web site of open source applications that have been tested for compatibility. Other vendors have specific validation programs for particular hardware and software configurations. Additionally, a software rating system has been developed to evaluate open source software.

Carnegie Mellon University, Intel, O'Reily CodeZoo and SpikeSource have devised a rating system intended to relieve some of the testing and evaluation challenges that often plague IT organizations in their pursuit of implementing open source. This initiative, known as Business Readiness Ratings (BRR), employs a scoring system that rates open source software according to 12 categories, such as its functionality, usability, quality, security, documentation and technical support.

BRR gives companies a trusted, unbiased source for determining whether the open source software they are considering is mature enough to adopt. There are more than 100,000 open source projects listed on SourceForge, SourceLabs, CodeHaus, Tigris, Java.net and Open Symphony. BRR helps organizations assess which open source software is best suited to their needs and enables them to share their findings within the open source community.

The goal of BRR is to promote the use and adoption of open source software. It is a tool that not only helps technology organizations select software but also assists open source developers in creating software geared toward the needs of enterprise consumers. For more information about the details of the rating system, visit http://www.openbrr.org.

Another helpful open source validation tool is the Navica Open Source Maturity Model (OSMM). The OSMM is a formal process to assess the maturity level of open source software depending on how scalable, manageable and supportable a given software product is. For more information, visit http://www.navica.com.

wide, MySQL is a key part of LAMP (Linux, Apache, MySQL, PHP/Perl/Python), a fast-growing open source enterprise software stack.

Novell. With its acquisitions of SUSE and Ximian, Novell provides a full range of Linux solutions for the enterprise, including a desktop and server OS, groupware, systems management, security and collaboration solutions. It also provides Linux-based solutions for identity management, Web services and cross-platform networking services, all supported by professional services, technical support and educational services. Novell created The Open Source Now Fund, a nonprofit corporation formed exclusively to assist companies developing software under the General Public License and nonprofit institutions supporting such companies.

OpenLogic. As a provider of software and services, OpenLogic helps organizations create and manage their own integrated, commercial-grade open source development and deployment environments.

Open Source Experts. Open Source Experts promotes open source by providing a directory of open source experts by region/country/state via their Solution Provider Indices.

OpenXource. OpenXource helps organizations define an open source strategy. The process includes meeting with the stakeholders in an organization to address marketing, sales, engineering, finance, legal and executive perspectives.

Optaros. Optaros is a consulting and systems integration firm that helps large enterprises solve business problems by providing services and solutions that maximize the benefits of open source software.

Red Hat. Red Hat plays a key role in several open source projects, some of which have become standard technology across the industry. The Fedora Project is a Red Hat-sponsored and community-supported open source project with the goal of working with the Linux community to build a complete, general-purpose operating system exclusively from free software.

SGI. SGI has long funded prominent contributors to open source development efforts. It helps sponsor the Samba project (a Windows-compatible file and print service that runs on Linux or Unix systems) and a port of Linux for SGI/MIPS machines. SGI open sourced GLX (OpenGL extensions to X11) and the XFS journaling file system, and launched an open source site (http://freeware.sgi.com). SGI has dropped most support for its proprietary Unix variant and is focusing its efforts on Linux for its high-end server products.

Sleepycat. Sleepycat Software makes Berkeley DB, a widely used open source development database. Berkeley DB offers programmers a highly efficient and scalable database that requires virtually no database administration. Berkeley DB is distributed under a dual license: an open source license that permits internal use and redistribution within open source applications at no charge, and a commercial license that enables customers to redistribute Berkeley DB within proprietary applications.

Sun Microsystems. Sun Microsystems has contributed to many open source development efforts. OpenSolaris involved the release of more than 1,600 patents associated with the Solaris OS. Additionally, Sun has released its licensing rights to Forte IDE for Java, the Mozilla Web browser project, Project Looking Glass, Java 3D technology (used by NASA for its command and control system for the Mars Rover mission), JDesktop Integration Components (JDIC) and JDesktop Network Components (JDNC). These are now all available to the Java developer community as part of javadesktop.org.

Trolltech. Trolltech is a provider of technologies for Linux and cross-platform software development including products such as Qt, a cross-platform C++ application framework, and Qtopia, an application platform built for embedded Linux. Qt has been used to build thousands of commercial applications worldwide, and is the basis of the open source KDE desktop environment. Qtopia is a widely used application platform for numerous Linux-based PDAs and Smartphones.

VA Software. VA Software is a provider of open source software, information and community support. VA Software has been a tremendous supporter of OSTG (Open Source Technology Group). One of the group's sites, SourceForge.net, is the world's leading community-driven media network and the largest open source repository.

Virtuas. Virtuas offers an array of professional services around open source software, from high-level consulting, architectural assessment, educational services and delivery and documentation services.

WindRiver. Wind River Systems is a global leader in device software optimization. Wind River is also very active in the Eclipse Foundation. Eclipse is an open source community whose projects are focused on providing an extensible development platform and application frameworks for building software.

Zope. Zope Corporation developed the Zope content management system, which provides Web sites with dynamic content creation and management tools, usable by both programmers and non-programmers. Its core technology is entirely open source and is powered by the open source Python programming language.

Where Can I Find Open Source?

There are a number of places on the Internet to find open source software.

BerliOS Source Well

The goal of BerliOS is to provide support for different interest groups of open source. BerliOS targets developers and users of open source software, including commercial software vendors and support companies. For more information, visit http://developer.berlios.de.

Codehaus

The Codehaus is an open source project repository with a strong emphasis on Java. Codehaus welcomes software with multiple licenses as long as at least one of them is a business-friendly open source license. Projects proposed to Codehaus are typically subject to a selection review process.

Darwin

Through the open source model, Apple allows developers to customize and enhance Apple software. Major projects include Darwin, the core operating system of Mac OS X, and the Streaming Server, which runs on a wide variety of platforms. For more information, visit http://developer.apple.com/darwin.

GNU

The GNU Project was launched in 1984 to develop a complete Unix-like operating system that would be free software. This is also the Web site of the Free Software Foundation, the principal organizational sponsor of GNU. For more information, visit http://www.gnu.org.

Freshmeat

Freshmeat maintains the Web's largest index of Linux, Unix and Palm OS software. Thousands of applications, which are mostly released under an open source license, are cataloged. For more information, visit http://www.freshmeat.net.

Linux Archives

Linux Archives, an advertising revenue-based Web site, provides a source of both Linux applications and distributions. It also provides a list of "Top 100 Linux Web Sites." For more information, visit http://www.linuxarchives.com.

Open Source Directory

OSDir is owned and operated by O'Reilly & Associates, a publisher of computer technology information including books, conferences and Web sites. OSDir is its open source portal providing Linux information and software. For more information, visit http://www.osdir.com.

Open Source Initiative

Open Source Initiative is a non-profit organization dedicated to managing and promoting the open source definition. OSI provides copies of approved open source license agreements. For more information, visit http://www.opensource.org.

OpenLogic

OpenLogic has collected over 170 mature, stable, integration-ready open source projects and packaged them with sample applications, robust documentation along with point-and-click installation package. OpenLogic provides quarterly updates in addition managing open source usage policies and legal exposure. For more information, visit http://www.openlogic.com.

SourceForge

SourceForge is the world's largest open source software development Web site. The mission of SourceForge.net is to enrich the open source community by providing a centralized place for open source developers to control and manage their projects. For more information, visit http://www.sourceforge.net.

Swik

Sponsored by SourceLabs, the Swik directory facilitates the sharing of information about open source projects and includes project documentation, download sites, reviews and descriptions. For more information, visit http://www.swik.net.

Chapter 3

Free and Open Source Software

As we enjoy great advantages from inventions of others, we should be glad of an opportunity to serve others by any invention of ours; and this we should do freely and generously.
— *Benjamin Franklin*

Open source is not only a tour de force in the software development world; it has become a cause célèbre for many organizations. If there are two things we notice about public licenses today, the first is the confusion surrounding them and the second is their abundance.

Because of this abundance, free software licensing has become a difficult and obscure topic. But this method of licensing is one of the distinctive and important things about Linux.

The term "free and open source software," or FOSS for short, has come to represent software that falls under one of two definitions: the Free Software Definition as defined by the Free Software Foundation (http://www.fsf.org), and the Open Source Definition of the Open Source Initiative (http://www.opensource.org). These licenses differ slightly, but they agree fundamentally on three freedoms:

- The freedom to copy
- The freedom to make derivative works
- The freedom to redistribute

Open Source Licensing

As a point of clarification within the open source community, the term "free software" generally tends to emphasize the rights of the software user. Such people may identify themselves as members of the free software movement officially represented by the Free Software Foundation (FSF). Richard Stallman is a leader of this group and the author of the prominent licensing terms associated with it, namely the GNU General Public License (all subsequent references of this licensing agreement will just use the acronym "GPL").

Other people prefer to argue the value of open source on another basis, such as its cost, security or reliability. Eric Raymond was one of the original founders of the term "open source software" and is widely regarded as a leader of this group known as the Open Source Initiative (OSI).

The free software group is often perceived as more ideological, and tends to argue for open source from a basis of political theory. The FSF has never been reluctant to point out that its goals were primarily social and political, not technical or economic. On the other hand, the OSI, which was formed much later (the term was coined in the late 1990s, whereas free software dates back to Richard Stallman's writings nearly a decade earlier), is more business-friendly.

The phrase "open source software" has largely come to designate that portion of the community which participates in making, distributing, and selling products and services facilitated by free software without specifically and directly embracing the political and social goals of the movement.

Eric Raymond once summed up this divide by pointing out that in the 1960's many radical groups agreed on their goals, but couldn't agree on the means to reach those goals. In the FOSS world, both sides agree on the means — public release of code — but disagree on the end to reach that goal.

There are many open source licenses of various kinds, and all of them agree absolutely on the nature of the first two freedoms. But the third freedom — freedom to redistribute — is trickier. Two prominent licenses, the GPL and the BSD (Berkeley Software Distribution), differ on this key point.

General Public License

Developed by the FSF, the GPL is the archetype and most influential of all open source licenses. First released in 1989, many of the most important FOSS programs of the past 20 years are licensed under the GPL, including the Linux operating system, the GCC compiler suite, MySQL database engine and JBoss application server. Freshmeat.net reported in 2003 that 72 percent of the 25,286 software packages it tracked are GPL licensed. The next two most popular licenses were the LGPL (4.47 percent) and the BSD (4.17 percent).

Last updated in 1991, the GPL is now being modernized. For the first time in 14 years, the Free Software Foundation will update its licensing, and when a draft of the new license is available, the debate will be contentious and will most likely take at least a year to resolve all potential disagreements with its new terms (see sidebar **The Rewriting of the GPL**). The license is being modernized to deal with new realities in the computing industry, such as widespread patenting of software, computers that will run only software that has been cryptographically signed and software services available over the Internet.

Scrutiny of the license is increasing as the free and open source software projects it governs have become more widely used by mainstream IT organizations. And even though the SCO Group is having difficulty proving the merits of its USD $5 billion lawsuit against IBM — alleging that Big Blue violated a contract by moving proprietary Unix software to open source Linux — the case has served to bring even more attention to open source licensing issues.

One distinguishing feature of the GPL is that it requires derivative works to also be distributed under the GPL licensing terms, thus ensuring that once software is released under the GPL, it will remain open source permanently. In other words, software that contains GPL software must be itself released under the license. In fact, if Microsoft wished to include a GPL licensed utility in Windows, the entire OS would need to be made open source.

While a GPL license cannot prohibit changes to the source code, it can limit how that modified code is distributed. The most common restriction specifies that any changes must be distributed as separate patches that can be integrated into the original source code (or ignored) at the discretion of the user.

Another method of achieving the same aim is to force modified code to carry a different name or version from the original. Both restrictions serve to establish the responsibility for software changes while preserving the brand or product identity.

Protecting Ideas

The intent of the GPL is to ensure software code remains publicly available, or free. The GPL serves a purpose that most legal drafters would do anything possible to avoid: it licenses copyrighted material for modification and redistribution in every one of the world's systems of copyright law. The terms of the GPL encourage continual improvement and development while preserving the control and protecting ideas of the original author of that code.

In order to do this, it is necessary to use copyrights, a method of protecting the rights of the creator. In fact, in most countries software you write is automatically copyrighted. A copyright license enables the author to allow use of his creation in ways that are acceptable to him. This license is a form of protection provided under Title 17 of the U.S. Code.

Different circumstances call for different types of copyright licenses. For example, most commercial software companies protect their assets by only releasing them in machine-readable (compiled) form and restricting their use by those accessing them.

On the other hand, beyond the legal permission that the GPL extends to those who wish to copy, modify, and share free software, the GPL also embodies a code of industry conduct with respect to the practices by which free software is distributed. Under the GPL licensing scheme, software developers and programmers generally agree to abide by a different understanding:

- It does not allow the use of their code in any proprietary software.
- It protects the identity of the author of the code.
- It provides free distribution of source code.
- It forces any work that includes any part of the code (such works are called derived works) to use the same copyright license.

Copylefting

The GPL gives the user three rights: 1) to copy the software and give it away, 2) to change the software and 3) to have access to the source code. The key requirement is that the user passes on these rights, unimpaired, to other users. This automatically means that any changes passed on by the user must be distributed along with the source code. It is intended that developers will register a copyright for their programs. This is a simple, yet effective procedure that guarantees legal rights to controlling the distribution of the software.

Ideology aside, the GPL is intended to be a pro-user license, unlike commercial licenses that are biased towards the vendor. But there are several other licensing agreements used with open source software: the LGPL (Lesser General Public License), which is a variant of the GPL, and various

BSD licenses (as discussed below). These licenses tend to be less demanding about conditions placed on code derived from the original source. The goal of GPL was to give users freedom and prevent GNU software from being turned into proprietary software. As a result, the term "copyleft" was invented.

Copyleft uses copyright law but flips it over to serve the opposite of its usual purpose — instead of a means of privatizing software, it becomes a means of keeping software free. The central idea of copyleft is that we give everyone permission to run the program, copy the program, modify the program and distribute modified versions but not permission to add restrictions of their own. For an effective copyleft license agreement, modified versions of the software also must be free.

The copyrighted program can be distributed in any way the copyright holder chooses: it can be turned into an OEM agreement and licensed to another vendor, or it can be sold outright to another vendor and still be distributed under the copyleft license. In essence, copyleft eliminates the middleman who takes away a developer's freedom.

If, however, the developer were to place the program under the public domain, it is free to all comers: anyone could take it, modify it, and copyright and sell the results, thus returning the software to proprietary ways. The primary difference between FOSS and a piece of work in the Public Domain is that under the Public Domain the original author has disclaimed the copyright in the work; no copyright exists. This is not true with FOSS.

Viral Licensing

The big issue surrounding the GPL is the "viral" licensing effect. The principle is that any code combined with GPL licensed software must be issued under the GPL. Some people regard this effect of the GPL as being viral, and it is a reason frequently given by developers unwilling to use the GPL licensing scheme. And in some cases it is difficult to comply with the GPL, especially when dealing with operating systems.

The BSD and MIT licenses offer a counter to the anti-proprietary effects of the GPL. These licenses puts no restrictions on whether you distribute the open source software outside your organization, modify the code or combine it with your code — the three cardinal sins covered by the GPL. In essence, the BSD or MIT license allows you to take the source code proprietary; that is, once you modify it, there is no obligation to redistribute the modified code (consequently you cannot put GPL code into a BSD or MIT binary). Thus, derivative works forbidden by the GPL are allowed by the BSD license. However, the downside of this is what is known as "forking."

It should be noted that not all open source licensing schemes utilize a reciprocity provision like the GPL or LGPL. As mentioned, these reciprocity provisions put a constraint on any subsequent redistributions of modified software code. The BSD and MIT open source licensing agreements do not maintain this same constraint.

Lesser GPL

The LGPL is an alternative form of copylefting. The provisions held by the GPL created several problems specifically for software library developers, leading to the creation of the LGPL.

Originally known as the Library GPL, it's now generally referred to as the Lesser GPL. Under this license, the libraries themselves and any derived works must be distributed under GPL-type provisions but software that merely uses the libraries can use another license. Many people writing libraries want proprietary programs to be able to call them, so for them the LGPL is a popular choice.

The LGPL is largely identical to the purpose and contents of the GPL. This means that the free copying, distribution and modification of software and libraries must be ensured. The source text — including the source text of modified versions — must be available to everyone.

If the libraries were subject to GPL, no programs other than those subject to GPL would be allowed to link these libraries. Programs using libraries subject to LGPL may be distributed subject to license terms and conditions, which can be freely selected. However, the source code for the libraries subject to LGPL must be available to customers so they can modify and re-link the program code.

BSD License

On the other end of the spectrum is the BSD (Berkeley Software Distribution) license, developed in 1977. The Computer Science Research Group at the University of California, Berkeley was doing a lot of research work on early Unix systems, and acted as a hub for the collaborative research community. The regents of the university developed a simple license for their work to encourage new research and adoption of the software.

The BSD license permits the free copying of software with or without the distribution of the modified source code as long as the copyright notice and the BSD license are included with its redistribution. Without written permission, neither the name of the university nor the names of the authors may be used for advertising or marketing purposes, and both parties are exempt from any legal claims and liabilities.

BSD suggests, but does not require, that modifications to source code be returned to the developer community, and allows derived products to use other licenses, including proprietary licenses. BSD licensed code also can be contained in, or can contain, code that uses other licenses. However, the BSD license does allow any software company to integrate BSD-licensed source code into one of its products and subsequently keep the code undisclosed.

The flexibility of this license has allowed companies to create proprietary products based on BSD code. Mac OS X, based on BSD Unix, is one example. The license is useful for companies wishing to encourage the broad adoption of their software in both the open source and proprietary worlds.

BSD has been used as the basic model for many other open source licenses. Known as Berkeley-style licensing, this model was used for the MIT Project Athena license (used for the X11 windowing technology, including all the contributions from Hewlett-Packard and Digital Equipment Corporation). The Berkeley-style license was also the model used in the early Apache community in 1995. The original Apache Web server was created out of work developed at the National Center for Supercomputing Applications, University of Illinois, and the license reflected the research base and collaborative development in that community (in 2004 the Apache 2.0 license was released specifically for this software).

MIT License

The MIT License is similar to the BSD license, except for the notice prohibiting the use of the name of the copyright holder. Many groups use the MIT license for their software, including MetaKit, XFree86 and X11.

According to the FSF's license list, the MIT license is more accurately called the X11 license because MIT has many licenses for software. However, the OSI refers to it as the MIT License, as do many other groups.

What is Forking?

Some companies, like TrollTech, MySQL and Sleepycat, use a fundamentally different approach with their licensing scheme. The guiding principle behind these companies' licensing terms is *quid pro quo* ("something for something").

The basic concept is that if you wish to derive a commercial advantage by not releasing your application under an open source license, you must purchase an appropriate "commercial" license from the licensee. By purchasing commercial licenses, you are no longer obliged to publish any modified source code.

Alternatively, OSI-approved licenses allow users to develop, modify and distribute their software freely (the OSI is the nonprofit group that reviews licenses and awards official open source status to those that meet their Open Source Definition). By licensing software this way, developers can take active part of the open source community. This is what some people call a dual license strategy. The user is free to use and distribute derivative works unless it is for a commercial application.

The Politics of Forking

So what is forking? Forking is the effect of having a software development project split into two independent development efforts from the original project. There are a couple of basic reasons for forking; the simplest is the software license itself. For instance, the BSD license enables developers to take code private and not make improvements public. Originally, Unix system vendors forked the Unix code base in order to promote and leverage their own hardware enhancements within the commercial IT marketplace.

Politics is the other basic cause of forking, such as when the developers of glibc (the C library in the GNU system and most systems with the Linux kernel) ignored Intel graphics requirements. Fortunately, libc, the forked version of glibc, got back together again with the release of glibc2. Unfortunately, BSD is still split, and has gone down the trail far enough that the divisions cannot get back together.

The lesson here is that there is a benefit in requiring modifications to be open source. Linux can serve as an example of the anti-forking properties of the GPL. It is the open source requirement — for the received code and all changes to it — that makes forking less likely.

If we look at the condition of BSD, we see that any time a developer may take the source code, modify it and distribute it in a closed version there is an absolute tendency to have the code fork, as demonstrated by the record. On the other hand, the GPL source tree shows a tendency to pull the branches together.

The various licensing agreements and their effect on forking and granting end-user rights are illustrated in Figure 3–1.

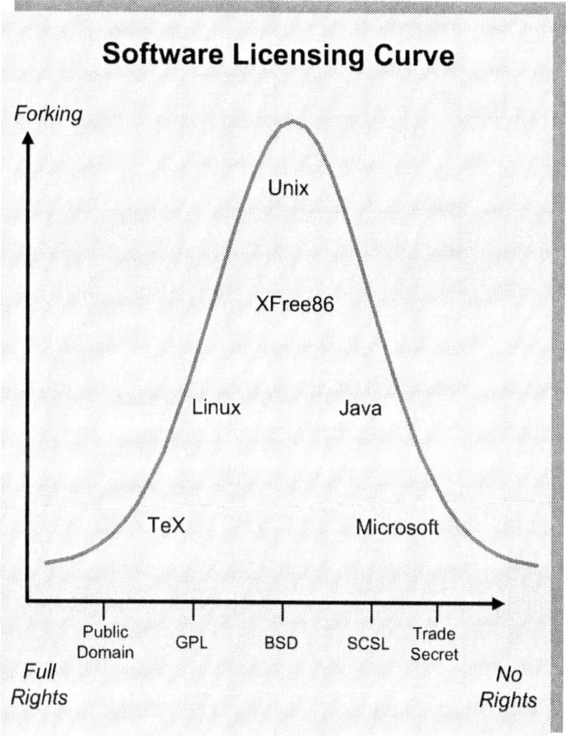

Figure 3-1. *Software Licensing.*

Proprietary Software & Dual Licensing

Companies open sourcing existing applications often create customized licenses, as Computer Associates has done with its Ingres database and the CA Trusted Open Source License. This allows third parties to incorporate Ingres into existing products as long as the Ingres source is included with the product.

Another popular scheme, adopted by MySQL, Trolltech and Sleepycat Software, is to release software under two licenses — usually the GPL and

The Rewriting of the GPL

It is estimated that approximately 70 percent of the 100,000-plus open-source projects listed on SourceForce.net were licensed under the GPL, which had its last major update in 1991. Since then, change in the software industry — such as the rise of the importance of software patent issues and questions about how the GPL handles derivate works — has made this update necessary.

Conflict between patent rights and Linux was inevitable because of the GPL's "liberty or death" provision about patents, which forbids GPL users from putting patent license restrictions on downstream distributes.

One option that the FSF is considering is making it necessary for organizations that distribute GPL software to pledge that they're also explicitly giving the right to use the patents found in their code. Under U.S. copyright law, there is an implicit right that lets users employ patents in this way. That right is not explicit, however, and it covers only U.S. customers.

The ongoing efforts and challenges associated with the rewriting of the GPL couldn't be better explained than how Eben Moglen summarizes it below:

> *Some copyright licenses are no doubt known, in the restricted circle of one firm or law office, as the achievement of a single author's acumen or insight. But it is safe to say that there is no other copyright license in the world that is so strongly identified with the achievements, and the philosophy, of a single public figure. Richard Matthew Stallman is a profoundly important figure in the history of his time, and the GPL is as representative of his ideas, and the effect those ideas had upon the world, as the literary output of any novelist, essayist, scholar, or public official. Mr. Stallman remains the GPL's author, with as much right to preserve its integrity as a work representative of his intentions as any other author or creator.*
>
> *Changes to the GPL, for whatever reason they are undertaken, must not retard the underlying movement in the*

direction of freer exchange of knowledge. To the extent that the movement has identified technological or legal measures likely to be harmful to freedom, such as "trusted computing" or a broadening of the scope of patent law, the GPL needs to address those issues from a perspective of political principle and the needs of the movement, not from primary regard for the industrial or commercial consequences.

The GPL serves, and must continue to serve, multiple purposes. Those purposes are fundamentally diverse, and they inevitably conflict. Development of GPL version 3 has been an ongoing process within the Free Software Foundation; Richard Stallman and I, along with our colleagues, have never stopped considering possible modifications. We have consulted, formally and informally, a very broad array of participants in the free software ecology, from industry, the academy, and the garage. Those conversations have occurred in many countries and several languages, over two decades, as the technology of software development and distribution changed around us.

Soon, the pace of that conversation will change, as a particular proposal becomes the centerpiece. The Foundation will, before it emits a first discussion draft, publicize the process by which it intends to gather opinion and suggestions. The Free Software Foundation recognizes that the reversioning of the GPL is a crucial moment in the evolution of the free software community, and the Foundation intends to meet its responsibilities to the makers, distributors and users of free software. In doing so, it hopes to hear all relevant points of view, and to make decisions that reflect the many disparate purposes that the license must serve. Its primary concern remains, as it has from the beginning, the creation and protection of freedom. It recognizes that the best protection of freedom is a growing and vital community of the free.

 Eben Moglen is professor of law at Columbia University Law School. He serves without fee as General Counsel of the Free Software Foundation, and is the founding Director-Counsel of the Software Freedom Law Center. You can read more of his writing at moglen.law.columbia.edu.

a commercial license, or a dual licensing model. Under the dual license strategy, a software company offers free use of its software with some limitations or commercial distribution rights and a larger set of features for a fee.

With the dual license approach, free use carries certain conditions. Typically, any modifications that are distributed must also be made public in source code form, and companies cannot use the free version as a component of any product or solution they commercialize. This prevents third parties from developing improvements that would rival the original open source software.

The dual license approach is not typically one integrated license. Instead, it is a business policy that permits a customer to choose one of two licenses: either the commercial license or, typically, the GPL.

So what is the incentive for dual license vendors to license software without charge? A free option facilitates new business in a number of ways, including improved customer awareness and faster adoption, stronger competitive positioning, and a large base of users to find bugs and recommend improvements to the software.

Proprietary software is not open source. It is owned by an individual or organization — usually the software manufacturer — and usually has legal copyright protection. The use of the software is subject to the terms of the owner's license agreement. These terms usually prohibit duplicating, disseminating and modifying the software. Software of this kind is sometimes offered for free on condition that the applicable terms of the license are adhered to.

OSI refers to the GPL, LGPL, BSD and MIT as the classic open source licenses. If you want to develop open source, consider the GPL for applications, the LGPL for libraries (and possibly for software used in service-oriented architectures) and the MIT license if you want your code incorporated into proprietary code.

Other Licensing Schemes

Currently, there are nearly 60 different open source license schemes. Many people and organizations have written their own software licenses. This is actually frowned upon the by the open source community because writing a license that does what you want involves many additional issues. Too often the wording is either ambiguous or people create conditions that conflict with each other.

Writing a license that would hold up in court is even more difficult. Luckily, there are a number of licenses already written and publicly available. Some of the features these licenses have in common.

- You can install the software on as many machines as you want.
- Any number of people may use the software at one time.
- You can make as many copies of the software as you want and give them to whomever you want (free or open redistribution).
- There are no restrictions on modifying the software (except for keeping certain notices intact).
- There is no restriction on distributing, or even selling, the software.

For a complete list, visit http://opensource.org/licenses. The following is an abbreviated list of these licenses. Most are compatible with the GPL.

Apache License

Version 2.0 is a free software license that is incompatible with the GPL because it has certain patent termination clauses that the GPL does not require. It is advisable not to use Apache licenses for software you write. However, there is no reason to avoid running programs that have been released under this license.

Apple Public Source License

Version 2 provides a free software license, incompatible with the GPL. It is advisable not to use this license for new software you write, but it is safe to use and improve the software released under this license.

Common Development and Distribution License (CDDL)

Sun Microsystems has emphasized its support for the open source software movement but criticized the GPL. It was acknowledged that these views about the GPL would likely be unpopular, but that Sun would continue to eschew the licensing model for future projects.

Sun Microsystems believes the GPL is tantamount to economic imperialism since it expressly limits choice by disallowing the inclusion of non-GPL code into GPL projects. Those who use the GPL as a foundation for proprietary software dislike having to give their intellectual property back into the world. As a result, Sun Microsystems has authored CDDL for its release of OpenSolaris.

The CDDL is a modified version of the MPL (Mozilla Public License) Version 1.1. Like the MPL, the CDDL is not expected to be compatible with the GPL, since it contains requirements that are not in the GPL. The primary difference between the GPL and CDDL is the latter allows developers to guard their work if they decide they want to. CDDL is open only to the point where developers start trying to take advantage of its being open source. Sun inherently prevents technologies of Sun origin from making their way into GPL licensed systems and software projects, such as Linux and the GNU tool set.

The decision not to open source everything in the license was the result of Sun not being legally able to release those parts of Solaris that it doesn't have full ownership of (such as the GNOME desktop), and also probably because Sun wants to maintain control of its software. This controversy over the GPL has led to the OSI to reform the system for using open source code under license. CDDL is an OSI-approved open source license.

Java Research License (JRL)

The JRL was created specifically for those who want to use Java technologies as subject matter for learning and research. This includes schools and universities as well as companies that are interested in investigating new products and services using Java technologies.

This research license is only for initial research and development projects, and can be used for Java.net projects among peers who have agreed to its terms. JRL is intended to simplify and relax the terms of the existing "research" section of the current Sun Community Source License (SCSL) used to evolve Jini technology.

Projects developed using this license must sign a commercial agreement and meet Java compatibility requirements if the project is released commercially. The JRL is intended for all Java platforms, profiles and standard extensions currently covered under Java SCSL licenses (e.g. J2SE, J2EE and J2ME).

Modified BSD License

This is the original BSD license, modified by removal of the advertising clause. It is a simple, permissive non-copyleft free software license, compatible with the GPL.

Mozilla Public License (MPL)

The MPL was developed in 1998 when Netscape made its browser open source. MPL contains more requirements for derivative works than the BSD license, but fewer than the GPL or LGPL. This is one of the first licenses created by a corporation, and that heritage shows through in its legal structure and depth compared to other open source licenses.

The MPL divides a software work into files, which are separated into (a) the open source part (called "Covered") and (b) anything the user adds. This arrangement allows developers to add their own files and distribute them with the Covered files, provided they do not modify the Covered files. If they do modify the Covered files, then they must distribute those modified files under open source MPL rules.

The MPL license makes it easy for proprietary and open source software to work together. If, for instance, the developer uses the published API to call the open source files, they can keep their own code proprietary. If they want to add some API calls to the Covered files, that's fine, too; they just need to share that part of the code.

Netscape Public License (NPL)

This is a free software license, not a strong copyleft, and incompatible with the GPL. It consists of the Mozilla Public License with an added clause that permits Netscape to use your added code even in their proprietary versions of the program. Of course, they do not give you permission to use their code in the analogous way. It is advisable not to use the NPL.

Artistic License

The Artistic License is more of an editorial than a strict software license. The author, Larry Wall (inventor of the Perl programming language), didn't want to get into legal trouble but he wanted to clarify his view of the GPL; consequently he wrote the Artistic License not so much to be legally binding but to encourage the "good" people.

With the Artistic License, you can modify the source code and take it private if you also supply the standard version of Perl with it. Equally, you must be careful that any modified file still works with the standard version.

Public Domain

Being in the public domain is not a license. Rather, it means the material is not copyrighted and no license is needed. Practically speaking, though, if a work is in the public domain, it might as well have an all-permissive non-copyleft free software license. Public domain doesn't mean a work is owned by no one; it means it is owned by everyone (It is BSD without restrictions). Public domain status is compatible with the GPL.

Sun Community Source License (SCSL)

Under the terms of the SCSL, Sun shares the rights to the source code among a community of developers to enhance and evolve Java and Jini technologies. The SCSL establishes responsibilities to ensure implementations are compliant and provides an incentive for innovation and invention by allowing licensees to create proprietary enhancements in their implementations, but with two significant obligations:

- Compatibility among deployed versions of the software is required and enforced through testing.
- Proprietary modifications and extensions including performance improvements are allowed.

These important differences and other details make SCSL a combination of proprietary licensing schemes and open source licensing models.

X11 License

This is a simple, permissive non-copyleft free software license, compatible with the GPL. Older versions of XFree86 used the same license, and some of the current variants of XFree86 do so as well. This license is sometimes called the MIT license, but that term is misleading, since Massachusetts Institute of Technology has used many licenses for releasing software.

Licensing Lingua Franca

To keep things in context in our discussion of open source software, there are salient terms that need clear definitions and understanding. For the purpose of clarity and accuracy, the following terms are presented and defined.

Commercial Software

Commercial software is developed by a business that aims to profit from it. "Commercial" and "proprietary" are not the same thing. Most commercial software is proprietary but there is commercial free software, and there is non-commercial non-free software. For example, MySQL is distributed under the GPL, but it is also sold commercially.

Copyleft

When software is offered under copyleft licensing terms, it is free software whose redistribution does not permit any additional licensing terms applied or implied. This means that every copy of the software, even if it has been modified, must remain as free software. In the GNU Project, almost all the software is copylefted, because the goal is to give users the freedoms implied by the term "free software."

Copyleft is a general concept. To actually copyleft a program, you need to use a specific set of distribution terms. In practice, nearly all copylefted software uses the GPL terms and conditions.

Free Software

Free software is software that comes with permission for anyone to use, copy and distribute it, either verbatim or with modifications. This means source code must be available. Free software is a matter of freedom, not price.

Note: Many languages have two separate words for "free" as in freedom and "free" as in zero price. The French have words like libre and gratuity, but unfortunately, we do not have an adjective that refers unambiguously to the concept of freedom. This is unfortunate, because such a word would be useful here.

Freeware

The term freeware has no clear accepted definition, but it is commonly used for packages that permit redistribution but not modification (and their source code is not available).

GPL

The GNU General Public License is one specific set of distribution terms for copylefting a program. The GNU Project uses it as the distribution terms for almost all GNU software. The GPL depends heavily on the Berne Convention, but it is written in a legal language very reminiscent of U.S. copyright law. A new version is being drafted (most likely to be released in 2007) to support the current software development environment by recognizing global copyright laws more explicitly.

GNU

GNU is software that is released under the auspices of the GNU Project. Most but not all GNU software is copylefted. All GNU software is free software.

GNU/Linux is a free Unix-like operating system that is either written by the staff of the Free Software Foundation or contributed by volunteers. Since the purpose of GNU is to be free, every single component in the GNU system is free software.

Non-Copylefted Free Software

Non-copylefted free software comes from the author with permission to redistribute and modify but adds additional restrictions to it. If a program is free but not copylefted, then some versions may not be free.

A software company can compile the program, with or without modifications, and distribute the executable file as a proprietary software product. The X Window System essentially does this.

The X Consortium releases X11 with distribution terms that make it non-copylefted free software. If you wish, you can get a free copy, however there are non-free versions. In fact, the developers of X11 charged for it for awhile before deciding to make it free.

Open Source Software

The term "open source software" is often used to mean the same thing as free software. However, this definition is not quite accurate. Open source software implies license restrictions that would be considered too restrictive for free software.

Public Domain Software

Public domain software is software that is not copyrighted. In some cases, an executable program can be in the public domain but the source code is not available. This is not free software since free software requires accessibility of source code. Most free software is not in the public domain; it is copyrighted, and the copyright holders have legally given permission for everyone to use it in freedom, using a free software license.

Public domain is a legal term that means "not copyrighted." Under the Berne Convention, which most countries have signed, anything written down is automatically copyrighted, including programs. If you want a program you have written to be in the public domain, you must take some legal steps to disclaim the copyright on it; otherwise, the program is copyrighted.

Proprietary Software

Proprietary software is software that is not free. Its use, redistribution or modification is prohibited, or requires you to ask permission.

Shareware

Shareware is software that comes with permission for people to redistribute, but optionally requires anyone who continues to use the software to pay a license fee. Shareware is not free software.

Chapter 4

The Complexity of Open Source

Time flies like an arrow; fruit flies like a banana.
— Groucho Marx

The primary objective of open source licensing is "to protect users' rights," but that protection comes at a price for IT because, like it or not, open source licensing does add complexity to any application development effort.

A majority of companies are using open source software. Some organizations may make an active and informed decision to use open source, but a surprisingly large number begin using open source without much visibility by management.

By inadvertently using open source, these organizations place themselves at risk of unintended violations of open source licenses. With the growth in open source software usage predicted to continue, it is important to understand the potential risks to your organization.

While many of the risks posed by open source are similar to those posed by proprietary software, open source software does have a number of unique risks. The chief legal risks relate to interpretation of the open source license and its claim of intellectual property infringement and, most importantly, the absence of warranties and indemnification within the license.

Law and Order on the Open Source Range

Is free software a subset of open source software? Most people use the terms interchangeably and usually use open source as a general term describing anything supporting open source or free software. However, those influential within the open source movement specifically do not discuss user freedoms, and since this is the central principle behind the free software movement, the two terms are considered to be quite distinct.

Despite these subtle differences between open source organizations, the truth is that free licenses are enforceable only under the current copyright laws. And since the GPL uses copyright law to benefit software users instead of vendors, as copyright law gets more powerful, so does your GPL rights. In fact, this will be a major concern with the efforts behind rewriting the GPL — updating the licensing so that it also uses patent law to protect users from lawsuits. Seeking to relieve patent licensing worries by the open source community, the biggest difference with GPL Version 3 is the inclusion of clauses on how to conduct patent defense.

Software developers and vendors need to remember that only a copyright holder who has code in the project in question has standing to bring a suit, and that although the work is considered copyrighted with no action on the author's part, the copyright must be registered before a suit can be brought.

Nevertheless, many software vendors and developers do not register their copyrights. A private organization known as gpl-violations.org (http://www.gpl-violations.org) is trying to correct this situation. The goals for gpl-violations.org are to:

Raise public awareness of the infringing use of free software, thus putting pressure on the infringers

Give users who detect or assume GPL-licensed software is being misused a way to report that misuse to the copyright holders. This is the first step in enabling the copyright holders to push for license compliance

Assist copyright holders in any action against GPL infringing organizations

Distribute information on how a commercial entity using GPL licensed software in its products can comply with the license

An Open Source Software Compliance Strategy

Open source does not impact all organizations in the same way or to the same degree. The risks posed by open source to your organization will vary depending on the way and the extent to which you use the software. Unlike proprietary software licenses, open source software licenses often do not require the payment of a fee or the execution of a signed agreement.

Typically, all that is required to enter into an open source license is the act of downloading and using it.

Many organizations discover their developers have been using open source within the IT infrastructure after the fact. It can even enter your organization via a component of a proprietary software package.

Like proprietary licenses, open source licenses impose legal obligations on the parties to the license. These obligations can be complex and ambiguous. Your organization's breach of these obligations (even unknowingly) can lead to automatic termination of the rights granted under the open source license terms.

Certain uses under a given license may impose few obligations on the licensee. Other uses may have potentially severe consequences, such as obligating the licensee to make publicly available the source code of proprietary software that is distributed with the open source.

Whether your organization is using open source or interested in preventing the use of open source, developing an open source software compliance strategy is an important first step.

To foster and control open source, it is in your best interest to form an internal team of technologists and attorneys whose role is to ensure your company's proper use of any open source software. Of first order is to establish an open source software compliance strategy. Of next importance is to publish a list of acceptable open source licenses so developers know before they download code whether the license is acceptable.

However, it is important to realize that open source software whose licenses fall outside your approved list might still be worth using. Most owners of open source copyrights can be dealt with individually. Many of the dozens of licenses listed on the OSI's Web site (http://www.opensource.org) include a clause suggesting the copyright holder may be willing to negotiate licensing terms directly.

For example, Sleepycat has signed more than 300 standard commercial licenses with individual companies. Since Sleepycat owns all the copyrights to its embedded database software, BerkelyDB, it is willing to negotiate special terms when appropriate. One caveat to this approach is that few people know how many copyright holders there are to all the parts of Linux, all of which are covered under the GPL.

The Federal Deposit Insurance Corporation (FDIC) has released guidance describing these risks as well as other strategic and operational risks relating

Campaign Against Software Patents

The Electronic Frontier Foundation (http://www.eff.org) and NoSoftwarePatents.com are two organizations that campaign against the use of software patents. They believe that software patents create more injustice than justice, and point out that only a small group of people in the patent system benefit from them-primarily large corporations. After all, software is already protected by copyright law. These organizations identify threats to our basic rights to educate the press, policymakers and the general public about civil liberties issues related to software technology.

Despite their efforts, numerous illegitimate patent applications make their way through the U.S. and European patent examination processes each year without adequate review. The problem is particularly acute in the software and Internet fields where we have seen patents applied on such simple technologies as:

- One-click online shopping (U.S. Patent No. 5,960,411.)
- Online shopping carts (U.S. Patent No. 5,715,314.)
- The hyperlink (U.S. Patent No. 4,873,662.)
- Video streaming (U.S. Patent No. 5,132,992.)
- Internationalizing domain names (U.S. Patent No. 6,182,148.)
- Pop-up windows (U.S. Patent No. 6,389,458.)
- Targeted banner ads (U.S. Patent No. 6,026,368.)
- Paying with a credit card online (U.S. Patent No. 6,289,319.)

Commenting on NoSoftwarePatents.com campaign's focus, founder Florian Mueller says that "many governments and others spread misinformation about software patents and the directive, and our campaign will relentlessly debunk the untruths."

Reputable organizations, such as Deutsche Bank Research, PriceWaterhouseCoopers and the Kiel Institute for World Economics, have already warned of the negative implications of software patents to Europe, indicating that copyrights protect innovators and software patents are used as weapons against innovators.

In September 2004, the European Parliament (http://www.europarl.eu.int) proposed a directive that would do away with software patents. And in July 2005 the European Parliament finally rejected the Computer-Implemented Inventions (CII) directive, which would have permitted the patenting of software.

Many dominant software companies backed lobbying efforts in favor of the ratification of the CII directive that would permit the patenting of software. Despite these efforts, the European Parliament reinforced the need for balanced legislation that ensures a competitive software industry, at least in Europe.

to the use of open source. For a good review of this subject, FDIC has published Risk Management of Free and Open Source Software. You can get this document by visiting http://www.fdic.gov.

Is Open Source a Legal Time Bomb?

Open source software may be a legal time bomb waiting to explode into a series of lawsuits, according to a study by the Alexis de Tocqueville Institution (ADTI). Based on studies conducted in 2002 and 2004, ADTI spotlighted alleged security concerns around the open source development model as well as challenged Torvalds' claim to have invented the Linux kernel. ADTI's critics have noted that Microsoft is one of the think tank's financial backers, a fact acknowledged by ADTI and Microsoft.

The new study, called Intellectual Property — Left? focuses on what author Kenneth Brown sees as a number of worrying legal issues that surround the open source development model. He argues open source is on a collision course with standard intellectual property law.

According to his report, users, developers and distributors are in conflict with traditional, staid intellectual property law. Among the potential conflicts are "licensing, attribution, anonymity, derivative works and indemnification."

Open Source Developers versus Corporate Employees

The ADTI study points out that many open source contributors work for corporations. These employees are beholden to strict employee invention/intellectual property agreements. Even if open source development is done in their spare time, they are potentially giving away company ideas, code and products to open source projects.

This opens up questions around the legal ownership of contributions and could even open an avenue for a "disgruntled employee" to give away company secrets by contributing them to open source projects, the report argues.

The ADTI report alleges that credit for the origin of Linux should go to projects such as Minix, authored by Andrew Tanenbaum. That report drew criticism from many quarters, including. Tanenbaum himself. "My conclusion is that Ken Brown doesn't have a clue what he is talking about," Tanenbaum wrote in a Web posting at the time.

Things are different now. Whereas patents originally covered only inventions, the U.S. now grants them on even the most obvious and general algorithms, ensuring that almost every program in use today — proprietary or open source — infringes on at least one patent. The only thing keeping software companies out of court is that the main holders of software patents are other software companies, and they fear retaliatory lawsuits (see **Campaign Against Software Patents**).

This is a problem for the open source community, as well as for startups that haven't patented anything yet. Worse, users can also be held liable for patent infringement, and few vendors will risk indemnifying their customers.

Copyright Threats Against Linux

A study conducted by Open Source Risk Management (OSRM), a company that is offering insurance against patent and copyright violations, has identified 283 patents that could pose a threat to users of the Linux operating system, including two dozen owned by Microsoft Corporation. Patent attorney Dan Ravicher, senior counsel for the Free Software Foundation, which promotes the use of free software, conducted the research.

Currently, Linux is the center of a pending multi-billion-dollar copyright infringement suit filed in 2003 by SCO Group against IBM. Of those patents, one-third are owned by companies that support the use of Linux and are unlikely to take legal action. Those companies include Cisco Systems, Hewlett-Packard, IBM, Intel, Novell, Oracle, Red Hat and Sony.

Of the remaining patents, however, 27 belong to Microsoft. The rest belong to companies or individuals who would have little to gain in making legal threats against Linux users in the hopes of reaching lucrative settlements.

Some analysts, however, are not convinced that users face a major legal threat from Linux, pointing to a recent court decision to throw out most of a lawsuit filed by SCO against DaimlerChrysler, and another separate decision to delay a suit against auto parts retailer AutoZone. Vendors distributing Linux in products are the more likely targets, not their customers.

SCO's actions have opened a Pandora 's Box of potential legal problems. There's no way to tell how the courts will rule on patent and copyright issues related to Linux use, and Linux backers such as IBM and Red Hat are offering only limited protection.

Fortunately there have been no successful patent suits stemming from the use of open source software. No patents that have been validated by a court were among the 283 identified by OSRM. About half the patents challenged in court are found to be invalid.

Royalty-Free Patents for Linux?

With financial support from IBM, Novell, Philips, Red Hat and Sony, Open Invention Network (OIN) is a company that is acquiring Linux patents and will offer them royalty-free. OIN is creating a new model where patents are shared in order to facilitate the advancement of the Linux operating system.

OIN plans to foster an open, collaborative environment that stimulates advances in Linux to ensure the continuation of innovation that has benefited software vendors, customers, emerging markets and investors. Patents owned by OIN will be available on a royalty-free basis to any company, organization or individual that agrees not to assert its patents against the Linux operating system or certain Linux-related applications.

OIN intends to spur innovation in IT and across industries by helping software developers focus on what they do best — developing Linux-related software — without the worry about intellectual property issues. Among Open Invention Network's initial patent holdings is a set of business-to-business electronic commerce patents that were purchased from Commerce One by JGR, a subsidiary of Novell.

OSRM plans to offer up to USD $5 million in coverage for legal costs associated with patent and copyright claims, for an annual premium of about USD $150,000. Consider the fact that IBM, for example, obtained a total of 3,248 patents from the United States Patent and Trademark Office in 2004. Most organizations with significant in-house Linux development and support expertise have processes in place to ensure that code contributed to open source software projects by staff members does not infringe on protected intellectual property.

Chapter 5

Linux and Linux Distributions

I'm doing a (free) operating system (just a hobby, won't be big and professional like gnu) for 386(486) clones.
— Linus Torvalds, 1991 in an e-mail to the comp.os.minix newsgroup

Although no one needs an operating system by itself, the choice of OS impacts the way your organization supports its applications and manage its data. The characteristics of an OS greatly affect the behavior of those applications along with the costs and risks associated with the organizations' application processing infrastructure. An OS will impact what cost an organization will bear for its hardware and application software; the cost and quality of system support it will receive; and the future streams of costs that it will incur supporting its applications. In effect, an operating system is very important to your organization, which is why your organization should begin adopting Linux.

Ready for Prime Time

Linux 2.0 arrived in June 1996 and included support for a number of new architectures but most importantly brought Linux into the world of multiprocessor machines. Subsequent major releases have expanded Linux support for new hardware and system types.

Linux 2.4 was notable for bringing Linux into the desktop space with kernel support for Plug-and-Play and USB (Universal Serial Bus). And version 2.6 of the Linux kernel, introduced in late 2003, provides more major improvements with support for both significantly larger systems — it supports up to

32-way processors and has even been tested on 64-way systems — as well as significantly smaller ones such as PDAs, MP3 players and other small mobile devices and consumer appliances.

Linux 2.6

There are three 2.6 Linux trees of code development: the mainline or stable kernel, known as 2.6.x, maintained by Torvalds; the 2.6mm, or staging tree, where technologies are tested before being added to the mainline kernel; and the 2.6.x.y kernel, for bug fixes.

The hierarchy in the 2.6 Linux kernel development is fairly flat relative to the earlier development efforts — there are smaller teams of experts working at a consensus level rather than having a primary maintainer. The number of kernel developers has also risen with the 2.6 effort. There are more than 1,000 unique kernel developers actively working on Linux 2.6.

Here is a quick look at the major initiatives associated with the Linux 2.6 kernel.

Multiprocessor Support

To make Linux a more acceptable kernel for larger computing environments, Linux now provides support for NUMA server designs. NUMA, or Non-Uniform Memory Access, is a step beyond SMP in the multiprocessing world and a major leap forward with lower design and manufacturing costs for systems that have more than four CPUs.

Whereas SMP systems tightly couple processors with memory, NUMA uses a loosely coupled approach that partitions memory into local and shared segments. NUMA provides a system that is much less expensive to design and manufacture than comparable SMP hardware designs.

Accessing shared memory induces latency since the memory bus speeds are significantly slower than the memory bus that conventional local memory uses (shared memory is accessed via fiber optic system interconnections between the cell boards and not the built-in memory bus the CPU chip complex utilizes). But since NUMA is much less expensive to manufacture than SMP systems, server manufacturers are beginning to adopt it. IBM's high-end xSeries servers utilize a NUMA system design.

Since it is much faster to access memory on the local CPU complex instead of memory contained on a completely separate memory cards, dealing with

NUMA system designs requires Linux to efficiently schedule processes so as to leverage local memory access patterns whenever possible.

There were many other internal changes made to allow Linux to support these new high-end SMP and NUMA system designs, and this is definitely an area of growth for the Linux kernel and one where Linux is rapidly improving. Over the course of the next year, we can expect to see many more improvements in support for these very high-end systems.

Processor Scaling

Linux 2.4 was reported to scale to 16-way processing, but for most applications it did not scale beyond eight CPUs. Linux 2.6 is capable of scaling easily to 32-way and even 64-way systems. But it is worth noting that a linear one-to-one relationship between the CPU count and throughput for all CPU counts is rarely achieved because one or more bottlenecks introduce serial constraints into the otherwise independently parallel CPU execution streams.

The most common Linux bottlenecks, involving contention among processors for access to shared resources, also apply to simple two-processor servers as well as to multiprocessor NUMA-based systems. These bottlenecks are usually insignificant on smaller systems but high processor counts make the bottlenecks increasingly visible and problematic.

Much of the work required to scale Linux to 64 processors involved improvements to reduce or eliminate lock contention — a state in which CPUs sit idle waiting for resources that are locked by another CPU. Because access latencies in NUMA architectures to remote memory are greater than for local memory, steps have be taken to ensure that CPU data structures used by each individual CPU are allocated in its local memory.

Other enhancements include the ability to pin a process to a particular CPU or set of CPUs (known as processor affinity or CPU binding). This is particularly useful on NUMA systems with high processor counts because it allows applications to scale without causing the additional latency when the kernel must communicate between physically separate NUMA nodes. When NUMA systems grow, CPU hop counts increase, interconnects become slower and memory management becomes critical. Linux, with help from IBM, now addresses these issues very effectively.

Kernel Locks

Any multiprocessor implementation in which resources are shared needs a way to lock those resources while they're in use in order to guarantee that only one CPU at a time can update shared data.

A simple, coarse-grained approach would be to have a single lock on the kernel, and require that any processor accessing the kernel first acquire the lock. Early Linux multiprocessor releases relied on a single lock, the Big Kernel Lock (BKL), as the primary synchronization and serialization lock for the kernel.

While this was not a significant problem for workloads on a two CPU systems, a single coarse-granularity lock is a major scaling bottleneck for systems with larger CPU counts. Recently, a number of open source projects have attempted to address the BKL bottleneck. One approach has been the preferential use of the XFS file system, which uses scalable fine-grained locking and largely avoids using the BKL altogether.

OS Scheduler

The 2.6 kernel incorporates a new scheduler. The OS scheduler is the part of the operating system that controls when a process runs and on which processor it runs (known as the global run queue). The previous CPU scheduler was efficient for uniprocessor and small multiprocessor platforms, but inefficient for large CPU counts and large thread counts.

Previously, the time it took to determine which processor went next was directly proportional to the number of processes running on the system. This is acceptable for an application that generates several hundred processes but on systems running tens of thousands of processes it is too slow.

The new scheduler — known as the O(1) scheduler — partitions the global run queue into multiple run queues. Now it takes a fixed amount of time to schedule processes, regardless of how many them the CPUs have to choose from. This has the effect of making performance much more linear and, as a result, makes Linux more suitable for large system deployments.

Another issue with the previous kernel's scheduler was that it would bounce processes between CPUs. In other words, a process would start running on one CPU but often finish on another one. This leads to additional overhead when transferring processes and processor states between CPUs, but the real problem becomes apparent when this happens on a NUMA system.

In this case, the memory the process was using on its original CPU may be very far from its new CPU. This causes the process to slow down because it has to wait longer for memory access. It also can degrade overall system performance as more data must contend for the memory bus. With this in mind, the new scheduler was designed to ensure that processes maintain "processor affinity" and minimize the bouncing from CPU to CPU.

Virtual Processors

Another major hardware advancement supported under Linux 2.6 is simultaneous multi-threading (SMT). Also known as Hyper-Threading (HT) by Intel, this is the ability for a single physical processor to masquerade at the hardware level as two or more CPUs. SMT allows separate processes, or threads, to execute in different parts of the CPU simultaneously. This is different from SMP, which allows separate processes to run on completely separate CPUs at the same time.

The new scheduler is aware of virtual processors and schedules tasks among virtual processors so as to not overburden the underlying single processor. This is all in addition to the scheduling that takes place among multiple (actual, not virtual) processors. This improves overall system performance in many cases, but also adds a slight scheduling complexity. The new kernel design now knows how to recognize and optimize SMT processor loads across both real and virtual CPUs.

It's worth noting that Linux was ahead of the market curve on supporting this new hardware feature transparently and intelligently.

Preemptable Kernel

The 2.6 kernel is now fully preemptable. Previously, a process running kernel code could not be interrupted by another process, even if it had used its entire time allotment as scheduled by the scheduler. By allowing the kernel to preempt itself, the system as a whole becomes much more responsive.

This is important not only for desktop systems full of interactive programs but for time-critical server applications. It should be noted, however, that a preemptable kernel doesn't necessarily make the system much faster. It just helps make sure that every process receives its fair timeslice, which gives the perception of a faster system across all users and applications.

Faster I/O

Waiting for a disk read is particularly painful for a server and often makes up a disproportionate amount of the total runtime (known as blocked I/O) of an application. Consequently, this is one the most important enhancements made to Linux. The 2.6 I/O subsystem has improved with asynchronous I/O, elimination of multiple copies to memory buffers while writing to disk, reduced contention for kernel locks and numerous other I/O driver enhancements.

One of the best enhancements for performance was with asynchronous I/O (or non-blocking I/O) in the kernel. Before the introduction of asynchronous I/O, processes submitted disk requests sequentially. Each I/O request would cause the calling process to sleep until the request was completed. Asynchronous I/O allows a process to submit an I/O request without waiting for it to complete.

This improves performance in two ways. First, because a process can queue multiple requests for the kernel to handle, the kernel can optimize disk activity by reordering requests or combining individual requests that are adjacent on disk into fewer, larger requests. Second, because the system does not put the process to sleep while the hardware processes the request, the process is able to perform other tasks until the I/O is complete.

New I/O Scheduler

The Linux 2.6 I/O subsystem has implemented a new I/O scheduler. The new scheduler allows administrators to tune the server to match its usage with three I/O behavior policies that attempt to cut down on unnecessary disk seeking, which is generally the slowest access for any hard disk drive. There is a fair queuing algorithm that is suitable for a wide variety of applications, especially desktop and multimedia workloads. It is the default I/O scheduler.

Complete Fair Queuing (CFQ) treats all competing processes equally by assigning each process a unique request queue and giving each queue equal bandwidth. It also promotes reads before writes. This is because I/O writes can wait, since the application does not need anything from the disk to continue processing.

Another I/O scheduling heuristic is known as the deadline scheduler, which was added specially for more disk-intensive applications such as databases. The deadline scheduler implements a per-request service deadline to ensure that no requests are neglected.

Anticipatory scheduling was the third improvement to the I/O scheduler. It is a very simple, though counterintuitive, modification. After processing a read request and sending the data back to the application, the I/O scheduler will wait (in milliseconds) to see if another read request gets processed.

Applications will generally request another I/O read request immediately after data is read. If such a request does come in during this wait period, the scheduler immediately sends it to the disk. Since the scheduler has not done anything else in this interim, the drive head is exactly where it was before the new request arrived.

By eliminating the seek operation normally necessary for the beginning of a read, the time required for several consecutive read operations is cut drastically. Some studies have indicated that the Apache Web server runs 50 percent faster as a result.

These I/O scheduling algorithms are selectable with boot options or at runtime.

Linux File Systems

The Linux 2.6 kernel provides support for two new journaling file systems: JFS (created by IBM) and XFS (created by SGI). These new file systems, along with the existing Ext3 (Red Hat) and Reiser (Novell) file systems, give Linux users a choice of four different journaling file systems. Also, the support for Microsoft's NTFS file system (which was added in Linux 2.4) has been improved in Linux 2.6.

NTFS support finally includes write support (the 2.4 NTFS code was read-only). Windows SMB file sharing along with the Novell NetWare affinity code are all inside Linux 2.6. This means Linux, Windows and NetWare can actually share a single file system, in terms of both reading and writing.

XFS File System is an extent-based, 64-bit journaling file system that is extremely well suited to the I/O requirements of HPC customers. It provides enhanced performance and robustness, and its fine-grained locking structure eliminates many of the scaling problems associated with the Big Kernel Lock. XFS combines the ability to support exceptionally large disk farms with rapid failure recovery and exceptional I/O throughput capabilities.

Coming in future stable Linux kernel releases will be Fuse, which makes it possible to implement a fully functional file system in a user-space program, as well as OCFS (Oracle Cluster File System), which will be the first clustering component to be added to the public kernel.

No-Install Linux

Some Linux distribution vendors provide live or bootable CD-ROM distributions. A live CD can be used to provide users with the ability to run a bootable Linux system on their desktop. They can use it to test and evaluate the user interface, applications and other facets of the Linux client before an actual client migration occurs — and this can be done without harming the host operating system that is already installed on the system.

Another benefit of no-install Linux is early detection of incompatible hardware and other potential device problems. The live CD can help validate proper hardware detection and device support and identify any issues prior to a complete Linux migration.

One notable live CD distribution is provided by Knoppix (http://www.knoppix.com). Knoppix is a bootable CD with a collection of Linux software. It can be used as a Linux demo, educational CD or rescue system, or adapted and used as a platform for commercial software product demos.

Security Extensions

Linux security has been enhanced in the 2.6 kernel in several areas. The entirety of kernel-based security has been modularized to allow for partitioning of superuser privileges, making a root account with access to all facilities and data optional, not required. Linux now can leverage hardware-assisted random number generation, not relying on just the entropy pool mechanism in prior releases. Finally, Linux has had an improved kernel-based firewall capability with the replacement of IPchains with the BSD-derived IPtables facility from the 2.4 kernel. This is just one example where code improvements from the open source community have been adopted by another open source project to the benefit of the greater good.

Better Memory Management

In an effort to provide better support for both large and small systems, the Linux 2.6 kernel's memory management code has been overhauled. For example, the Linux 2.6 kernel can run on architectures lacking a memory management unit (MMU), a unit that is inside PCs and servers but often not incorporated into embedded devices like PDAs and cell phones.

A translation lookaside buffer (TLB) is a CPU hardware structure that maps virtual memory addresses to real physical addresses for recently referenced memory pages; it serves as a quick-reference index to the pages the system is most likely to need. When memory changes make the TLB entries invalid, its contents are flushed and reloaded with current information.

Since all processors have shared memory access, a TLB flush on one processor must be propagated across the system. This can be a time-consuming operation, particularly on systems with large processor counts.

Several changes have been incorporated into the Linux kernel to reduce the impact of the TLB flush bottleneck. First, the memory management system is designed to minimize the frequency of TLB flushes. Once a TLB flush does happen, the system is able to determine which processors have executed code that makes their TLBs invalid, and only include those TLBs in the flush routine. This can reduce the time required to complete the system-wide flush operation substantially.

Freeing shared memory becomes especially difficult, as the OS must make sure that no other process — not just the process that originally requested the memory — is also using it. In order to avoid this problem, the Linux 2.6 kernel keeps a per-page list of processes in addition to the normal per-process page list. This technique is much faster than checking the page table of every running process.

Linux Instances and Virtualization

The Linux 2.6 kernel allows the Linux kernel to run as a user-space application. In other words, Linux can now be run from inside a running Linux OS (user-mode Linux). Linux 2.6 has a set of system calls that lets another kernel be loaded by the current executing kernel.

Another technology to run multiple operating systems at the same time on the same Linux server is known as Xen. Xen is the open source hypervisor software being developed at the University of Cambridge in the United Kingdom.

Xen has garnered so much attention that its authors have now formed a company, XenSource, to support it. Xen is backed by Hewlett-Packard, IBM, Sun Microsystems and others that want to standardize virtualization under Linux. AMD, IBM and Intel are even building virtualization hooks into their next-generation chips that Xen will be able to leverage.

The inclusion of Xen in the Linux kernel is very significant. Essentially this means that every Linux kernel, from any distribution, will support Xen as its virtualization technology. This type of logical partitioning is a feature found in IBM mainframes as well as various Unix midrange and enterprise servers from IBM, Sun Microsystems and Hewlett-Packard.

OS Miscellany

Other improvements in the 2.6 kernel include support for IPv6, SELinux (or tiny Linux), iSCSI, NFSv4, IA-32 stack/buffer overflow resistance, software suspend and many others. A new feature called address space randomization is designed to help block the effectiveness of viruses. A number of drivers, such as those for DVB, USB, networks and sound chips, have had major updates.

Linux contains a file system event monitoring mechanism known as inotify. Inotify is a fine-grained asynchronous mechanism suited to a variety of file monitoring needs, including security and performance.

Most Linux distributions are already shipping with the latest kernel enhancements. As with most Linux kernel upgrades, all of these new features have been accessible for awhile, but were only available as patches for earlier Linux kernel releases. For example, the Native POSIX Thread Library has been available on the 2.4 kernel from many sources, even though it was actually part of the 2.6 kernel development effort.

Many improvements in the Linux 2.6 kernel favor enterprise applications. Organizations will see significant performance and reliability improvements in a wide range of computing uses for Linux, from mobile devices, desktops and data centers to advanced telecommunications applications. The new kernel is a huge step forward for Linux and Linux applications.

For more information regarding kernel development and future enhancements, vist http://www.lwn.net.

Linux Roadmap

The Linux roadmap continues with the release of the 2.8 kernel. Along with better balanced SMP scaling, the 2.8 kernel will have NUMA and clustered file system enhancements. It will see the introduction of dynamic hardware reconfiguration, Infiniband drivers and OS partitioning.

OS checkpoints and restarts will be introduced. Checkpoint and restart are mechanisms for protecting operating systems and enterprise applications from computer failures by taking a snapshot (the checkpoint) of the system and data at critical points. If the system or process crashes, it can be restarted from the most recent checkpoint file, without having to go back to the beginning and rerun everything. But while the concept is easy to understand, the technical mechanism to checkpoint and restart an operating system or application is quite complex.

FUSE (File System in User Space), Reiser 4 network-based file system and version two of the Oracle Cluster File System will be included in the next release; and due to the modularity of Linux, vendors are able to incorporate these new features into their core distribution quickly.

The next major release of Linux will result in an operating system that provides complete application availability for all business and technical requirements.

Linux Distributions

What is usually referred to as Linux is more accurately called a "distribution." Linux distributions are prepackaged collections of software, generally comprising the kernel and various other components. Most major distributions include a graphical desktop environment and a user-friendly installation program.

The Linux Standard Base (LSB) project attempts to standardize distributions to minimize the changes that may affect portability. As a workgroup within the Free Standards Group, an independent, non-profit organization supported by the Linux development community, the aim of LSB is to define standards designed to achieve maximum compatibility of all distributions and prevent divergence among the Linux systems.

The purpose of standardization is to facilitate work for both software developers and distributors. The majority of Linux distributions available today tend to meet the Linux Standard Base definitions and requirements. For more information, visit http://www.linuxbase.org.

A distributor (such as Red Hat or Novell) is a company that packages a Linux distribution for commercial purposes. They don't technically resell the software license, but rather sell a subscription service for support and maintenance.

The move into enterprise-class software drives and separates the distributions. These distributions cost more but include more enterprise class fea-

What About UnitedLinux?

UnitedLinux LLC began in May 2002 as four Linux vendors — SUSE, Turbolinux, Caldera (now part of The SCO Group) and Conectiva — joined to create a standardized, industry-certified and robust enterprise version of the open source operating system. Unfortunately, its four original partners have now undergone a number of significant changes.

SCO threw the partnership into a tailspin when it filed its now infamous lawsuit against IBM, alleging that IBM illegally contributed SCO's System V Unix code to Linux. Then, Tokyo-based Turbolinux underwent ownership changes and largely pulled out of the U.S. market, causing more instability for the united effort. And, finally, Novell bought SUSE, essentially merging the founding member of UnitedLinux as part of its OS product strategy.

Industry analysts agree that UnitedLinux failed to meet most of its goals. The idea was that the four partners could jointly develop SUSE Enterprise Linux and be able to cut their overall development costs.

But in hindsight it would have been better for users for UnitedLinux to begin from the Linux Standard Base project (http://www.linuxbase.org), which is developing a set of standards to increase compatibility among Linux distributions and enable Linux software applications to run on any Linux-compliant system.

tures and multiple levels of support, from bug fixes to 24x7 help desk support. Enterprise class distributions will include:

- Optimized release cycles of 12 to 18 months and version support for three to five years or more
- Independent software vendor certification platform
- Enterprise-class features and support such as dynamic I/O link management
- Longer integration and testing cycles

- Improved SMP and NUMA support
- 24x7 global enterprise class support offerings

Completing Linux

In the vast majority of cases, Linux applications are compatible with all distributions of Linux. When a new Linux kernel is released, it is uploaded to the main Linux kernel site (http://www.kernel.org). The distribution companies then package the kernel and provide it as an update on their own Web sites.

Distributors take the kernel as is. This includes all changes and fixes that are contributed by members of the development community. Often distributors will add updates with specific features to support their business needs. As a result, the distributions share much in common.

For example, each distribution comes with two major desktop GUI interfaces: the K Desktop Environment and GNOME. To the end-user, they are functionally equivalent. Choosing one over the other is a matter of personal preference. Both of these Linux desktops are similar in function to the graphical windowing that Microsoft provides with Windows. For developers, the difference between the desktops is the set of tools and libraries that each supports.

When buying a distribution, the customer does not buy Linux itself. Instead, the customer pays for a combination of operating system, utility programs, installation programs and documentation created by the distributor. The purpose of these distributions is to reduce administrative efforts on the part of the user. Distributions are received either as a set of CDs or as a download license key.

Pursuant to the GPL, which applies to many programs and the operating system kernel used under Linux, distributors also supply the source code of the corresponding programs. This enables users to recompile the software when problems arise and to modify the software in line with their specific requirements.

Compatibility of the Linux versions and standardization of the various distributions will be important issues in the future. Fortunately for Linux, the Free Standards Group was formed in 1998 to promote standards for open source software. FSB organizes workgroups for LSB, OpenI18N10 (formerly Linux Internationalization Initiative), LANANA (The Linux Assigned

Names and Numbers Authority), OpenPrinting, Accessibility, DWARF and Open Cluster. For more information, visit http://freestandards.org.

Linux Distributions

There are at least 386 available versions of Linux packages. Besides the pure operating system, most of these distributions contain many other software packages including Web servers, database management systems, mail server, firewall, proxy server and directory services.

The following distributions were selected because of their widespread market adoption.

Asianux

Asianux is a Linux distribution co-developed by Chinese Linux vendor Red Flag Software Co. Ltd. Japanese Linux vendor Miracle Linux Corporation and Korean Linux software vendor Haansoft Inc., targeting the enterprise Linux platforms in Asia.

Red Flag Software, Miracle Linux and Haansoft distribute and market Asianux without any modifications to the Linux distribution package for China, Japan and Korea markets. New products such as Red Flag 5, Miracle Linux and Haansoft Linux will be based on Asianux, each distribution bundled with localized features for their respective country. For more information, visit http://www.asianux.com.

CentOS

CentOS is an enterprise-class Linux distribution derived from sources freely provided to the public. CentOS conforms fully with the upstream vendors' redistribution policies (CentOS mainly changes packages to remove upstream vendor branding and artwork.) For more information, visit http://www.centos.org.

Debian GNU Linux

The Debian Project is a worldwide group of volunteers whose endeavor is to produce a completely free Linux distribution. Various processor types are supported, including Intel IA, Alpha, ARM, Intel IA-64, Motorola 68k, MIPS, PA-RISC, PowerPC, SPARC, IBM S/390 and Hitachi SuperH.

Debian motivated the formation of Software in the Public Interest (SPI), a New York-based non-profit organization. SPI was founded to help Debian and other similar organizations develop and distribute open hardware and software. Among other things, SPI provides a mechanism by which The Debian Project may accept contributions that are tax deductible in the U.S. For more information, visit http://www.debian.org.

KNOPPIX

KNOPPIX is a Linux distribution that boots and runs completely from CD/DVD media. It includes the most recent Linux software and desktop environments, with programs such as OpenOffice, Abiword, The Gimp, Konqueror, Mozilla, Apache, PHP, MySQL and many other open source programs. Knoppix is based on KDE desktop and Debian Linux.

KNOPPIX can be used as a productive Linux system for the desktop, educational CD or rescue system, for testing Linux compatibility, running a firewall or router or bootstrapping a Linux installation, or as a platform for commercial software product demonstrations. It does not require an installation process to a bootable hard disk drive. For more information, visit http://www.knoppix.com.

Mandriva

In November 1998, several young Linux devotees met on the Internet and created Mandrakesoft. In 2005, Mandrakesoft was changed to Mandriva after its merger with Conectiva. With corporate headquarters in Paris, Mandriva offers a set of GNU Linux and open source software including more than 2300 applications. This Linux distribution has since become an international reference in open source software.

Mandriva Linux is the most international Linux distribution because its installation is supported in more than 40 languages. In August 2001, after having established itself as one of the world leaders in open source and the Linux software industry, Mandrakesoft became the first Linux company listed on a European stock market. For more information, visit http://www.mandriva.com.

MontaVista

MontaVista Software provides an open source platform allowing system designers to innovate across a wide range of application processing infrastructures. It provides software developers with a commercial-grade Linux-based operating system that can be used in many applications environments ranging from communications infrastructures to consumer electronics. For more information, visit http://www.mvista.com.

Red Hat

Founded in 1994, Red Hat provides the most popular Linux distribution in North America. It is well known for its Red Hat Package Manager (RPM) for installing and maintaining its components. Red Hat offers development, deployment and management tools for Linux and open source environments ranging from embedded devices to enterprise servers. The Red Hat Linux distribution also is the basis for several other Linux distributions.

Red Hat has introduced the Open Source Architecture program, which provides a roadmap for open source technologies and capabilities. Red Hat's enterprise solutions are offered primarily for technology organizations and are backed by a proven certification process. For more information, visit http://www.redhat.com.

SUSE

Founded in 1992 to adapt the international Slackware distribution to the demands of the German market, SUSE Linux originated in Nuremberg, Germany. SUSE distributions include an integrated installation and administration system known as YaST (Yet another Setup Tool).

SUSE provides enterprise Linux distributions that are chiefly designed for IT organizations. Novell acquired SUSE (as well as Ximian) in 2003. For more information, visit http://www.novell.com.

Turbolinux

Turbolinux is particularly popular in the Asia Pacific markets since it supports both Japanese and Chinese languages. Turbolinux distributions are designed from the ground up specifically for enterprise computing and were the first to conform to internationalization standards to help simplify development of applications that require multiple language support. For more information, visit http://www.turbolinux.com.

Ubuntu Project

The Ubuntu Project is sponsored by Canonical Ltd., a company owned by South African entrepreneur Mark Shuttleworth. (Ubuntu is a word from the

African Nguni language family, meaning humanity, caring and harmony). Canonical focuses on selling services rather than selling the Ubuntu distribution itself.

Ubuntu is on the bleeding edge of Linux development, incorporating the latest kernel and versions of GNOME and Evolution. For more information, visit http://www.ubuntulinux.org.

Linux Distributions

Distribution	Developed By	Server / Workstation/ Groupware	Platforms	URL
Asianux	Miracle Linux, Tokyo, Japan Red Flag Software, Beijing, China Haansoft in South Korea	S, W	AMD, Intel, IBM OpenPower	http://www.asianux.com http://www.miraclelinux.com http://www.redflag-linux.com http://www.miraclelinux.com
CentOS	Open Source Software	S	AMD, Intel, S390	http://www.centos.org
Debian	Ian Murdock; Open Source Software	S, W	Alpha, Intel, PPC, SPARC	http://www.debian.org
KNOPPIX	Klaus Knopper, Germany	W	AMD, Intel	http://www.knoppix.com
Fedora	Linux Community; Red Hat Sponsored	W	Intel	http://www.redhat.com/fedora
Mandriva	Mandriva, SA Paris, France	S, W	AMD, Intel, PPC	http://www.mandriva.com
MontaVista	Sunnyvale, CA	Embedded	PICMG	http://www.mvista.com
Red Hat	Red Hat, Inc. Raleigh, NC	S, W, G	AMD, Intel, PPC, S390	http://www.redhat.com
SUSE	Novell, Inc. Provo, Salt Lake City	S, W, G	AMD, Intel, PPC, S390	http://www.novell.com
Turbolinux	Turbolinux, Tokyo, Japan	S, W	Intel, S390	http://www.turbolinux.com
Ubunta	Isle of Man, South Africa	W	AMD, Intel, PPC	http://www.canonical.com
Yellow Dog	Loveland, Colorado	W	PPC	http://www.terrasoftsolutions.com

Figure 5-1. *Linux Distributions.*

Yellow Dog

Supported by Terra Soft Solutions, a leading developer of integrated PowerPC Linux solutions, Yellow Dog is a complete Linux distribution designed for the Apple Mac hardware platform, from iMac G5s to Mac minis.

Yellow Dog Linux is a Fedora-based operating system tailored for PowerPC computers that provides a unified KDE and GNOME desktop environment. For more information, visit http://www.yellowdoglinux.com.

Figure 5–1 shows the list of market-leading Linux distributions. For a complete list, visit http://www.linuxiso.org.

OpenBSD

Theo de Raadt is a pioneer of the open source software movement and a huge proponent of free software. De Raadt makes an open source operating system called OpenBSD. Unlike Linux, which is a clone of Unix, OpenBSD is based on an actual Unix variant known as Berkeley Software Distribution (BSD). BSD powers two of the best operating systems in the world — Solaris from Sun Microsystems and OS X from Apple Computer.

There are three open source flavors of BSD — FreeBSD, NetBSD and OpenBSD. OpenBSD is best known for its security features. De Raadt says BSD could have become the world's most popular open source operating system, except that a lawsuit over BSD scared away developers, who went off to work on Linux and stayed there even after BSD was deemed legal.

Where Can I Get Linux 2.6?

There are plenty of places to look for Linux distributions. Perhaps the best-known places are http://www.distrowatch.com and http://www.linuxiso.org.

It's easy to become overwhelmed by all the Linux distribution permutations. Each has a niche and offers varying levels of driver and technical support, application management, ease of installation, various market segment support and funding. However, when looking for the right Linux distribution, keep the following considerations in mind.

You should not buy anything that you could get somewhere else for free. You should just pay for the support provided to you. Since the price of distributions is small, it may be a good idea to put two different providers in competition and select the one that gives you the best support.

Experience shows that we all have a tendency to consider the first distribution that works as "the best" because we do not try any other distribution after we have Linux up and running. Almost every distribution claims to be the first in its category and has one magazine or another that endorses that idea for the same reason.

Chapter 6

The Consistent Approach

Sometimes I lie awake at night, and ask, "Where have I gone wrong?" Then a voice says to me, "This is going to take more than one night."
— Charles M. Schulz

As the saying goes, there is safety in numbers. And with Linux, this couldn't be more true. The more Linux is deployed, the more fans it attracts. Companies the have jumped on the open source bandwagon cite major advantages and cost savings associated with their migration. But what do you need to know before taking a leap into the brave new world of Linux-based computing?

The question companies must answer in order to migrate to Linux is simple. Which pieces of the corporate computing architecture have become commodities? Web servers are already there — open source Apache software has more than 60 percent of the Web server market. And other computing solutions are quickly following suit as proprietary software hits development dead spots, and stops changing and improving.

For many, this now includes word processing, spreadsheets, databases, presentation software, desktops, network devices, firewalls, load balancers, terminal servers and application and database servers. Figure 6–1 illustrates various areas where Linux is being deployed.

The Process

One of the first tasks companies must initiate is commissioning a pre-migration study to identify technical concerns and business impact risks. The out-

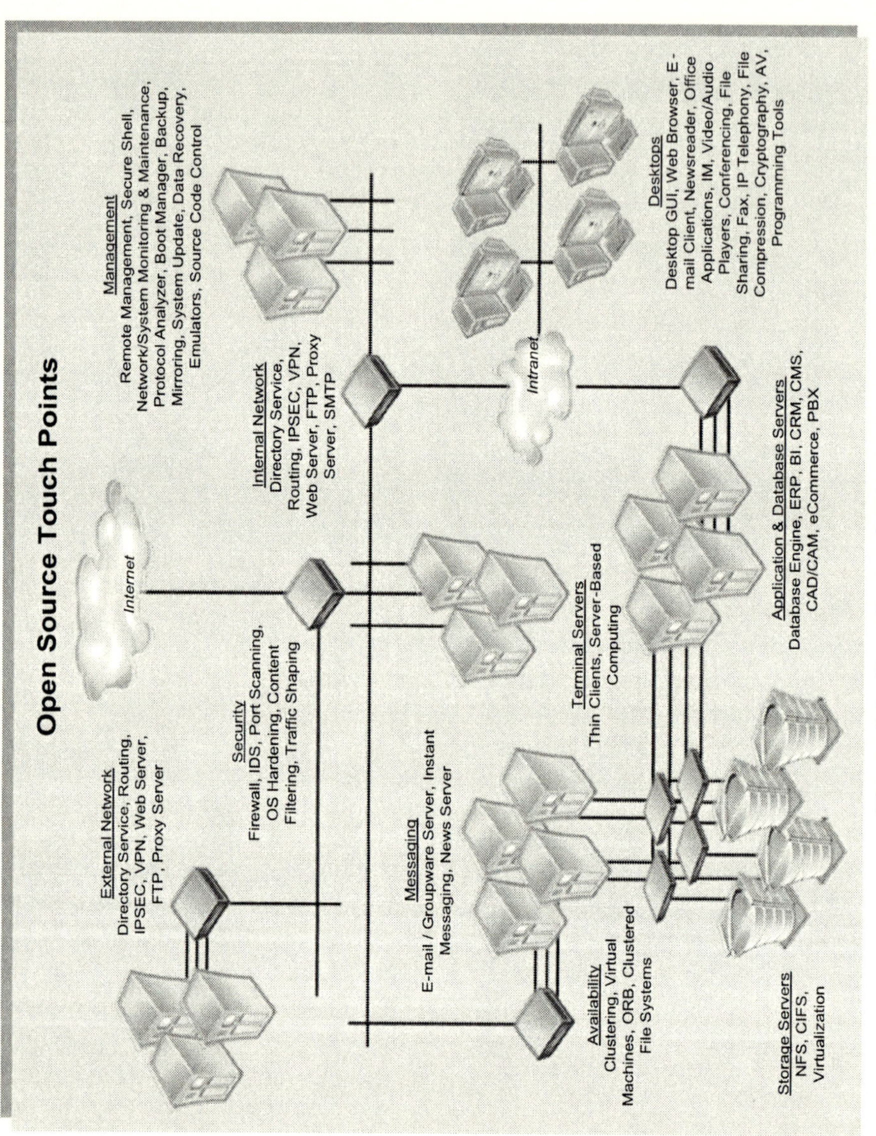

Figure 6-1. Open Source Deployments.

come from this analysis is a final agreement of an overall migration plan. The migration plan will most likely be a long-term strategy that provides a gradual transition and slow integration of Linux.

Companies would be well advised to seek out similar organizations that have migrated or are in the process of migrating to open source software before and during this process. It is important to explore their successes as well as their migration issues.

Even though no two Linux or open source migration efforts are identical, the experience gained from companies that have migrated to Linux will help identify common migration problem areas and risk management requirements. Figure 6-2 illustrates the Linux migration process. Each step builds

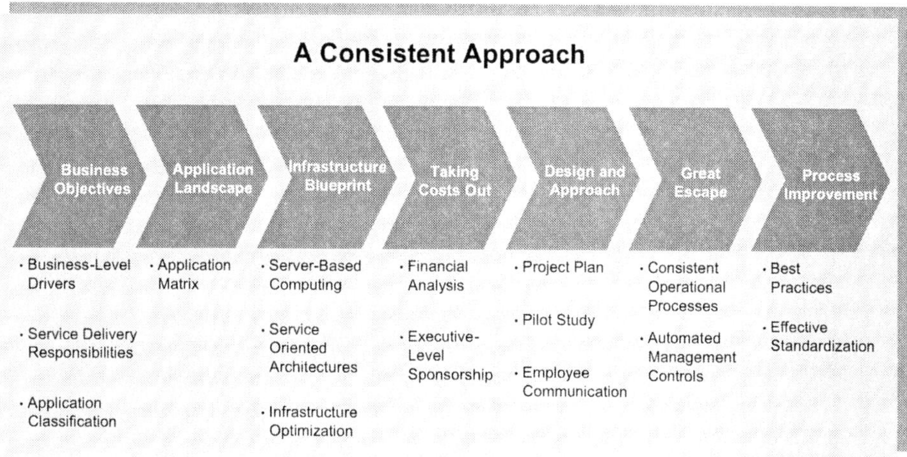

Figure 6-2. *The Methodology.*

upon the next, creating a solid foundation necessary for the migration process.

There are Seven Keys of successful Linux and open source adoption and migration efforts. They are fundamental to structured system analysis and design principles. Part Two of this book will explore each of these Keys, providing critical success factors, best practices and financial investment analysis. Adhering and adopting these Keys, or principles, will not only guarantee a successful migration but more importantly, will provide a migration effort that provides a more cost-effective, scalable and reliable computing environment.

Introduction to The Seven Keys

Fundamentally, we are beginning to see an evolution of information technology — an IT movement away from productivity-based models to a more information-based paradigm. This shift will allow businesses to have access to the right information, at the right time, and at the right price.

But why are many IT organizations still reluctant to migrate from their legacy computing platforms? Why do customers hesitate to move away from their Unix or Windows environment, instead of taking advantage of the clear cost savings of open source and Linux?

There are many reasons why companies find it difficult to move away from their Unix and Windows infrastructures. Most customers find it problematic to pursue a platform migration while still maintaining current business operations. There are learning curves, the fear from the "unknown," no clear way to test and evaluate a Linux migration, and simple resistant to change. Enter The Seven Keys.

The Seven Keys for Linux and open source adoption is an execution strategy — a series of initiatives along with their corresponding outcomes. The seven function-point process is predicated on critical underlying adoption principles. First, it is imperative to understand your organization's business initiatives (Key #1), finding the pragmatic balance between those applications that represent parity services for your organization and those that provide a competitive advantage.

If, after examining the current application environment (Key #2), it is shown that Linux and open source can be directly applied to your business and its computing requirements, then with the proper Linux infrastructure blueprint (Key #3), Linux and open source can spawned new approaches and methods for deploying your application infrastructures.

However, to be successful using this new computing paradigm, you must secure management commitment and executive-level sponsorship. And the best approach to get management support is through an objective financial analysis ensuring proper validation and justification for the business-level objectives (Key #4).

The success of the migration rollout is dependent on the organization understanding the importance for Linux and open source. Your organization must conduct pilot studies and build interoperability labs that provide proper training, usability studies and technical validation (Key #5). If a migration project is going to be delayed or completely canceled, it is done during the pilot study.

As with any new computing environment, performing a controlled and well managed rollout is critical to the success of the project. Linux and open source adoption requires forethought on how to manage logistics such as scheduling servers and data to be migrated, notifying users of planned outages, responding to user inquiries and having processes to resolve reported software problems and errors (Key #6).

Finally, it is important to identify process improvements, consistent management and operational processes (Key #7). The business and technology organization must take all reasonable steps to use established methods of success, accurate financial analysis and the use of process improvement and controls.

An Exploration in Discovery

Part II of this book is devoted to an exploration into the Seven Keys, delving into the most important aspects with Linux and open source computing. It provides background information and relevant resource material behind the seven-function-point methodology.

The Seven Keys comprise the following:

1. **Defining Business-Level Objectives.** Understanding what the ideal computing infrastructure is for an organization is the first step to creating an information technology paradigm shift. The success criteria and business-level drivers that are necessary for a company to be competitive in the marketplace provides the foundation for building a more cost-effective computing environment, and having a paradigm shift occur.

   Open source databases, standards-based services, server-based computing and service-oriented architectures provide the building blocks for utility computing and a successful business computing infrastructure, but the future outcome and success is dependent on the business objectives behind the effort. Tying the business value drivers and goals is critical for the success of the project.

2. **Surveying the Application Landscape.** Organizations considering Linux and open source must understand the current application base including the strengths and weaknesses surrounding the current application infrastructure. Without an analysis of the current application environment, the business values and economic savings from Linux cannot be recognized.

   It is important to understand that Linux is not an all-or-nothing proposition. It can be slowly added into your data center by gradually replacing network service functions. It can be deployed within the infrastructure with the rollout of a new business application.

   Organizations can install Linux desktops, but keep users accessing Windows Office applications. Companies can deploy Linux desktops and Linux applications, but segment these users to an affinity group, such as transaction workers or technical workstations. Establishing a paradigm shift often involves conducting a controlled and managed rollout.

3. **Designing the Infrastructures Blueprint.** Linux has risen with the advancement of new computing technologies for business applications. It enables sophisticated data management solutions such as advanced clustering, gridware and blade computing architectures.

   Linux can be instrumental in the data center as application servers, network services or other management functions. Equally, Linux can provide a low-cost, maintenance-free desktop environment. The application blueprint is the basis for the paradigm shift with Linux.

4. **Finding the Right Project.** The organization must secure executive-level commitment and sponsorship for the migration project. Without proper management support, a paradigm shift will not be achieved.

   Executive-level sponsorship is obtained with an objective financial analysis ensuring the effort is objectively validated against the business-level objectives.

5. **Ensuring Project Success.** The success of the migration rollout is dependent on the organization understanding the importance of Linux. Organizations must conduct pilot studies and build interoperability labs that provide proper training, usability studies and technical validation.

   If a migration project is going to be delayed or completely canceled, it is done during the pilot study. Pilot studies are an important Key since they act as the primary gating factor for achieving a paradigm shift.

6. **Performing the Great Escape.** It is important to identify process improvements and consistent management and operational processes. One of the largest costs that organizations face is dealing with hardware and software inconsistencies. IT organizations often face problems with servers because their configurations vary from server to server and location to location.

   It is important that the migration process include the ability to create a consistent server image, to have automatic hardware configuration and software installation, and to perform quality assurance tests.

7. **Practicing Process Improvement.** The business and the technology organization must take all reasonable steps to use established methods of success, accurate financial analysis and the use of process improvement

and controls. Enforcement of Linux and open source adoption "best practices" sets in operation the new computing paradigm.

Change management is an important aspect of continuous process improvement because, at its core, it seeks to address the people aspect of any project. The goal of change management is to ensure the success of program changes by assessing and addressing the impact of those changes on the organization.

If there is one overarching message that readers will learn in the next part of this book, it is that Linux adoption requires a process. And it is important that the process be broken down into digestible project tasks where the real work is accomplished. But remember, projects and related project tasks require ongoing review, updating and continuous process improvement.

Migrating your business processing environment to a Linux and open source computing model offers significant cost savings and performance improvements. While most Linux and open source projects will migrate smoothly, best practices and an approach based on business risk mitigation helps future migration projects have minimum risk and maximum return.

PART II

Linux and Open Source Adoption

Linux has emerged as a credible alternative for businesses that rely on application computing solutions and business computing environments. With the introduction of both open source and commercial Linux software, including databases, Web and application servers, middleware, infrastructure software, and management tools, it is apparent that Linux offers a complete end-to-end software solution.

Linux and open source account for approximately 70 percent of all Web servers and transmit nearly two-thirds of all Internet e-mail. In fact, most Internet infrastructure applications are first developed on the Linux platform and, perhaps not surprisingly, run best on Linux.

Linux is proving to be the preferred and dominant operating environment for many of the world's newest and largest supercomputers. A group that keeps track of the top 500 supercomputers in the world estimates that Linux powers 60 percent of those systems, displacing Unix, which used to be the most popular operating system for high-performance computing.

Open Source Equivalents

Open source applications such as Samba and OpenLDAP provide reliable user and directory services. CUPS is a tried-and-tested print service that cost-effectively addresses the requirements for a complex print environment. There are e-mail server alternatives that enable full-scale replacement of Microsoft Exchange. There are a number of system management alternatives that are freely available, alleviating the cost pressures of implementing traditional monolithic framework products such as HP OpenView or Computer Associates Unicenter. There are free database management products such as MySQL, PostgreSQL and EnterpriseDB. And this list of Linux-based equivalents continues for every application, database and infrastructure software category.

But why are businesses hesitant to move away from proprietary Unix and Windows environments, instead of taking advantage of the clear cost savings of an open source Linux environment? Why are many technology organizations still reluctant to migrate from their legacy computing platforms?

There are many reasons why companies find it difficult to move away from their Unix and Windows infrastructures. Most organizations find it problematic to pursue a platform migration while still maintaining business operations. There are learning curves, the fear from the unknown and simple reluctance to change.

The Business Challenge

Linux presents a new business challenge for organizations. The key question and ultimate business concern is this: "Is there a better way to jumpstart and radically accelerate Linux and open source adoption?" The short answer is, yes. What follows in Part II is a time-tested approach to successful Linux and open source adoptions. Part II provides the direction and introduction for a new way of delivering business application solutions for your company. More specifically, it is precisely the Seven Keys in Part II that provide the secret for success with this new computing paradigm.

Part II highlights the project methods of the Seven Keys for highly successful Linux and open source adoption. The specific steps of this methodology are presented in more detail in the Appendix, but the concepts, technical background and business rationale is highlighted in Part II. After reading the material presented in this book, organizations will be well prepared to embrace and widely adopt Linux and open source computing for their business computing environments.

Key #1

Defining the Business-Level Objectives

To create a Paradigm Shift, have a clear vision of your ideal computing environment.

Key Overview

Understanding what the ideal computing infrastructure is for your organization is the first step to creating an information technology Paradigm Shift. The success criteria and business-level drivers that are necessary for a company to be competitive in the marketplace provides the foundation for building an adaptable and highly cost-effective computing environment.

The basis for creating a Paradigm Shift is understanding the discrete business functions that are necessary for the organization to thrive. Linux and open source provide an enabling technology — how your organization leverages it is up to you.

Chapter 7

Laying the Foundation

Thank you John, Paul, George and Ringo for your demo, but we don't find your music suitable at this time.
— Decca Records, 1962

So what really does an operating system do for you?

Whether it's investing in supportability, creating better scalability, avoiding vendor lock-in, future-proofing your environment or reducing the total cost of ownership, an OS is extremely important to building an underlying system infrastructure; and with Linux, it is with its wide range of available tools and applications, broad implementation of open standards and protocols, low deployment cost and, perhaps most importantly, the thriving community of end-users and developers and rapid cycle of bug fixes and innovation that flow from the open source nature of the software.

In his book, *The Google Legacy*, IT consultant Stephen Arnold claims Google can put more horsepower under its hood more cheaply than competitors, thanks to its use of commodity servers and a customized version of Linux. Mr. Arnold claims Google not provides a search engine, but a supercomputer that delivers applications with good performance and cost effectiveness.

Supporting Application Workloads

The move of the industry's hardware and software vendor community to port their products to Linux is exactly the kind of industry support that lends credibility to the power of the open source software movement. Linux on the IA (Intel Architecture) platform has emerged as a viable alternative to Unix and Windows for enterprise computing. Linux running on X64 systems (moniker for 64-bit IA-compatible hardware) has risen in rank among the other processing platforms in the datacenter.

However, the key to realizing the benefits of Linux begins with careful consideration of where to deploy it, understanding why to deploy it in those roles, managing its expectations and monitoring its results. Successful Linux and open source adoption requires good alignment between the requirements of the application workload and the attributes of Linux.

The Heated Debate

The debate is long-lived. What qualities of Linux and open source products make them a good choice at this point in computing history?

Today's enterprise computing environment is a heterogeneous mix of hardware, operating systems and applications, making it more important for organizations to choose hardware and software that is flexible and adaptable. And Linux, by its very nature, is designed, influenced and constantly modified for this exact type of environment, providing a platform of universal use and adaptation.

Open source programming is rapidly spreading. As evidenced by the rapid adoption rate of Linux, Apache, MySQL, PHP, Java and Mozilla, it is widely accepted that open source software is more reliable, provides better performance and is more secure than its proprietary alternatives.

What is even more significant, the functionality unique to the open source approach is its ability to easily interface with other systems. The protocols incorporated in Linux are open, defined and published. By contrast, commercial software is closed. There is no access to source code and no ability to shape the software's functionality according to your organization's needs.

IT organizations are realizing that software in general requires a service-centric approach. With Linux and open source, applications and resources are treated as a service, having interfaces that are defined according to industry standards, enabling them to exchange information and provide flexibility to treat applications and the underlying infrastructure — as well as the business processes — as components that can be mixed and matched at will.

Linux and open source computing have created a disruptive shift in the computing ecosystem and are driving significant change both from a technology and a business perspective. Every major computing initiative is being impacted by this Paradigm Shift

Yet, Linux is a resource that requires a different decision methodology. To be successful with Linux and open source, your organization must have software decision-making discussions as well as adopt open source dynamics. Your organization must clearly understand the valid business reasons for moving to this platform. Bottom line: There must be a compelling reason to change.

Defining Valid Business Reasons

There are many valid business reasons to consider when embracing Linux and open source software. As a preferred operating system for many organizations, Linux and open source are chosen for the following reasons.

Invest In Supportability. Linux scales from the smallest devices to large multiprocessor systems and mainframes — no other OS provides this breadth of coverage. And since Linux was intended from its introduction in the early 1990s to deliver a Unix-like experience, it inherently addresses high availability, reliability, performance and supportability.

Build Better Scalability. Linux is a driving factor for both horizontal scaling and grid computing. By using commodity-based components, Linux can build large clusters that can be managed and controlled as a single system image. And with grid computing these large clusters can be shared as if they were one large, virtual computer. By leveraging lower-cost computing nodes that can cost-effectively scale your business applications, your organization is equipped to meet any workload your end-users can throw at it.

Avoid Vendor Lock-In. Control of software is important for corporations. Software alone accounts for most proprietary vendor lock-in. Linux forces organizations to learn how to work with the open source community further avoiding vendor lock-in. The more your organization uses and deploys solutions based on open standards, the greater is its vendor independence. Fortunately, Linux and open source are built on widely accepted industry standards.

Future Proof Environment. The goal of the Linux community is to develop standards that promote compatibility, enabling Linux applications to be supported on any compliant system. This decreases the cost for your organization to change its applications or application vendor. By using industry standards as a basis of selection for the best solution for your company, you will find that those solutions provide the right balance between cutting-edge innovation and proven industry approaches and strategies.

Improve Infrastructure Stability. Since the Linux kernel is developed from the combined effort of many industry development groups and standards committees, software components have been designed to interoperate efficiently, securely and more reliably.

Obtain Better Software Quality. One of the most important aspects of Linux and open source is that it has a large community of developers working on it. This method of development leads to higher quality software by leveraging the expertise of developers and end-users around the world. Open source development improves software quality through open peer review as well as providing a natural mechanism for rapid software fixes.

Reduce Total Cost of Ownership. Linux provides a tremendous cost savings in both capital and operational expenses. By avoiding the use of proprietary hardware and its associated high-priced software, Linux provides a low cost of computing with the broad availability of open source applications and support for commodity-based hardware. Whether the cost savings needs to be achieved on the desktop or in the data center, Linux and open source provides a vast selection of applications to reduce your total cost of computing.

Improve Application Performance. Linux is valued as a high-performance operating system due to its modular design and lightweight kernel footprint. Integer and floating-point performance improvements from Intel and AMD help Linux achieve the best performance benchmarks in the industry. And because Linux is the primary development platform for new and advanced technologies such as application grids, high-performance clusters and scalable file systems, it's no wonder these technologies run faster on a Linux operating environment.

Establish Better Security. Linux has received a significantly greater level of peer review than any proprietary code base. And since Linux does not incorporate obscure, proprietary protocols or services, it's inherently easier to make it more secure.

Find the Pragmatic Balance

Every technology choice should be based on the business applications it will support. With Linux and open source projects, this couldn't be more true. Organizations must find a pragmatic balance between the technical and business objectives of the applications.

It is imperative to understand what the IT goals are for your organization. Often these goals are mere ideals, but can become tangible objectives for the company. There are many objectives and goals that a computing infrastructure can provide. The importance of this list of goals is to ensure your organization understands "what it wants" from Linux and open source (see Figure 7–1).

Understanding these objectives helps bridge the traditional communications gap between technology and business decision makers, providing a common framework for understanding projects and the business value they deliver. Once this is understood, the Paradigm Shift begins.

Spend time with your executive management staff and peers. As shown in Figure 7–2, analyze cost allocations and recurring fixed expenses. Then evaluate the IT decisions related to your cost outlays. Are IT costs returning value to the business? This analysis will properly align your technology organization with the business side of the company, and ultimately improve its competitiveness in the marketplace.

Today's IT Imperative

- Better alignment with business groups
- Less waste — more reuse
- Reduce costs
- Streamline operations
- Better support for business growth opportunities

Figure 7-1. *IT Objectives.*

As a rule, it is helpful to include both near-term and long-term objectives. It is not uncommon to list goals that are part of a longer-term strategy, such as establishing your organization's five-year infrastructure plan. The goals of having ongoing flexibility and agility are valued more highly than one-time efficiency gains. Figure 7–3 lists today's acceptable goals as well as valid business reasons for pursuing a Linux and open source project.

Value-Driven Information Technology

Most organizations skip the important step of defining just what it is they're measuring. Before you can leap into a Linux and open source project, you must first focus on identifying what kinds of processes are of true business value to the organization. Just what are the business needs you are seeking to support and drive? The precursor to this value quantification is application categorization.

The first step within this decision-making framework is to bring clarity and focus to the project selection process. In order for IT and executive management to understand the importance of your Linux initiative, it is necessary

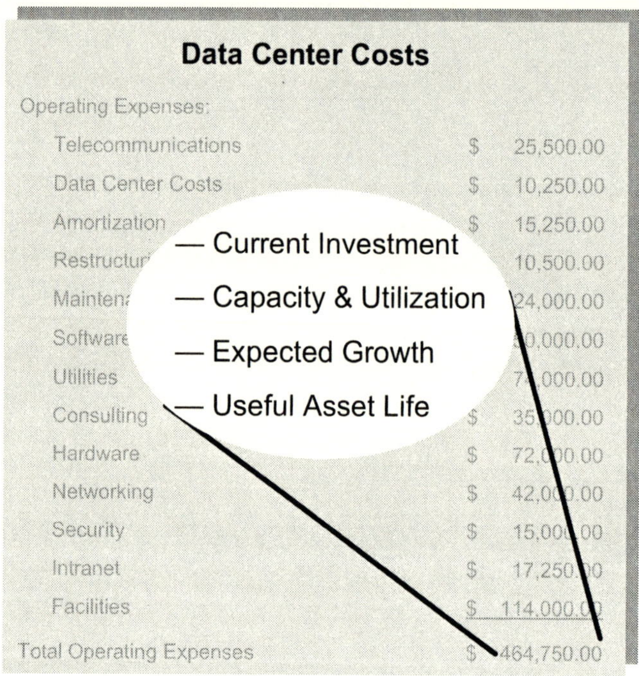

Figure 7-2. *Understanding Budget Allocations.*

to identify projects according to business need. Once projects have been classified, it becomes a simple process to determine which applications are unique to the organization (meaning they are extremely differentiating) and which are parity applications (meaning that they don't have to be better than any other business, they just can't be any worse).

For most companies, applications are easily segregated between those providing a "competitive advantage" and "mission-critical." That is, IT applications either advance the business organization competitively in the marketplace or they just help the business keep pace with the industry.

Once you have your organization's business application identified and categorized, you have a new and powerful basis for determining where your technology investments should be going. Linux initiatives are successful when the organization understands what it needs from the IT organization. As Figure 7–4 illustrates, value-driven information technology is about focusing on those applications that matter to the organization.

Critical Success Factors

Linux favors a targeted approach to adoption. It is unusual to find open source software deployed across an entire enterprise. Instead, use is limited to select business functions, departments or divisions.

Linux and open source initiatives should target computing environments identified as "mission-critical." New hardware required for these environments must significantly outperform or undercut the cost of existing systems. Mission-critical applications provide a continual business value and processing function to the organization. Generally, these applications are very typical among most companies.

Business-Line Objectives

- Must be scalable
- Must be flexible
- Must enable rapid deployments and *ad hoc* changes
- Must be cost effective and provide a timely return on the investment
- Must enable low labor headcount
- Must be secure and trustworthy computing environment
- Must provide a reliable infrastructure platform

Figure 7-3. *Aligning With Business Goals.*

In order to operate a business, the IT organization needs to provide generic processing functions such as Web, application and terminal services; system and network management processes; user and networking functions; file and storage systems; database repositories; information security applications; desktop environments; desktop productivity applications; and messaging systems.

In finding the pragmatic balance, the first area to look at is those applications that represent parity services for your organization. For these projects, it is not necessary to add any software or hardware uniqueness or add innovation to the application or application components since they do not add significant differentiation to the business. If the intent is simply to match the industry's best practices, then these projects should be the first ones

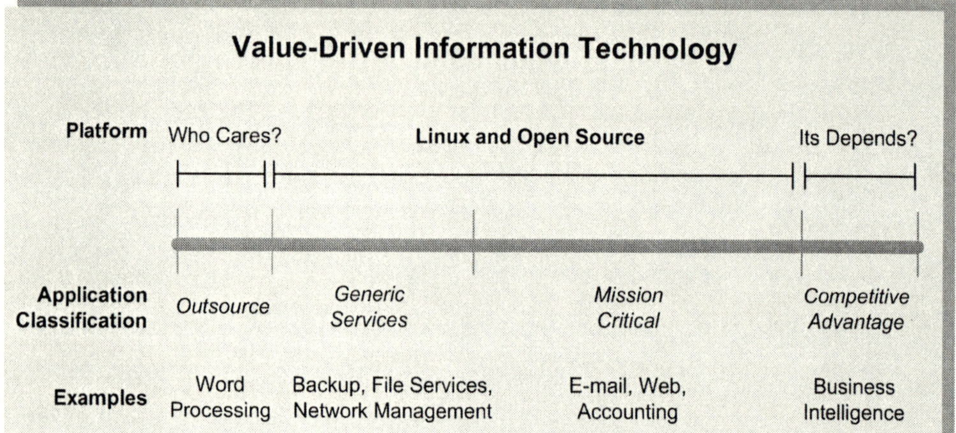

Figure 7-4. *Being a Value-Driven IT Organization.*

considered for Linux and open source alternatives. The next chapter will delve into more detail in identifying those applications within your organization.

Even though parity projects do not provide a competitive advantage or some sort of uniqueness for your company, that's not to say they are any less important to the organization. It still requires them to be highly reliable, available and scalable. They must deliver a satisfactory level of performance and not be difficult to manage. It simply means they should be built, installed and maintained as generically as possible. The value generated from parity projects can easily be reduced if they get overly complicated and require too many company resources.

The application category that matters most to the organization is IT functions providing a "competitive advantage" to the company. These business applications provide information processing functions that differentiate the company from other businesses in the marketplace. This is generally a much smaller set of applications within the application landscape (discussed further in Chapter 8) that might require support from many computing environments, not just Linux and open source.

Linux projects often fail because IT and business executives focus on projects that don't generate a positive return for the organization. Projects fail because companies focus on Linux for Linux's sake, and not for valid business-level reasons. Using a prioritization system that classifies projects by the value they bring to the business ensures the right resources are given to the right projects. This is extremely important for Linux and open source initiatives.

Key Takeaways

It is essential to clearly understand the business reasons why your organization is behind the movement toward Linux and open source. The answer is: It depends on the business and strategic planning your company's management team has already laid out. Business and technology decision makers must work together to define clear standards and justify exceptions based on cost breakdowns and the business value that is expected to be delivered.

Carefully consider why you want to move to this computing model. With this understanding, your organization can better manage its expectations and monitor its results. By aligning and supporting your IT and business goals, your organization has a better understanding of IT's service delivery responsibilities and, correspondingly, has a better handle on its priorities for Linux and open source projects. Developing a decision-making framework for projects brings more focus to the IT project process.

Most IT activities are either differentiating or parity processes. They either advance the business competitively or just help it keep pace with the rest of the market. Identifying business priorities around each project allocates the appropriate amount of resources — staffing, capital investment and time — to each project. By prioritizing and classifying these decisions, the executive management, business and technology organizations can examine them more objectively.

Key #2

Surveying the Application Landscape

The computing application real estate must be surveyed and documented to pave the way for the Linux and open source Paradigm Shift.

Key Overview

Applications are the focal point for successful Linux adoptions. Whether the applications run on the desktop or are hosted in the data center, the Paradigm Shift is about how an organization delivers its business applications. Linux enables an infrastructure that delivers these applications reliably and securely.

Chapter 8

The Application Landscape

Knowing when to get off the old curve and jump onto the new is the secret of staying ahead of the competition.
— Richard Foster, Creative Destruction, New York Times Bestseller

The application landscape represents the most expensive piece of computing real estate in your organization. By surveying this landscape, organizations can uncover potential opportunities for Linux and open source. The purpose of a Linux-based computing infrastructure is to provide a reliable substrate for business applications to run on. It is important to remember that applications are the only reason the Linux infrastructure exists in the first place.

Companies must take a look across the infrastructure to find out where Linux fits best in the organization. The most optimal way of doing this is building an Application Matrix.

Conducting an Application Survey

An Application Matrix is central to any open source or Linux effort. It is essentially a detailed understanding of the business computing environment. This includes a complete discovery of the hardware and software components, their relationship with each other and their relationship back to the business services they support.

It is recommended to use automated discovery and a service impact models to help determine these relationships. Discovery helps to identify what is in the computing infrastructure, what the settings and configurations are and should be, and how each business service component is linked within the business environment.

Why Standardize?

Increase Agility
- Ability to leverage staff skills which improves overall utilization of personnel
- Reduces new project complexities

Increase Revenue Opportunity
- Faster time-to-market from IT efficiency gains
- Builds competitive edge due to simplified infrastructure

Reduce Risk
- Reduces complexity, skill requirements and risk
- Ensures common processes for security and disaster recovery

Reduce Costs
- For every OS eliminated, as much as 20 percent recurring costs can be eliminated

Figure 8-1. *Reasons to Standardize.*

How many different databases, operating systems and hardware configurations are actually deployed in your computing infrastructure? How many custom applications, management tools, drivers and application interfaces does your organization support? What development tools are used and how often are design elements reused to accelerate application development?

The answers to these questions enable your organization to build and deploy a Linux and open source foundation that can help it move toward a simpler and more standardized environment — an environment with a limited number of design patterns, configurations, components and services. Figure 8–1 shows why standardizing is important for your organization.

An Application Matrix identifies the interrelationships and dependencies of components, or groups of components, in the infrastructure. Appendix A provides an example of an Application Matrix.

Building an Application Matrix

The process of creating an Application Matrix provides an ideal opportunity to review business systems and client software with respect to identifying proprietary vendor lock-in (subsequently documenting the high costs associated with them). It also provides an opportunity to review and quantify security vulnerabilities. It is a perfect time to review business application performance and availability noting both planned and unplanned downtime associated with the current underlying computing infrastructure.

The Application Matrix should include:

- The Application name, version number and contact information of its support personnel
- How many users require access to it
- Details about the operating environment, including system and third-party software
- Details about the underlying hardware infrastructure, including interfaces and peripherals
- The configuration of the storage fabric and storage arrays supporting the application infrastructure
- OS components, including patches and maintenance releases
- Requirements for accessing the applications outside the internal networks

The Application Matrix collects application infrastructure details, establishing the processing environment baseline. Fortunately, most of this information is easily collected in an automated fashion using asset inventory tools. Discovery helps to identify what is in the computing infrastructure, what its settings and configurations are and should be, and what business service each component is linked to within the business operations. As illustrated in Figure 8–2, an application assessment provides a detailed baseline of the computing infrastructure.

The Application Matrix is not only needed for creating a plan of action, but much of it is required to be able to construct a valid cost of ownership model. In summary, the Application Matrix helps to ensure that the choices made today provide the capabilities that are required in the future.

Application requirements involve an understanding of the overall requirements for application scalability, availability and operational management and controls. In order to define an application's scalability requirements, it is important to understand the application workload characteristics. This includes both current workload requirements as well as an estimated projection of future workload requirements. Projections should be made over multiple time periods.

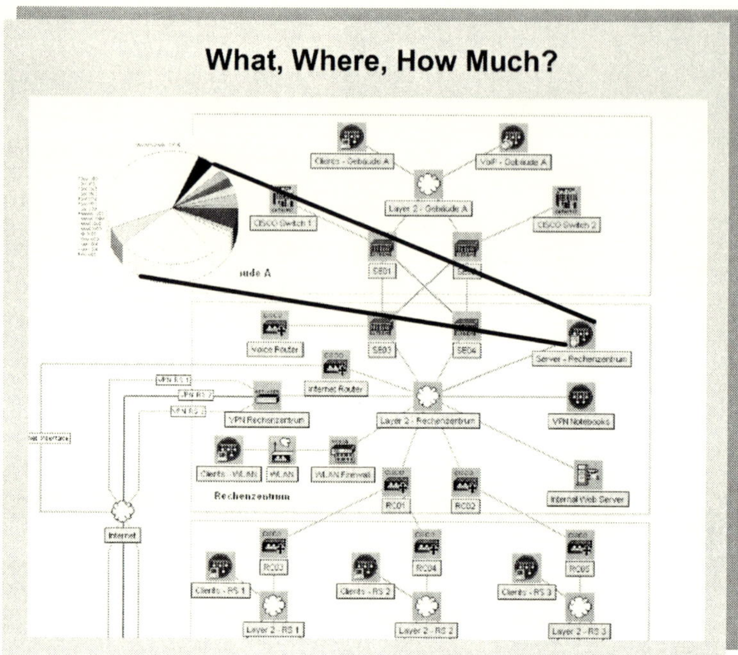

Figure 8-2. *Knowing Your Network Environment.*

The main issue is to determine:

- What matters most to the application?
- What sets of application metrics capture the criteria against which the system is evaluated?

Availability requirements are an important consideration in order to develop the proper infrastructure recommendation. Availability requirements are often stated in terms of service level agreements (SLAs). Operational considerations must be understood in order to provide an application environment that is easy to support and maintain. A good understanding of these trade-offs and their impacts to an existing or new application is crucial to the upcoming migration effort (see Figure 8–3).

Application Selection

Software for Linux is plentiful — there are more than 10,000 stable open source software products. There are multitudes of Linux touch points within an application landscape (see Figure 8–4). The best method for pinpointing potential Linux and open source applications for your organization is identifying industry standards used in your current computing environment. For most organizations, the industry standards being used would allow the company to substitute any proprietary software for open source applications such as Apache, Mozilla, NFS, OpenLDAP, OpenSSH, OpenSSL, Perl, PHP, Python, Samba and Sendmail.

Scope Definition

- What are your key applications?
- What dependencies do they have?
- Who are your key users?
- Which functions are most important?
- What are the necessary features during active operation?
- Which alternatives are available as open source?
- What are the functional differences?
- What must be taken into consideration during migration?
- What are the repercussions of the potential integration of other vendor product lines?
- What are the top business and technology priorities?
- What are the tradeoffs among priorities, such as achieving cost reduction or improving infrastructure flexibility?

Figure 8-3. *What Is the Scope?*

Obviously there are thousands of commercially available Linux-supported applications, databases, network and systems tools, security packages, messaging applications and desktop alternatives, but there are just as many freely available open source counterparts, including open source alternatives that have commercial sponsorship. Just looking at the sidebar **Open Source Software Categories**, it is easy to see how Linux and open source can provide valid application alternatives for your organization.

The process of determining which applications should be targeted for an open source platform is an ongoing process that depends on a number of factors. The best approach toward application selection is first obtaining a clear understanding of the strengths and weaknesses of your current applica-

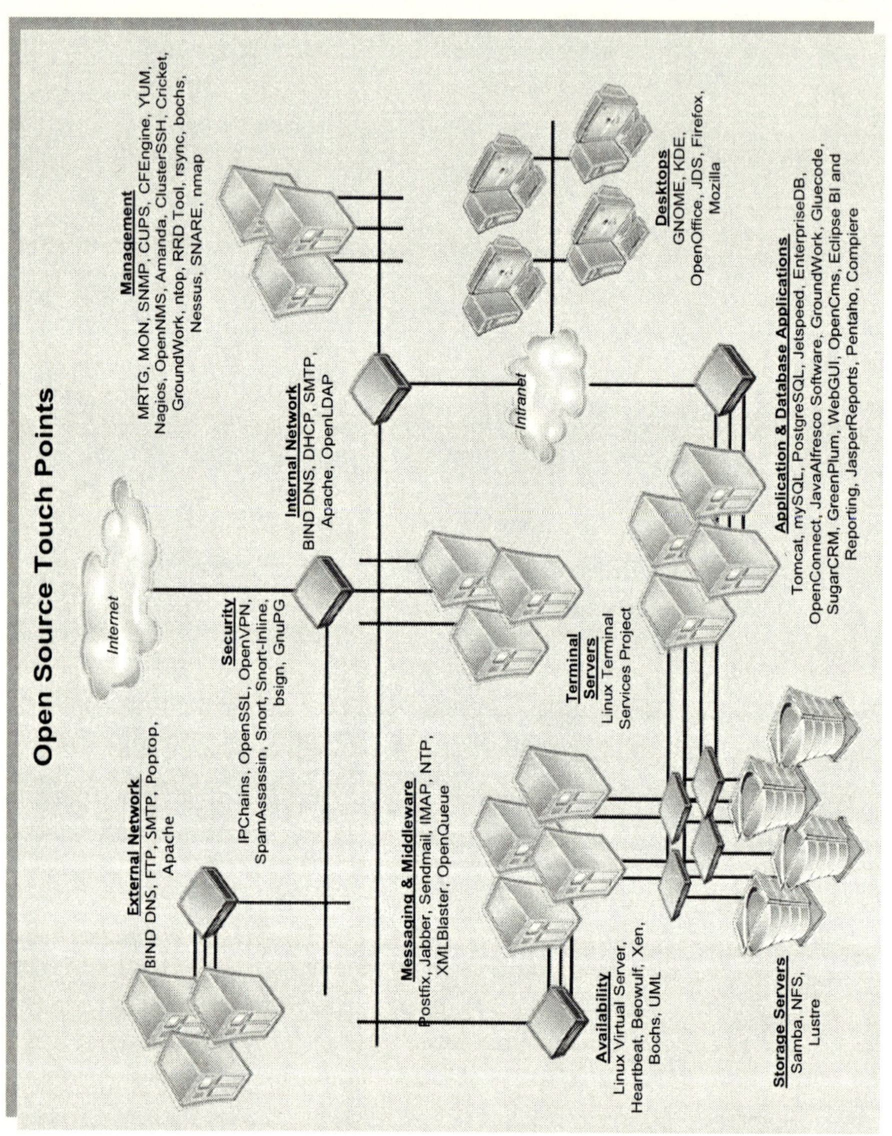

Figure 8-4. *Open Source Deployment Examles.*

tion environment. Obviously, anywhere there tends to be a perceived weakness in the application computing environment is an excellent area to consider using a Linux-based alternative.

Moving to Linux and open source must provide some sort of advantage to the organization. If there is no "value add" associated with moving away from your current application environment, then there is no reason to migrate. A Linux and open source strategy is about improving your application processing environment. It's about increasing your application service availability. It's all about getting more performance out of your systems. And it's definitely about lowering your cost of computing.

The goal is to identify the best fit for Linux in your organization. For most organizations, the best approach is to first adopt commercially developed Linux applications. After the organization becomes familiar with the process of deploying, managing and supporting these applications, it can begin to experiment with open source solutions. The first step in looking at Linux applications starts with answering questions specific to your application environment, such as:

- Where is there application support for Linux?
- Does it provide complete application functionality?
- What are your most price-sensitive environments?
- Are there end-of-life environments that require a refresh?
- Are there simple applications that can be hosted in a utility environment?
- Are there environments that are trying to escape vendor lock-in strategies?

For applications that have no Linux or open source equivalents, a thin-client environment (see Chapter 10) provides a non-disruptive way of providing access to these applications until they can be replaced with Linux and open source equivalents. A combination of open source and proprietary applications is not uncommon. The goal is to create an optimal business computing environment.

It is important to understand that Linux-based computing is not an all-or-nothing proposition. Linux can be gradually put in service in the data center by systematically replacing network functions. Or the process can begin with the deployment of open source solutions for a new business application. Organizations can install Linux desktops but keep users accessing Microsoft Office applications. Or companies can deploy Linux desktops and applications but segment these users to affinity groups such as back-office or transaction users. It's all a matter of control and process.

As outlined in Figure 8–5, there are critical success factors that do influence the success of your organization's adoption of Linux-based business applications. Following the Seven Keys will no doubt improve upon this success. Below is a list of popular infrastructure and middleware services that should be apart of your open computing reference architecture. Most are provided in all Linux distributions.

Critical Success Factors

- Focus on initial deployment costs (both hardware & software)
- Focus on ensuring application stability
- Avoid exotic hardware configurations
- Avoid software bloat (select only the applications absolutely required)
- Assess all compatibility issues (consider use of Terminal Services for native Microsoft application access)
- Provide training and workshops
- Continually highlight long-term benefits to the organization

Figure 8-5. *Critical Success Factors.*

Apache

Apache is an open source Web server that is developed and maintained under the auspices of the Apache Software Foundation. Apache is the most prevalent Web server on the Internet garnering appropriately 70 percent market share of the Web server install base according to the NetCraft Web server survey (http://www.netcraft.com/survey). For more information, visit http://www.apache.org.

Axis

Apache Axis is SOAP toolkit for software developers. SOAP is a XML-based protocol that is universally accepted W3C (World Wide Web Consortium) standard backed by Microsoft, Sun Microsystems, IBM and HP. For more information, visit http://ws.apache.org/axis.

CUPS

CUPS (Common Unix Printing System) is the de facto printing service for all major Linux distributions. CUPS is designed for cross-platform print sharing across IP networks. CUPS supports all popular print service protocols, such USB, Parallel, JetDirect, IPP, LPR/LPD, Socket/AppSocket and CIFS. It is uncommon to find a printer that is not supported with CUPS on Linux. For more information, visit http://www.cups.org.

DHCP

DHCP (Dynamic Host Configuration Protocol) is an Internet protocol for automating the configuration of computers including the assignment of TCP/IP addresses, subnet mask, default router, and other configuration information including the addresses for printer, time and news feeds. For more information, visit http://www.isc.org.

DNS

DNS (Domain Naming Service) is a global naming service for the Internet. DNS provides hostname-to-IP address mapping as well as lists the mail exchange servers accepting email for each domain. BIND (Berkeley Internet Name Domain) is the most commonly used DNS server on the Internet. For more information, visit http://www.isc.org.

Geronimo

Geronimo is a J2EE-based application server based on the Apache open source license (this license is less restrictive than the JBoss LGPL). For more information, visit http://geronimo.apache.org.

Jabber

Jabber is an XML-based protocol for instant messaging providing one-to-one chat, multi-user chat and presence (although not limited to IP communications, it has become synonymous with IP applications such as VoIP and Instant Messaging). Jabber provides a secure, ad-free instant messaging alternative to IM services such as AIM, ICQ, MSN and Yahoo. For more information, visit http://www.jabber.org.

JBoss

JBoss is an J2EE-based application server based on the open source LGPL license. JBoss, Inc. provides royalty-free software for its active development community, but also provides the ability for organizations to purchase professional support services. For more information, visit http://www.jboss.org.

Jetspeed

Jetspeed is an open source implementation of Java Portlet Standard that leverages Java, XML, RSS or SMPT content. Jetspeed aggregates information from multiple sources and provides a common structure and framework for these data sources and applications. For more information, visit http://portals.apache.org.

Linux Terminal Server Project (LTSP)

LTSP enables thin client computing by allowing applications to execute on servers and display their output on the desktops (a.k.a. thin client computing). For more information, visit http://www.ltsp.org.

Linux Virtual Server (LVS)

LVS is a scalability and availability solution. LVS provides advanced IP load balancing and failover functionality as well as application-level load balancing and cluster management. LVS is implemented in the Linux kernel. For more information, visit http://www.linuxvirtualserver.org.

NFS

NFS (Network File System), originally developed by Sun Microsystems, provides heterogeneous, network-based file sharing allowing systems to mount disk partitions across an IP network. For more information, visit http://nfs.sourceforge.net.

Network Time Protocol (NTP)

NTP is used to synchronize the system clocks on servers with a high degree of accuracy (millisecond precision). For more information, visit http://www.ntp.org.

OpenLDAP

OpenLDAP is an open source implementation of the LDAP (Lightweight Directory Access Protocol) standard. OpenLDAP comes with a complete set of tools that allows the implementation and deployment of an LDAP-based directory. OpenLDAP provides a standard-based authentication mechanism to query information about users, directories and resources. For more information, visit http://www.openldap.org.

Samba

Samba is an open source implementation of Common Internet File System (CIFS). Samba allows you to consolidate Linux, Unix and Windows systems and is critical for mixed environments since it can synchronize user passwords between these environments. For more information, visit http://www.samba.org.

Struts

Struts, from the Jakarta Project, is a development framework for Java servlet applications. The Struts framework is designed to give you modularity and loose couplings with application development. For more information, visit http://struts.apache.org.

Squid

Squid is a proxy caching server for Web clients. It provides caching of Internet objects such as HTML, FTP, SSL, WCCP, provides HTTP server acceleration and caching of DNS lookups. Squid also is useful for providing network bandwidth controls and load balancing services. For more information, visit http://www.squid-cache.org.

Tomcat

Tomcat implements the Java servlet and the Java Server Pages (JSP) specifications (JSP code is Java code embedded within an HTML page). The Tomcat servlet engine often is used in combination with an Apache Web server. For more information, visit http://jakarta.apache.org/tomcat.

Open Sourcing Your Application Environment

Once your organization is successful with Linux applications, it should quickly begin investigating the use of open source solutions. There are many areas within the application infrastructure where open source solutions provide extremely reliable and highly secure alternatives. Common uses for open source include Web servers; firewalls; system and network management; security management; file and print servers; portals and Web applications; reporting and analytics; e-mail; and DNS. As highlighted in Figure 8–5, there are multiple open source alternatives readily available.

The most common area to begin deploying open source solutions is usually closer to the network layer of an application stack. This would include the areas illustrated in Figure 8–4, such as the external and internal network, security and management "touch points." Even though these touch points might be ancillary to a primary business application, they are extremely important to any applications' availability and functionality. The deployment of any open source solution should be done in such a way that it provides a highly available service.

Application Middleware and Databases

The next area to consider for open sourcing your application environment is with application middleware and databases. The open source community is very serious about the application development market. The Apache Software Foundation (ASF) is spearheading this effort with the launch of the Synapse initiative, an open source effort to produce a common, standardized way to broker services across a network. The Synapse initiative is an open source project to develop an interoperable framework for Web services infrastructure software, including an enterprise service bus, Web services brokers and Web services management products.

Businesses increasingly rely on these middleware components to connect applications and databases to complete business processes and deliver an application service. If your organization is serious about Linux and open source, the first step is to adopt an open source reference architecture for application development, as illustrated in Figure 8–6.

Database Alternatives

The Linux database segment is the fastest-growing segment of the database market. Because organizations can put together Linux servers utilizing open source and commercially developed Linux databases, resulting in a much less costly application database infrastructure, this Linux-based software segment has seen more development and improvements than other software categories.

There are many commercial database products available for the Linux platform. Most commercially available Linux databases are supported by the ISV application community and thus present virtually no risk. Open source database alternatives provide functionality almost identical to commercially available database products.

Commercial Linux Databases

Commercially available Linux databases are numerous. Almost every commercial database vendor has a version of its database for Linux. This is in large part because most database vendors use POSIX-compliant software development techniques, which make for a fairly straightforward migration to Linux. Additionally, the market for Linux databases is rather large con-

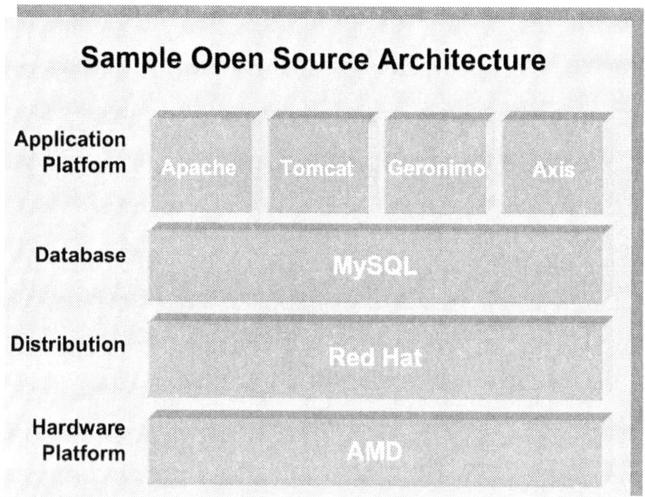

Figure 8-6. *Common Operating Environment.*

sidering the broad landscape of hardware support from mobile devices to SMP systems to NUMA architectures to S/390 mainframes.

The three most popular commercial database vendors are IBM, Oracle and Sybase. Each of these vendors has had a database product line on many OS platforms for more than three decades, which has allowed them the time to fully develop a scalable and highly available database environment including a rich set of development tools, administrative packages and ISV application support.

IBM DB2. IBM was an early supporter of Linux and continues to demonstrate technology and market leadership on this platform. Enhancing DB2 for Linux environments and exploiting the Linux kernel has been an important part of the continuing evolution of DB2 UDB.

IBM has delivered native 64-bit editions of DB2 and it has been optimized for all major Linux platforms. IBM supports the broadest range of high-end Linux platforms including the new 64-bit systems from Intel and AMD as

Open Source Software Categories

There is an open source alternative for virtually every Windows, Unix and Linux application in the marketplace. The following is a list of software categories where open source applications are freely available. There are many open source solutions available for each category. Revisit the section in Part I titled **Where Can I Find Open Source** to learn where to find and download these solutions.

Desktop Applications

Animation
Antivirus
Boot Rescue Tools
Business Presentations
CAD / CAM / CAE
CD / DVD
MP3 / MPEG4
Database Development
IDE
Desktop Publishing
Desktop Windowing
Disc Volume Encryption
Disk Defragmentation
Email / PIM / Groupware
Fax
File Compression
Flash Creation
Game Programming
GIS Solutions
Graphic Editor
Graphical Libraries
Graphing / Charting
Hard Disk Utility
HTML / DHTML Editor
Image Processing
Instant Messaging Client
IRC / IM Client
Java Development Tools
Network Diagramming
News Reader
Office Productivity
PDF Viewer
Personal Finance
Programming IDE
Project Management
Scanner Software
Scientific Applications
Speech Recognition
Spreadsheets
Statistical Analysis
Text Recognition (OCR)
TV Tuner
Video / Audio Conferencing
Visual Basic
Web Browser
Web Mail
Web Server
Windows Emulators
Windows Network
Word Processor
XML Editor

Server Applications

Backup Software
Business Intelligence
Clustered File Systems
Clustering and High Availability
Configuration Management
Content Filtering
Content Management
CRM
Cryptography
Data Synchronization
DHCP Servers
Directory Service
DNS Servers
Ecommerce Software
ERP
File Sharing
Firewall
FTP Client / Server
Gridware
HTTP Servers
Intrusion Detection System
IP Telephony
IPSEC
J2EE Application Server
Journal File Systems
Network Management
Network Routing
Object Request Broker
Port Scanning Detection
Private Branch Exchange
Protocol Analyzer
Proxy Server
Real Time Control
Relational Databases
Replication
Security Scanner
SMTP Servers
Spam Filter
SQL Databases
SSL
Stream Text Processing
SVG Viewer and Editor
System Configuration
System Management
System Update
Terminal Server

well as the zSeries (S/390). DB2 ICE (Integrated Clustering Environment) is a turnkey clustered DB2 hardware and software solution.

Oracle Real Application Cluster (RAC). Oracle RAC remains the only database technology in the industry that can leverage a cluster of IA-based Linux servers into a scalable and fault-tolerant platform. (The latest release is known as Oracle RAC 10g.) Oracle RAC can scale up to 100 servers in a single cluster and with Oracle Enterprise Manager Grid Control it is a simple environment to monitor, provision, clone and patch.

Oracle's key innovation is a technology called cache fusion. Cache fusion enables nodes on a cluster to synchronize their memory caches efficiently using a high-speed cluster interconnect. The key with RAC is that cache fusion enables shared data access by all nodes in the cluster (data does not need to be partitioned among the nodes). Oracle is the only Linux database with this capability due to Oracle's clustered file system (OCFS). Oracle has contributed the source code for OCFS to the open source community.

Sybase Adaptive Server Enterprise (ASE). Adaptive Server Enterprise for Linux is a highly scalable, high-performance Linux-based database engine. Sybase was among the first industry leaders to endorse the Linux platform — the company first released its flagship database for the Linux platform in 1999. Today, all core Sybase products run on Linux.

Sybase SQL Anywhere Studio is the industry's first mobile and embedded database for Linux, providing the same robust features and full technical support as other Unix and Windows platforms. Sybase's Linux versions support a broad range of hardware from workgroup servers to monitoring systems to edge servers to point-of-sale devices.

Open Source Databases

What most organizations discover is that database performance is much better with open source. Currently, the only drawback to open source databases is that they are not quite as scalable as commercially available databases. Yet open source databases can replace the majority of all database deployments today since most database applications do not require such large scaling. Below is a list of the most popular open source, Linux-based database servers in the industry.

EnterpriseDB. EnterpriseDB is based on PostgreSQL and designed to run applications written specifically for Oracle database applications, providing organizations with dramatic cost reductions in both application migration and skills re-training. The solution includes EDB Database Server, the

RDBMS engine, EDB Studio, a console for developers and DBAs, and EDB Connectors, which provide access to EnterpriseDB 2005 from JDBC, ODBC, .NET, ESQL/C++, PHP, Perl and Python. For more information, visit http://www.enterprisedb.org.

Firebird. Firebird is a relational database offering ANSI SQL-99 and SQL-2003 features based on the open sources of InterBase from Borland. Firebird provides a fully featured database environment that also works well on Unix and Windows platforms. Firebird is available in Classic and Super packaging. The Super version is more suitable for high volume environments as well as where most of the database early development occurs. For more information, visit http://firebird.sourceforge.net.

MySQL. MySQL is part of LAMP (Linux, Apache, MySQL, PHP / Perl / Python), a fast-growing open source enterprise software stack. Fuelled by the Internet boom, MySQL is widely used on many Web sites. MySQL has incorporated many high-end database features, although it still lags some enterprise-level database functions such as views, triggers and stored procedures. However, due to its popularity, there are many tools and applications that work with MySQL. MySQL achieved international recognition when SAP made MySQL their SAPDB database (MaxDB). MaxDB is a full-featured, mature DBMS. For more information, visit http://www.mysql.com.

PostgreSQL. PostgreSQL is an open source object-relational database management system providing most features present in large commercial DBMSs. PostgreSQL has most features required in an enterprise-level database, as well as a number of other unusual and potentially useful features: user-defined types and operators, table inheritance, partial and expressional indexes (indexes defined on only part of a table, as limited by a condition or created on the output of expressions) and multiple stored-procedure languages including the native PL/SQL, PL/PHP, PL/Perl and PL/Python. For more information, visit http://www.postgresql.org.

Other Open Source Databases

Ingres
http://ca.com/opensource

Interbase
http://freshmeat.net/projects/interbase

SQLite
http://freshmeat.net/projects/sqlite

GNU SQL Server
http://freshmeat.net/projects/gnusqlserver

Key Takeaways

You must examine your application computing infrastructure to find out where Linux and open source fit best in your organization. The most optimal way of doing this is building an Application Matrix to ensure that the choices you make today provide the capabilities that are required in the future.

Successful Linux and open source initiatives adopt the principle that it is not an "all or nothing" proposition. That is, you don't have to convert all your desktops to Linux, just those that are deemed suitable for the organization. You don't have to host Linux across your datacenter, just on those platforms where it makes the most sense.

Surveying the application landscape and understanding where Linux and open source fits within your organization provides the basis for a highly successful project.

Chapter 9

Today's E-mail Dilemma

The two basic principles of Windows system administration: for minor problems, reboot; for major problems, reinstall.
— Anonymous Windows Administrator

Restoring the balance of power between customers and vendors, along with gaining greater flexibility, transparency and freedom of choice, have been key drivers for Linux adoption and the open source movement, creating one of the biggest disruptive shifts in the industry. The advantages that Linux offers to an e-mail infrastructure — reliability, security, price per performance and freedom from proprietary vendor lock-in — strike at the very heart of the issues plaguing e-mail systems today.

The increased interest in Linux e-mail is linked to two trends. The first trend is that organizations have moved up the stack from a focus on using Linux just for the network infrastructure to a focus on using Linux for business-critical applications. The second trend is that many organizations are unhappy with their current e-mail systems and are now in the process of evaluating potential alternatives. The problems surrounding e-mail that customers are trying to solve play to the strengths of Linux. And this is exactly why this chapter discusses Linux-based e-mail solutions.

State of the Industry

There is a mature, consolidated e-mail market that is dominated primarily by Microsoft Exchange (Lotus Notes/Domino and Novell Groupwise are second and third). And, unfortunately, Microsoft creates a tight coupling between its "e-mailer" and other supporting infrastructure components. For instance, there is a tight interdependence between MS Exchange, MS Outlook and MS Active Directory, not to mention the interdependence on the underlying Windows platform that is required for the desktop and server platforms. The consequence of this interdependence is higher cost and greater complexity.

By not having a choice with the selection of e-mail infrastructure components and supporting applications, organizations invariably face vendor lock-in. Companies dealing with proprietary ecosystems bear a higher cost from the requirements of planned obsolesce, frequent hardware and software upgrades, higher administrative costs dealing with security and reliability, greater cost due to inflexible licensing policies and a larger investment in hardware equipment to meet scalability requirements.

E-mail Basics

To better understand how Linux can effectively replace a MS Exchange environment, it is necessary to explain how e-mail systems work. The basic principles behind Internet e-mail involve the use of three components: MUA, MTA and MDA. The mail is generated by a Mail User Agent (MUA). It is then passed to a mail server, which has to decide whether it can deliver the mail locally or whether the mail must be passed to another server. Each server consults a local configuration file together with information from DNS servers (known as MX records). The mail is passed from server to server until one of them decides that it can deliver the mail locally. When this delivery is complete, the mail is then available to a MUA.

The Mail Transport Agent (MTA) accepts connections from other mail servers and MUAs via the Simple Mail Transport Protocol (SMTP). If the mail is not for local delivery it is then sent by the MTA to another server. If the mail is for local delivery it is passed to a Mail Delivery Agent (MDA) where it is saved in the user's local mailstore. Sendmail is a common MTA.

The MUA is the package that most people think of as "e-mail." This is the client software that runs either on a Web server or directly on the desktop. The MUA handles protocols such as SMTP for mail delivery and IMAP or POP for mail retrieval. Where there is a requirement for strong end-to-end security, the MUA is also responsible for data encryption and creating digital signatures for e-mail messages. Figure 9–1 illustrates these concepts.

A Standards-Based Approach to E-mail

Organizations that have deployed other infrastructure and applications on Linux, such as Web servers and databases, are well positioned to migrate

Replacing Microsoft Exchange

There are essentially two approaches to Linux-based e-mail. The most elegant approach, at least from a technical perspective, is implementing a pure Linux end-to-end e-mail infrastructure by deploying both Linux mail user agent (MUA) and mail delivery agent (MDA) software. Most solutions that provide both Linux MUA and MDA also provide connectors that allow integration with other e-mail MUA (i.e. MS Outlook).

Another alternative, which is gaining popularity, is just implementing a Linux-based MDA. That is, preserve the e-mail MUA and switch out the proprietary MDA. Usually this approach appeals to organizations that have implemented MS Exchange since most other MDA, such as Lotus Domino or Novell GroupWise, are fully supported on the Linux platform.

Another approach is using an e-mail portal that implements the Internet Calendaring or the Scheduling Core Object Specification known as iCalendar. In reality, this is really an extension of the previous alternative.

There are many excellent choices that provide a pure end-to-end Linux e-mail solution. More than likely there is a very adequate e-mail solution bundled in your Linux distribution. One of the most popular Linux e-mailing packages is Evolution.

Evolution or Novell Evolution (formerly Ximian Evolution, prior to Novell's 2003 acquisition of Ximian) is the official personal information manager and messaging solution for GNOME. Primarily sponsored by Novell, Evolution combines e-mail, calendar, address book and task list management functions, and can connect with other e-mail MDAs such as Novell GroupWise and MS Exchange.

Organizations that have already deployed MS Outlook clients might want to consider those solutions that are designed to replace MS Exchange. By replacing MS Exchange, you are also replacing the need for (and vulnerabilities of) Windows. These solutions provide native Microsoft Messaging API (MAPI) support.

By supporting MAPI, these solutions enable support for the majority of Outlook functionality. Preserving the MS Outlook installed base can be a practical approach for some organizations, but that does mean continuing to individually configure and manage a Windows desktop as well as paying a MS Outlook client license fee.

There are several products that provide integration with MS Outlook such as Scalix, Samsung Contact, CommuniGate, Novell's Openexchange and Sun Microsystems' Java System Calendar. Both Scalix and Samsung Contact are based on licensed versions of Hewlett-Packard's OpenMail. These MS Exchange replacements also provide Webmail access, which allows your organization to gradually migrate away from the cost of licensing and deploying MS Outlook clients. These solutions also support any POP and IMAP clients such as Evolution, Mozilla Mail, Eudora or Outlook Express. (Most also support wireless e-mail access to devices such as BlackBerry.)

One good reason an organization may want to use these MDA alternatives, instead of going with a complete end-to-end Linux-based e-mail solution, is because of the various desktop clients they need to support. In organizations that have a mixture of Windows, Linux and Mac desktops, a Linux-based MDA is an ideal solution to provide the flexibility of having different e-mail clients, while preserving full function and synchronized access to their e-mail, calendar, contacts and shared folder data. But perhaps a better overall solution in that situation is to use a server-based, platform-independent Webmail interface.

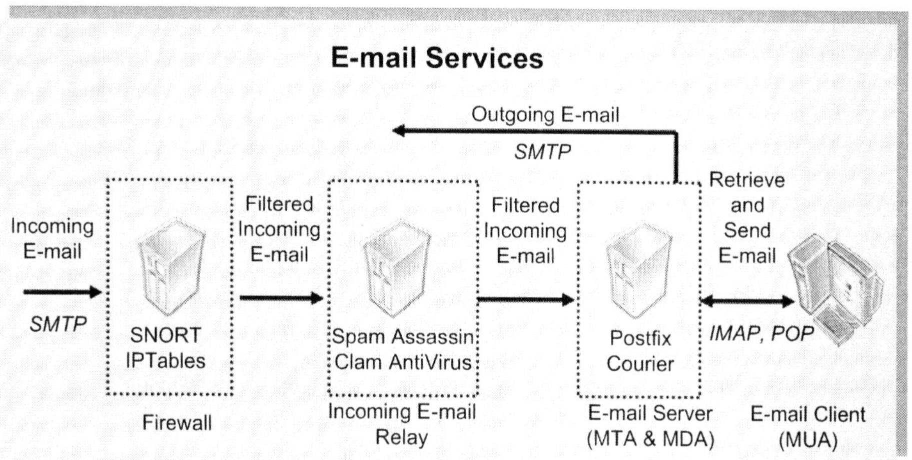

Figure 9-1. *E-mail Infrastructure Components.*

their e-mail infrastructure to Linux. A well-designed e-mail system that fully exploits the power of Linux allows organizations to reduce costs by leveraging commercial and open source tools for building an e-mail infrastructure. To keep abreast of open source projects, SourceForge (http://www.sourceforge.net) and Freshmeat (http://freshmeat.net) offer a wealth of information on e-mail clients, filters and transport agents.

Linux and open source infrastructures provide a high degree of flexibility, allowing organizations to better manage their e-mailing solution according to their business and technical needs. Fortunately, Internet e-mail has been developed and based upon open industry-standard protocols and APIs ideal for a Linux-based infrastructure.

A key requirement for Linux e-mail systems is that it should provide full-function support for the desktops and e-mail clients already in use. Sharing calendaring and contact information with other organizations requires Linux e-mail alternatives to support these common e-mail and groupware features.

Linux E-mail Solutions

Linux e-mail solutions can be implemented in various ways. The primary method of implementing a Linux e-mail alternative is to replace the MDA (i.e. MS Exchange). By replacing the e-mail server, MUA clients (i.e. MS Outlook) can transparently connect to the Linux e-mail server.

Alternatively, the Windows client can be replaced and users can connect to the e-mail server via a Web browser. Web-based e-mail provides the advantage of anywhere, anytime access through an Internet browser. Web-based e-mail clients offer the same familiar desktop application features, including a three-pane user interface, pull-down menus and drag-and-drop capabilities for e-mail access.

When the Linux e-mail server is used to connect to existing MS Outlook clients, it connects via MAPI (a proprietary API and protocol that delivers e-mail and calendaring functionality to the MS Outlook client). The popularity of MS Outlook has elevated the importance of native support for MAPI. Fortunately, most Linux-based e-mail solutions support the MAPI protocol and can easily replace MS Exchange without disruption to existing MS Outlook clients.

Linux e-mail solutions support all the Outlook features, such as:

- Integrated e-mail, calendar and directory services
- Rich Text Format (RTF) formatting
- Free/Busy directory calendar lookup
- Client- and server-based rules
- Delegates for mail and calendar
- Folder management, storage and sorting
- Public distribution lists
- Message properties: sensitivity, priority, expires by, flags
- Tasks and task delegation
- Offline folder synchronization
- Full Outlook address book and contacts
- Auto-preview of messages
- Public folders
- Event-driven notifications

Probably more important in the long run, however, is the support for industry standards such as SOAP and XML. These protocols play an important role in the evolution of a robust messaging architecture. Both standards help facilitate the move away from proprietary standards to the deployment of an open and componentized messaging architecture. Linux e-mail systems naturally exploit the power, flexibility and ease of integration that SOAP and XML offer.

The Linux Advantage

One of the most powerful features of a Linux-based e-mailing solution is the availability of Web e-mail clients. Known as Webmail, these Web-based e-mail clients provide many benefits. Webmail uses Web browsers and the HTTP (or HTTPS) protocol to access e-mail. For organizations, this is a very attractive alternative since it facilitates a server-based computing paradigm.

Not only does this simplify virus containment, archiving requirements, data protection processes and end-user support services, it greatly reduces the overall costs of an enterprise-wide e-mail infrastructure. Webmail does not require the support and maintenance of an e-mail client on the desktop. Webmail is attractive since end-users get the convenience of accessing their e-mail via the Internet. Obviously, a caveat with Webmail is it does require Internet connectivity and, consequently, does not support an offline mode like a client-based e-mail application.

Linux e-mail solutions provide a rich Web client that supports functions such as drag-and-drop, cut-and-paste and drop-down menus as well as calendaring and advanced collaborative features. With the support of secure and fast Web browsers such as Mozilla and Firefox, a feature-rich, desktop-grade e-mail Web client is an attractive alternative to MS Outlook. However, it is important that Linux e-mail solutions are built around a reliable e-mail infrastructure as outlined in Figure 9–2 to ensure high availability and reliability.

The specific advantages of Linux for an e-mail infrastructure are:

- Native, full-function support for open standards, as well as de facto industry standards such as SMTP, POP, IMAP, MAPI, SOAP and XML
- The use of Linux tools for e-mail system management
- Easy integration with other open source technology
- Linux file system-based message store
- Full-function support for the desktop and e-mail client of choice, including platform-independent Web clients
- A secure foundation that is significantly less vulnerable to security threats
- Reusability of existing Linux infrastructure investments
- A hardware-independent, open source platform
- Integration with the wide range of open source products such as directory, security, backup and storage, instant messaging, calendaring and scheduling, and collaborative applications

Open Source to the Rescue

In fact, there are a number of open source e-mail infrastructure services already deployed on the Internet. If your organization is not currently using any of these solutions, this provides a great opportunity to begin embracing the viability of open source computing.

A Reliable Linux E-mail Solution Should...

- Have multiple mail servers in active standby or in a load-balancing configuration
- Be attached via either SAN, NAS or iSCSI (storage system must be highly available)
- Use a centralized user directory that the mail server can refer to for account information and authorization (must be highly available)
- Have multiple mail relays and mail exchangers to queue the mail in case the network is temporarily not reachable

Figure 9-2. *E-mail Requirements.*

Clam AV

Clam AntiVirus is a GPL anti-virus toolkit. Clam AV provides e-mail attachment scanning using a flexible and scalable multi-threaded daemon, a command line scanner and a tool for automatic updating via the Internet. For more information, visit http://www.clamav.net.

Courier

Courier is an open source MTA that supports IMAP, POP3, LDAP, SSL and HTTP. Courier provides Encrypted SMTP, IMAP, POP3, Webmail and mailing list services. For more information, visit http://www.courier-mta.org.

Postfix

Postfix is an open source mail transfer agent (MTA) intended to be a faster, easier to administer and more secure alternative to Sendmail. Postfix is the default MTA in many Linux distributions and is included in the latest releases of Mac OS X. For more information, visit http://www.postfix.org.

Sendmail

Sendmail is by far the most widely used MTA. It processes approximately 70 percent of e-mail messaging traffic on the Internet. Sendmail has a long history with the Internet and has continued to evolve over the years. Sendmail is currently under the ownership of Sendmail, Inc., a company formed by Eric Allman, the original and lead software developer. For more information, visit: http://www.sendmail.org.

SpamAssassin

SpamAssassin is regarded as one of the most effective open source e-mail spam filters available. SpamAssassin is freely available under the Apache License. For more information, visit http://spamassassin.apache.org.

Key Takeaways

It is imperative that you rethink what your organization truly "needs" versus what your current applications "provide." Do you need basic e-mail service with calendaring? Would Webmail provide a better solution for your organization? Do you need a solution that can coexist in a multi-vendor e-mail environment? Does -e-mail drive other business-related processes that could leverage industry standards such as SOAP, XML, SSL or LDAP? With Linux and open source, it is important to understand what you require from your applications to support your business requirements.

Linux e-mail alternatives offer a cost-effective, secure, reliable and flexible solution when compared to other proprietary messaging systems. And e-mail is just one example of how business applications can be re-hosted to provide a robust and cost-effective solution for your organization. Whether you need a desktop client application that is easier to manage and control, or you require a more reliable, more scalable server-based application, open source software can be substituted for your proprietary business applications. However, it is up to you to determine and select which applications can be effectively re-hosted on Linux to provide better reliability, performance, flexibility and cost savings for your organization.

Chapter 10

Desktop Linux

Desktop Linux is no longer a technical challenge — it's a marketing challenge.
— Mitch Kapor

Many believe the desktop is the killer "app" for Linux. The *raison d'etre* for Desktop Linux primarily stems from the high licensing cost for the Microsoft Windows operating environment that includes an extensive ancillary set of office and other supporting applications that must be purchased to make Windows useful.

Desktop computing is one of the largest cost components for most organizations, and after businesses factor in the cost of server-based productivity applications that are associated with the desktop as well as the support costs, updates, security patches and mandatory hardware upgrades, the reasons for a Linux-based desktop become very compelling. For this reason, a dedicated chapter on desktops and desktop infrastructures is provided.

Companies are now realizing that the majority of their users are light producers or consumers of information, and that these users do not require all of the advanced features of an MS Office. Unfortunately, few ever use all the embedded functionality provided from a typical Windows desktop. And perhaps even worse, Windows users are continuously faced with MS Office application releases, maintenance and support fees, not to mention the hardware upgrades that are usually associated with it. Figure 10–1 highlights why organizations are switching from the Windows desktop standard.

Top Five Reasons Why Businesses Are Considering a Windows Alternative

1. Concerns about Windows security vulnerabilities
2. High cost of keeping Windows secure
3. High processing requirements for Windows, MS Office and applications
4. Ongoing frustration with Windows stability and reliability
5. Dissatisfaction with the cost and complexity of Windows licensing

Figure 10-1. *Disappointments with Windows.*

Desktop Computing Maturity

A Linux desktop deployment is different from a Microsoft Windows environment in that with the Linux desktop, every company can leverage a slightly different approach and deployment strategy. With Windows, most companies deploy it completely across the organization with no regard to customizing user functionality. Microsoft loves this approach since companies are consuming more Microsoft software licenses even though a significant portion of them are not warranted. This requires companies to invest in more desktop hardware than what is really necessary, not to mention the higher software licensing cost that organizations will pay as a result.

With Linux desktops, the desktop deployment is significantly different. Not only can organizations reduce the hardware investment for the organization, they can tailor the desktop configuration according to the employee's needs. This is because of the inherent flexibility that Linux brings to desktop computing.

Desktop productivity suites have now become commodity products. In an effort to out-feature other office application suites, Microsoft has single-handedly made desktop software a commodity since most of the newer features are functions that are rarely if ever used by the majority of desktop users. That is, most of the functionality now being provided with the standard MS Office suite is inconsequential and, as a result, office productivity suites have reached a level of product maturity.

Desktop Usage Models

There are four broad classifications of desktop users: transaction, power, knowledge and Internet. Each type of user operates under a different usage model and, consequently, can leverage a specifically tailored Linux desktop configuration.

At one extreme there will be power users dependent on a range of desktop applications whose features are used extensively. At the other end there are employees who make frequent but relatively shallow use of a desktop's total functionality.

Transaction Users

There are many subtypes of transactional workers but, in general, transaction workers are defined as users who use one or more fixed transaction applications, such as working at the Help Desk, providing order entry services or performing shipping and receiving operations. Transaction workers generally need access to e-mail, but not to many other business or office applications to perform their day-to-day tasks.

Power Users

Power users are defined as workers who have a deep knowledge of their office applications and use most, if not all, of the advanced features they offer. Power users include personnel such as IT professionals, engineers and software developers. They require access to e-mail as well as other office applications but primarily they need a high performance and custom desktop in order to perform their job responsibilities.

Knowledge Users

A knowledge worker is defined as a user who primarily needs access to office applications. Examples of knowledge-based workers include company managers or executives, financial analysts or field sales personnel. Knowledge workers can perform their job responsibilities solely by using an office suite of applications.

Internet Users

An Internet user operates primarily under a read-mostly usage model. These desktops are fixed function configurations that can operate either online or offline by providing access to e-mail, Internet or fixed content applications (e.g. kiosks).

Figure 10–2 illustrates these basic desktop usage models.

It is important that each company investigate the desktop environment looking not only at departmental categories but identifying and categorizing which personnel use the knowledge-, transactional-, Internet- or power-oriented usage model. Examining and categorizing employee usage model

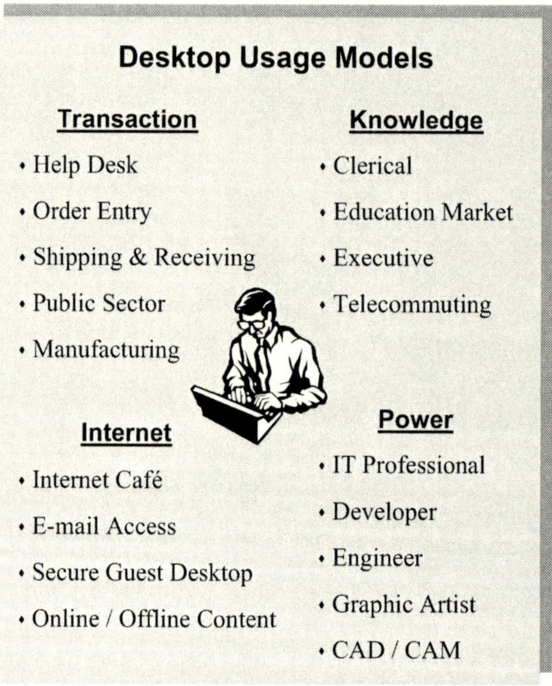

Figure 10-2. *Desktop Usage.*

requirements is the first step to creating an information-based desktop paradigm. Cost-effective alternatives can then be identified with training and support requirements.

The Basis of the Linux Desktop

Many users' only direct experience with computers is through their desktop or laptop computers running basic client applications, such as a Web browser, e-mail reader, word processor, spreadsheet or presentation software (a.k.a. office suite), and all of these must have a graphical user interface and be supported by an underlying graphical environment that, when bundled together, is affectionately called The Desktop.

Microsoft Windows outputs content using a method known as GDI (Graphic Device Interface). This creates a standard output facility that all Window applications can leverage. Windows also provides a set of standard widgets such as buttons, checkboxes, radio buttons and menu boxes. A standard API is provided as part of the system libraries to enable their use, which also allows developers to build their own widgets. In short, you can think of Windows as providing a tightly controlled set of building blocks for its applications. This provides the visual consistency that is familiar to all Window users.

With the Mac OS, Cocoa and Java applications utilize the Quartz subsystem to draw windows and other visual objects. It composes these objects just as the Windows graphics subsystem does; however the Mac OS discourages working outside the user subsystem API and instead encourages developers to strictly follow Apple's user interface guidelines. At a slight cost to mutability, this results in a desktop that is very consistent, not just within itself but also across all Mac applications.

The Linux Graphical System

The Linux desktop, in contrast, is drawn by a number of different programs and graphics libraries. The X Window System is the basis for the Linux GUI (as well as the Unix GUI). Applications use the X protocol to tell the display subsystem what to draw. The display subsystem, more commonly called X server, is responsible for dealing with all display and input events.

The application is called X client, for it requests the X server to draw things on its behalf. An implementation of a software framework for X clients and servers is available from the X Consortium (http://www.x.org). It includes X libraries that programmers can use to work with the protocol API.

By itself, the X protocol is a bit complex and tedious for application programmers to work with directly. The X protocol is actually a network protocol that provides the ability to work with graphical displays over a network

MS Office Alternatives

OpenOffice (OO) is an office suite, an open source project and a community. Compatible with all other major office suites, OO is free to download, use and distribute. The large open source community contributes to its development and support at http://www.openoffice.org.

OO is a multi-platform office productivity suite that runs natively on almost every operating system. It encompasses the key desktop applications, including word processing, spreadsheet, presentation manager and graphical drawing applications that support a variety of file formats and are compatible with MS Office. (The default output file format is Adobe PDF.) Since OO directly supports XML, it is interoperable with most other office applications.

OO provides user-expected productivity tools and ease-of-use functionality. OO provides autopilot guides (similar to MS wizards) that provide automated assistance while creating and working within documents as well as a stylist (similar to MS styles) that provides font and layout consistencies throughout a document. Typically, OO files are half the size of MS Office formats. With its well-documented APIs and SDK, OO can be easily extended and modified according to any business needs.

Writer is the word processor. It is full-featured and, for most tasks, can supplant MS Word. Features include styles, autocorrect, autoformat, autopilots, font special effects, advanced search and replace, database integration and object embedding. MS Word documents can be imported and re-exported. Writer lacks a macro recorder, but instead offers a script-style programming language called OfficeBASIC.

Calc provides a suitable replacement for MS Excel. Although it does not offer a complete replacement to all the features and functions, Calc does provide a broad range of spreadsheet functionality including 2D/3D charting and "what if" analysis. With Calc's DataPilot technology, data from databases can be cross-tabulated, summarized and manipulated.

Impress is the presentation application for OO. It is able to import and export MS PowerPoint files and, function for function, is on parity with MS PowerPoint. Impress provides slide transitions and the ability to use lecture notes as well 2D/3D clip art, special animation effects and high-impact drawing tools. Impress can interpret MS PowerPoint presentations providing full functional support. It supports a complete range of presentation views (Drawing / Outline / Slides / Notes / Handouts).

OO also offers a graphics and diagramming tool called Draw. Draw provides sophisticated graphics rendering and photo editing including features such as texturing, lighting effects, transparency and perspective manipulations.

StarOffice 7 Office Suite is Sun Microsystems' commercial product built on OpenOffice.org's open source code. It enhances OO with an integrated database called Adabas D, includes a licensed, commercial-quality spellchecker and thesaurus, and contains additional clipart images, sample templates and document filters. For more information about the features of StarOffice, visit: http://wwws.sun.com/software/star/staroffice.

Open Source Resources

The Desktop Linux Consortium. DLC is a vendor-neutral association that promotes interests and raises awareness of desktop Linux's emerging role. For more information, visit http://www.desktoplinuxconsortium.org.

DesktopLinux.com. The DesktopLinux Web site provides a focused desktop Linux-related news portal and forum. For more information, visit http://www.desktoplinux.com.

Linux Terminal Server Project. LTSP provides terminal services for thin clients, providing a Linux server-based computing solution. For more information, visit http://www.ltsp.org.

RDesktop. Rdesktop is an open source client that supports Windows Terminal Services by implementing the Remote Desktop Protocol (RDP). For more information, visit http://www.rdesktop.org.

as well as for a local OS. For this reason, developers generally do not work directly with the X protocol, but rather with widget toolkits. Popular widget toolkits are Motif, Qt from TrollTech, and GTK+.

It is the window manager (WM) that is responsible for how the X protocol looks and how it interacts on a desktop. Its primary responsibility is to provide the consistency between applications that is known as "look and feel." The WM provides an environment that makes life easier for end-users, such as dragging and dropping objects from one application into another, as well as providing the overall graphical interface for the desktop. Fortunately for Linux, freedesktop.org was formed to encourage cooperation and provide basic guidelines on how the various open source desktops for the X Window System should interoperate.

Linux Desktops

Two large, dynamic open source projects, KDE and GNOME, offer complete desktop environments that include a file manager, desktop administration tools and a broad range of applications ranging from simple games to complete office productivity suites. Both desktops offer a polished, mature and stable desktop environment. It should be noted that there are many other Linux desktop alternatives. For a directory of additional Linux desktops, visit http://www.desktoplinux.com.

The choice between GNOME and KDE is one of personal preference, but generally the choice is dictated by which Linux distribution is being deployed. Both desktops provide a functionally rich and easy-to-use desktop environment with interface personalization that is very similar to MS Windows.

The debate over which desktop is better was originally focused on the fact that KDE was not true free software. KDE was started in 1996 and, to make a graphical desktop environment, the KDE developers needed a programming toolkit. At that time, no free programming toolkit was available, so KDE utilized the Qt toolkit made by a Norwegian company named TrollTech.

However, Qt was not free software, creating an emotional debate within the open source community. Thus the argument over which desktop is better involved some philosophical issues. In reaction to the licensing turmoil presented from the inclusion of commercially based software within open source, Trolltech created the QPL (Q Public License), which was recognized by the open source community in 1999.

Although this step by Trolltech seemed to soften the debate at first, it was heated up again by an announcement in August 2000 at the LinuxWorld Expo that Sun Microsystems, Hewlett-Packard, Red Hat, Turbo Linux and others would support GNOME as the standard desktop for Linux.

Your selection criteria for choosing which Linux distribution to use could be based in large part on how closely the default desktop provided by that distribution meets your desktop functional requirements.

KDE

The K Desktop Environment project is the work of an open group of developers that now has 4.5 million lines of code and represents 400 person years. It provides a full-featured Windows-style desktop and application environment for Linux as well as for other Unix operating systems.

Widely heralded as a technological breakthrough for the Linux desktop, the standards-compliant Konqueror has a component-based architecture that combines the features and functionality of MS Internet Explorer and MS

Windows Explorer. KDE also provides an office suite known as KOffice (KWord word processor, KSpread spreadsheet, KPresenter presentation, Kivio flowcharting and diagramming, Karbon vector drawing, KChart charting, Kexi data management).

KDE maintains exceptional compliance with the Linux desktop standards. KWin, KDE's window manager, complies completely with the Window Manager Specification (wm-spec). Konqueror and KDE comply with the Desktop Entry Standard (desktop-entry-spec). KDE complies with the X Drag-and-Drop (XDND) protocol as well as with the X11 session management protocol (XSMP).

SuperKaramba (http://netdragon.sourceforge.net) provides the ability to fine tune the KDE environment. For a complete listing of the numerous applications available for the KDE desktop, visit http://www.kde-apps.org. For more information about KDE, visit: http://www.kde.org.

OpenOffice vs. Desktop Linux Offerings

OpenOffice at the moment appears to have more traction over KOffice and GNOME Office for Linux desktop users. This is primarily due to its compatibility with MS Office. There are other choices, however, that provide almost complete MS Office alternatives, such as Crossover Office from Codeweaver (http://www.codeweavers.com).

CodeWeavers' goal is to make Linux a fully Windows-compatible operating system. It is the leading corporate backer of the Wine Project (http://www.winehq.com), an open source software initiative that is re-implementing the Windows API, allowing CodeWeaver to run MS applications including the MS Office suite.

GNOME

GNOME is part of the GNU project and the Free Software Foundation (FSF). Miguel de Icaza started the GNOME project in 1997 and, by 1998, the project had more than 200 programmers contributing code. Miguel and Nat Friedman also co-founded Ximian (acquired by Novell). The original purpose of the GNOME project was to provide a user-friendly suite of applications and an easy-to-use desktop that is entirely open source.

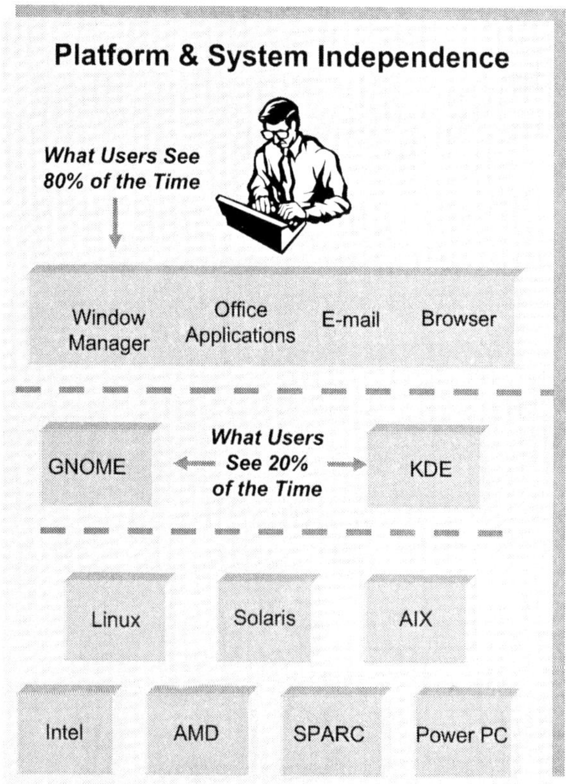

Figure 10-3. *Difference Between Platform and System.*

The major components of GNOME are the GNOME desktop, GNOME development platform, GNOME Office (AbiWord word processor, Gnumeric spreadsheet, GIMP image manipulation and GNOME DB data management), e-mail application and Internet browser. GNOME includes many other desktop applications such as GStreamer media handling and Bluefish HTML editor. For even finer tuning of the GNOME desktop, GDesklets (http://gdesklets.gnomedesktop.org) provide many options to add custom applications, or "desklets."

GNOME is the default desktop for Red Hat, Mandriva, Novell and Sun Microsystems. For a directory of GNOME-compatible applications, visit http://www.gnomefiles.org and http://www.gnomedesktop.org. For more information about GNOME, visit: http://www.gnome.org.

Other Desktop Derivatives

There are many commercial and open source Linux desktop derivatives. These products leverage the core pieces of GNOME and KDE to deliver specialized versions of a Linux desktop. All major Linux distributions provide a desktop environment based on GNOME, KDE or both. Figure 10–3 illustrates the basic concept of platform and system independence with a Linux desktop environment.

There are desktop environments being developed and released monthly so it is almost impossible to provide an accurate listing. Some of the new and intriguing alternatives are desktops that are trying extremely hard to replicate Windows (at least visually). These alternatives, including XPde and Lycoris (now owned by Mandriva), try to re-create the Windows XP interface to the pixel.

Among the more popular alternatives are Bluecurve, Java Desktop System (JDS), Linspire, Red Hat Desktop, SUSE Desktop and Xandros. Sponsored and developed by Sun Microsystems, JDS consists of a fully integrated desktop client environment including the GNOME desktop, StarOffice productivity suite, Mozilla browser, Evolution e-mail and calendar client, and Java 2 Standard Edition as well as the SUSE Linux operating system.

Bluecurve is a desktop theme for GNOME and KDE created by the Red Hat Artwork project. Bluecurve includes part of GNOME, KDE, Metacity, GTK+ and XMMS. Linspire — formerly known as Lindows but changed due to legal pressure from Microsoft over its Windows trademark — is based on the Debian distribution. Linspire targets consumer users with a full-featured and very user-friendly desktop environment based on KDE.

Xandros provides an enhanced KDE environment and delivers support for Active Directory, Codeweavers Crossover Office and StarOffice.

Migrating to Desktop Linux

Linux desktops work extremely well and are very cost-effective. However, it is important to realize that the most important requirement is the desktop applications that the organization and its users require to perform their daily tasks.

Figure 10–4 lists the most common reasons you will hear when considering a Linux desktop. Generally, the top five barriers for a Linux desktop migration are:

- Software availability and compatibility issues
- Usability and supportability of the new environment
- End-user acceptance of and resistance to change
- The cost and challenge of end-user training and support
- The cost and challenge of running critically needed Windows applications

Many organizations have found a number of useful processes for making this transition practical. Many start by replacing applications (and not the operating system underneath) with open source replacements. For example, an organization can easily switch to Mozilla for the Internet browser and e-mail reader as well as OpenOffice.org for the office suite without disrupting

What You'll Hear

- All my files are in Microsoft format
- I need to access legacy applications
- We can't afford to make this change
- Everyone only knows how to use Windows
- We only know how to manage Windows desktops
- Linux is too difficult

Figure 10-4. *Typical Excuses.*

the underlying operating environment. Table 10–1 lists the open source applications that can be utilized in a Windows environment.

Alternatively, organizations can replace the operating system with a Linux distribution, but continue to run Microsoft Windows applications via thin client computing. Then they can slowly replace applications with open source alternatives. Just about every significant Windows application has a Linux native counterpart.

Organizations can also move their infrastructure to a Web-based computing architecture and completely alleviate the concern around the underlying client operating system. Desktop Linux benefits from the ongoing trend to deliver software as a Web-based service.

The graphical user interfaces of most desktops have tended to converge on a fairly standard "look and feel" that reduces problems for end-users moving from one system to another. Even in light of similarities, end-user training will still be required to help people deal with the things that are different.

Desktop File Formats

Format	Proprietary	Open Source
.bmp	MS Paint	The GIMP, Ksnapshot
.jpeg	Adobe Photoshop	The GIMP
.doc	MS Word	OpenOffice Writer StarOffice SWriter
.pdf	Adobe Acrobat	Xpdf (to read) OpenOffice/StarOffice
.ppt	MS Powerpoint	OpenOffice Impress StarOffice Simpress
.xls	MS Excel	OfficeOffice Calc StarOffice Scalc
.avi, .mpeg	MS Media Player	Xine

Table 10-1. *File Formats.*

More importantly, training helps end-users get the most out of the new desktop environment.

Thin Client Computing

The desktop PC is perhaps the greatest drain on IT resources in terms of capital and time — yet few organizations could run their businesses without them. The shift from existing desktop environments to Linux has also triggered a shift in the desktop computing models that are being deployed by organizations.

As illustrated in Figure 10–6, there are three major types of desktops.

Thin Client. A desktop that is always connected and is usually built around the components of a Web browser utilizing a portal-based application infrastructure. Unlike a traditional desktop PC, which maintains a local copy of an operating system as well as its locally installed applications, a thin client is powered by a back-end server infrastructure. It is the server infrastructure that runs the applications with output transmitted across the network and displayed on the client. This reliance on a centralized server has led to the alternative term server-based computing.

Slim Client. A desktop that is intermittently connected and is usually built around client-server applications to Java components in a portal-based solution. Desktop processing is done remotely and locally. Slim clients are capable of running applications either on a back-end server or via the desktop.

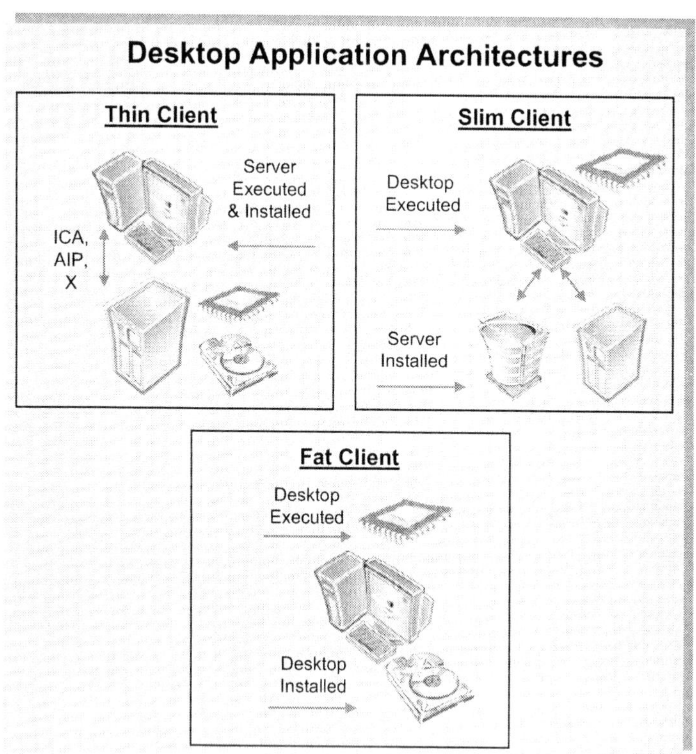

Figure 10-6. *Desktop Deployments.*

Fat Client. A desktop that has full offline capabilities with most applications locally installed and executed. Fat clients execute most, if not all, of their applications locally with the desktop maintaining the application configuration.

Table 10–2 highlights the most salient aspects of thin, slim and fat desktops.

Kill Your PC

The Linux desktop opportunity will be a mix of fat, slim and thin clients. The fat client is the dominant model of computing and has been since the advent of the PC some 25 years ago. With thin and slim models, desktop computing becomes completely transportable. That is, the desktop is inconsequential to the ability to use business applications, access business data, manage the desktop configuration, control virus detection and provide desktop administration.

Thin and slim clients use the network to access data and applications from servers rather than storing data or using processing power at the desktop.

Linux Is Ready, Corporations Are Not

Linux is definitely ready for the desktop, but it seems corporations are not quite ready for Linux. It's hard for most companies to make a business case to switch from Microsoft Windows in favor of the Linux desktop. The Linux desktop is stable, secure and very capable, but Linux resembles Apple Computer's Mac OS X¾ another capable desktop OS that does not enjoy widespread corporate adoption.

Most experts agree that the main reason for this slow rate of conversion is people. Since the majority of corporate end-users and technology staff are already trained on the Windows platform, a sudden migration to Linux would seemingly drive up costs. The fear in large corporations is lost productivity, even though Linux would offer a much lower cost to the bottom line.

The best time for a company to migrate to Linux on the desktop is when it is thinking about upgrading to the next release of Windows. Most agree that it's just about as much work to migrate to a new Windows edition as it is to switch over to Linux, especially considering that most PCs require hardware upgrades to support the newer Windows versions.

On average, organizations save between 20 percent and 30 percent on administrative costs, 50 percent on hardware, and 80 percent on licensing by switching to a Linux desktop. Best of all, most organizations have found that Linux stretches the lifecycle of desktop hardware by at least one or two years.

Besides providing a much lower cost of ownership, a Linux desktop affords organizations the tremendous advantage of a standards-based file format for office applications. Thanks to the efforts of OASIS (Organization for the Advancement of Structured Information Standards), OpenDocument is an XML-based file format standard that covers the features required by text documents, spreadsheets, charts and graphics. Linux office suites that support OpenDocument include OpenOffice, StarOffice, KOffice and IBM Workplace.

Thin clients require less administration, reduce maintenance, upgrade and support costs, and have a longer asset life than traditional desktop configurations. In terms of asset management, thin clients are the easiest desktop model to control, protect and manage.

Desktop Application Architectures

	Thin Client	Slim Client	Fat Client
Performance	Medium	Medium to Low	High
Serviceability	Excellent	Good	Poor
Cost / Unit	Medium	Medium to Low	High
Management Cost	Low	Low	High
Ease of Deployment	Very Easy	Very Easy	Complex
Licensing Costs	Low	Low	High
Scalability	High	High	Low

Table 10-2. *Desktop Deployment Characteristics.*

Any desktop computer can be converted into a thing client, even if the desktop system is several years behind current PC technology. There are also many purpose-built devices that are optimized for thin-client computing.

Most business software applications, such as word processors, spreadsheets, Internet browsers and e-mail applications, run equally well on thin clients as they do on the traditional desktop. In fact, these applications actually run much better in most cases due to the larger processing capabilities of the application servers compared to that of a typical desktop configuration.

The back-end servers that thin clients rely on are known as terminal servers. They get their name from the fact that these servers act as the graphics terminal for the thin clients. Terminal servers manage the desktop session including authentication, authorization and the graphics display. (Thin clients that support the X11 protocol are also known as X terminals.)

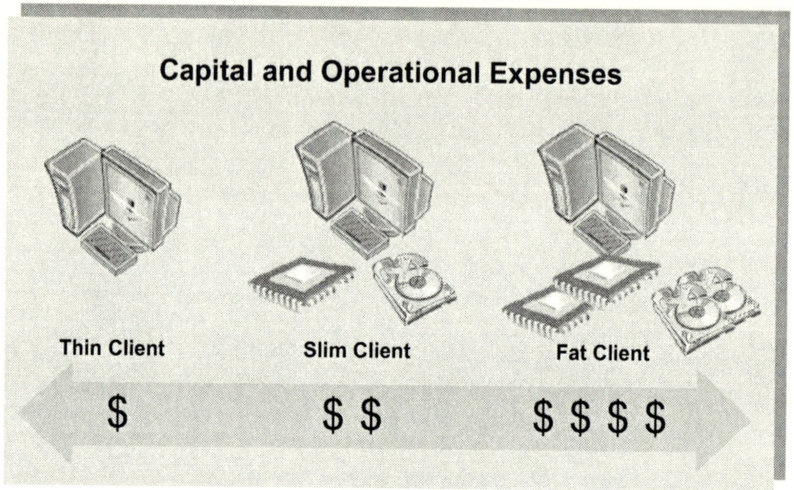

Figure 10-7. *Cost Comparison.*

By deploying thin clients and installing applications on centralized terminal servers, organizations instantly improve the quality of application service delivery and support, as all application management and desktop support is performed from a centralized, secure location. Because applications and data reside on centralized servers, the security and reliability offered by thin-client solutions are higher than what can be offered by a traditional desktop PC. Figure 10–7 illustrates the relative cost structure of the three types of desktop configurations.

Windows Application Access

No computing solution would be complete unless it offered seamless access to Windows applications. Through Linux-based thin-client computing solutions, Windows applications are easy to integrate via remote display software and terminal services. For example, CrossOver Office from CodeWeavers allows users to run MS Office applications, among other applications, all from a Linux server — without having to pay Microsoft operating system licensing fees. For data access, NFS and Samba provide an efficient method for data consolidation and interoperability with Microsoft file systems and printers.

Principally, there are three methods for integrating Microsoft applications into a Linux computing environment. One method is using a Windows Terminal Server and leveraging the Remote Desktop Protocol (RDP). RDP is the native connection method to a Windows Terminal Server. A competing protocol is the Independent Computing Architecture (ICA) developed by Citrix Systems.

Other alternatives for accessing Windows applications from Linux desktops involve some form of emulation. Within the emulation category, there are solutions that require a Microsoft Windows license and those that do not. Solutions that do not require a Microsoft OS license provide a completely rewritten Windows API. Based on the Wine Project (Wine stands for "Wine Is Not an Emulator"), these solutions rely on a translation layer that is capable of running Windows applications on the Linux OS by using a Linux implementation of the DLLs that Windows programs can execute.

The third alternative involves X86 emulation or providing a virtual machine (VM). These solutions actually emulate the X86 instruction set, thereby translating Windows applications into the corresponding Linux machine code (a.k.a. virtual machine). Most Windows applications are supported since they are running under a native Windows operating environment. However, VM, requires a full copy of the Windows operating system and a license for each user, in addition to a license for the emulator.

Bochs was the first open source X86 simulator. Bochs supports emulation of the X86 processor including memory, disks, display, Ethernet, BIOS and other common hardware peripherals. Many guest operating systems can be run using the emulator approach, including DOS, Windows, BSD, OS X and Linux.

Appendix D provides more information regarding the integration of Microsoft into a Linux desktop environment.

Server-Based Computing

Making technology decisions at a corporate level can result in significant cost savings for organizations. Having end-users run applications from a central server means everyone runs the same version of the same program. System administrators can deploy new applications quickly and easily, making them instantly available to the organization.

With server-based computing there is no need to manage desktops because all the system configuration information resides on the servers. Virus attacks can be localized and quarantined on an infected server rather than proliferated throughout the network to every desktop. This type of desktop computing is known as server-based computing. Server-based computing reduces support staff and software licensing costs for desktop systems.

For application upgrades, administrators need only to install software on the server, not the client machines. This reduces the need to upgrade existing PC hardware, as they only need the power to run the client-side software that links to the application servers. A central data repository allows users access to reliable and timely data from anywhere, in real-time.

Server-Based Computing

- Everyone runs the same application
- Upgrades happen simultaneously
- Near instant application deployment
- Data resides on secure servers; viruses are much easier and faster to quarantined quickly
- Greatly reduced support, purchasing and licensing costs for desktop and applications
- Can retrieve your data and run your applications from any desktop system

Figure 10-8. *Advantages of Server-Based Computing.*

Power consumption of a thin-client device can be up to 90 percent less than that of a traditional desktop PC. For example, a Sun Ray thin-client device manufactured by Sun Microsystems uses 15 watts compared to 120 watts for a basic PC — and this does not include the cooling that's necessary to counter the effects of this wattage. At 15 cents per kilowatt hour, a company with 10,000 employees would save more than USD $1.5M a year. The power savings alone completely offsets the cost of the thin-client devices, which are completely silent, maintenance free and have an expected life span of more than three times that of a desktop PC.

There are many reliable thin-client devices and software. Companies such as Neoware, Wyse and Sun Microsystems make extremely cost-effective thin-client devices that leverage a server-based application computing infra-

Display over IP (DOIP)

It's inevitable that pervasive and high-bandwidth capacity will eventually allow most of what happens on a desktop to migrate to the network. Why upgrade your PC if you can rely on network bandwidth to deliver your needed functionality as a service? You don't need to upgrade your TV set and the same should apply to your PC. DOIP is to a PC as XMRadio is to a CD player.

Essentially, DOIP is a PC that never gets upgraded and whose processing and intelligence are accessed remotely, not locally. DOIP might not be perfect for all applications, but it works well where Google.com works well, such as over a reliable broadband network. Eventually, DOIP will benefit from our telecommunications infrastructure having ubiquitous network coverage-even on an airplane.

structure (see Table 10–3 for additional thin-client solutions). Figure 10–8 highlights the most important aspects of server-based computing.

Hot Desking

Virtual Network Computing (VNC) software makes it possible to view and fully interact with one computer from any other computer or mobile device anywhere on the Internet. In essence, it provides a basis to deploy a server-based computing architecture. VNC software is cross-platform, allowing remote control between different types of systems.

VNC is remote control software that allows the capability to view and interact with one computer (the server) using a simple program (the viewer) from another computer. The VNC server can be configured to provide a Java viewer over HTTP, so you can use any Java-enabled Web browser on any operating system as a VNC viewer — all without having to install local software.

The VNC server acts as a virtual frame buffer managing the screen image of the application, but does not show the image on the server's graphics display. The VNC viewer interacts with the VNC server to obtain the frame buffer image in order to display it on the viewer's graphics terminal.

Advantages of Thin Clients...

Thin clients provide many advantages to your organization. For starters, all applications and user preferences can be configured to persist on the network. Known as hoteling or free-seating, this desktop model has not been viable for organization using solely Windows desktops. With a Linux-based computing infrastructure, it is possible for users to share Windows, Linux or Unix desktops in a successive fashion. Other advantages include:

1. Software licensing costs are significantly reduced.
2. Capital costs for desktop hardware are reduced.
3. Minimal setup time is required for installation of the desktop.
4. Desktop software rollouts are less expensive.
5. Desktop hardware has a longer useful life span.
6. Hardware upgrades are not required in order to run new applications.
7. Data resides on servers where it can be easily managed and controlled.
8. Users benefit from having a roaming desktop environment.
9. Increased administrative efficiency ensures servers are properly protected and secure.
10. Maintenance costs are reduced due to higher reliability of desktop hardware.
11. Desktops have no moving parts, causing fewer components to fail.
12. The cost to secure systems from viruses and worms is reduced.
13. Desktop equipment is completely immune from viruses.
14. Virus protection is more effective because fewer systems need protection.
15. Cost of software tracking, maintenance and upgrades is reduced.
16. There's no need to reload software on desktop equipment due to corruption.
17. Any application can be run without regard to OS, hardware or software dependencies.
18. Obsolete PCs can be redeployed.

19. Application performance is improved by having very powerful servers running the applications instead underpowered desktop PCs.
20. Power consumption is reduced-thin clients require up to 90 percent less energy than PCs and require no cooling.
21. Thin clients are smaller, lighter and quieter.
22. Thin clients are more tolerant of hostile environments (temperature, humidity, dust).
23. Thin clients are not as susceptible to being stolen as desktops or laptops.
24. If thin clients are stolen, there is no risk of company data being exposed.

Linux Desktop Resources	
• Citrix Systems http://www.citrix.com	• NoMachine http://www.nomachine.com
• Ericom Software http://www.ericom.com	•Tarantella. http://www.sun.com
• Mercury International http://www.thinanywhere.com	• ThinSoft http://www.thinsoftinc.com
• Neoware http://www.neoware.com	• ThinTop Technologies http://www.thintop.com
	• Wyse http://www.wyse.com

Table 10-3. *Desktop Vendors.*

The advantage of VNC is that the application session remains available even when a user disconnects from the VNC viewer (i.e. relocating from one location to another). With VNC providing a persistent desktop, there is no need to log in or log out of your application; instead, just access the application where it left off the last time it was running in the VNC viewer. This is known as "hot desking."

With the efficient design of VNC, few resources are required by the VNC viewer since most of the processing is done by the server. As a result, VNC is a great technology for making a thin-client solution. VNC is open source software that is supported on most platforms.

Building a Business Case

It is often perceived that migrating a desktop environment to Linux is a costly and labor-intensive process. It is true that these migrations often bring a number of risks and concerns. However, there are ways of managing a Linux desktop migration that can significantly mitigate these issues.

First, it is important to be clear as to why you are considering a Windows alternative. Suggesting that Windows should be replaced because of an ideological objection to Microsoft or the IT department's enthusiasm for the open source model are not very objective business reasons. In order to secure proper sponsorship and endorsement, it is best to be able to provide objective and quantitative data relating to:

Frequently Asked Questions

Will a Linux desktop support Windows applications?

It's always better, faster and more stable to run applications that are native to the operating system. Windows applications will never run as well under any other OS as they do under Windows. There are Linux-based applications to replace most Windows applications. For example, instead of using Microsoft Word, a very good replacement is available with Koffice or OpenOffice Write.

Where can I find Windows application equivalents for Linux?

There are many places to find Windows application equivalents. The best places to start are the SourceForge and Freshmeat portals. SourceForge (http://www.sourceforge.net) and Freshmeat (http://www.freshmeat.net) are the world's largest open source software development Web sites.

What if I have no choice but to use Windows programs?

If you must use Windows applications on a Linux desktop, you can dual boot your system and actually run Windows and its applications, or you can run an emulator environment like Win4Lin or VMWare. Optionally, your organization can deploy thin clients allowing a server-based infrastructure to run Windows, but have desktop clients access them remotely.

How can I deploy both Windows and Linux desktops?

Where a larger pilot deployment of Linux desktops is required, it may be convenient to keep file and authentication services under Windows. Samba's Winbind provides an easy way to link the two environments. Deploying Samba within the current environment causes no changes to the existing client base.

- A reduction of security-related business risk
- A reduction in operations costs
- A reduction in software license and upgrade fees
- Better service to end-users
- Improved performance and stability

From the high-level cost-benefit analysis, it should be possible to determine the feasible scope of a migration project. The ease with which a particular group may be migrated can be assessed by considering the following:

- How many Windows applications do they depend on?
- How many of these will also run on Desktop Linux?
- For those that won't run on Linux, is there a Linux-compatible alternative?
- Is it feasible to run the application in thin-client mode?
- Is there a strict dependence on third-party applications, plug-ins or devices that are only supported on Windows?
- Has the organization intensively developed custom applications based on native Win32 APIs and/or programming environments, such as Visual Basic or .NET?
- Is the organization dependent on Microsoft Office compatibility?

One of the biggest surprises with Desktop Linux is the broad set of management tools that are built into the operating system. As a result, one of the biggest risks is trying to create an exact duplicate of a Windows-oriented computing environment instead of exploiting the capabilities that Linux has to offer. From a standardization point of view, the Linux desktop is currently a very fast-moving target since it is experiencing a lot of software development. It is important to keep a close tab on the developments that are ongoing. Your organization may be suddenly surprised that Desktop Linux has removed all roadblocks that existed previously.

Key Takeaways

One approach is thinking how to best leverage the infrastructure to provide the necessary business applications. Cost-effectiveness is not enough to make Linux a serious threat to Windows on corporate desktops. Desktop Linux shows a better financial picture when it is leveraged along with terminal services and server-based computing.

To be successful with Desktop Linux, it is helpful to have access to Microsoft applications, but how the organization accesses them might be cause for a change. Having the ability to run Windows applications via server-based computing is often much more cost-effective. Linux desktops can run Microsoft applications natively using a thin-client computing architecture.

It is important to break down the barriers to Linux desktops. The biggest obstacle typically becomes the end-users who must adopt it. It is important to provide training, success stories or peer pressure to get the organization over the Linux migration hump.

Key #3

Designing the Infrastructure Blueprint

Infrastructure optimization lays the foundation for a Paradigm Shift.

Key Overview

Linux and open source enables advanced data management solutions and delivers a low-cost, maintenance-free processing platform, but application clusters, workload grids and blade computing provide the infrastructure that empowers the underlying Linux operating environment.

With the proper Linux infrastructure blueprint, a Paradigm Shift is created. Linux and open source have spawned new approaches and methods for deploying enterprise-class application infrastructures.

Chapter 11

Infrastructure Optimization

Things may come to those who wait, but only the things left by those who hustled.
— Abraham Lincoln

Business requirements do not speak to infrastructure requirements. Today, the goals of ongoing flexibility and agility are valued more highly than one-time efficiency gains. Every organization must address the major sources of cost and complexity that exist in their computing environments. But by optimizing the infrastructure and its operations, you can spend less on deploying and maintaining your computing investment. And, best of all, improve your odds with successful Linux and open source adoption.

Building an Infrastructure Blueprint

The purpose of establishing and maintaining an application computing infrastructure is to build a solid and reliable substrate for business applications to run on. It is important to remember that applications are the only reason the Linux infrastructure exists in the first place.

Infrastructures are built to be used broadly and heavily. They need to be accessible to organizations that need to use them and they need to support the demands of many end-users. A Linux infrastructure will not last if it is not flexible enough to provide economic incentives throughout the range of application services it supports.

It is increasingly important for companies to have an infrastructure that is flexible, dynamic and extensible. The cost of using an infrastructure and the value it delivers determine its cost efficiency. Most organizations today admit their use of computing resources is inefficient. Legacy systems can be difficult to change and expensive to maintain.

A Paradox in the Making

The most effective infrastructure is one that is built from its inception with the understanding that flexibility and stability need to be balanced. Flexibility facilitates usage and availability of resources while stability provides for a reliable, safe environment that supports the business lifestyle.

It's almost a paradox — stability is preserved by limiting change and flexibility is created by enabling change. This is probably one of the biggest reasons Linux and open source have become top priorities in many organizations. Linux-based computing addresses these problems by providing an adaptive software infrastructure that makes efficient use of low-cost servers. By scaling out with servers in small increments, you get performance and reliability at a lower cost.

The Rise of Utility Computing

One of the watchwords of today's computing infrastructure is utility computing. These technologies provide hardware and operating system abstraction — eliminating the reliance on vendor-specific hardware and software. Utility computing enables stable and commoditized scale-out application architectures allowing many servers to be provisioned as a single virtualized computing environment available for any business application.

If you consider today's challenges in the data center, organizations are dealing with server bottlenecks and hot spots, management issues with multiple servers, server utilization inefficiencies and inefficient business processing pipelines. Utility computing provides a remedy for these problems.

The vision of the utility computing model is now shared throughout the industry, although some industry leaders have already coined new terms for it such as Computing on Demand, Adaptive Computing, N1, Organic Computing and Ubiquitous Computing. Figure 11–1 illustrates the model these system vendors are trying to achieve.

Utility computing represents a wholesale shift in the computing industry. Utility computing is about moving the availability of computing resources into a grid-like compute environment where business applications are available through the grid. It enables the provisioning of application services on-demand based on their specific quality of service requirements.

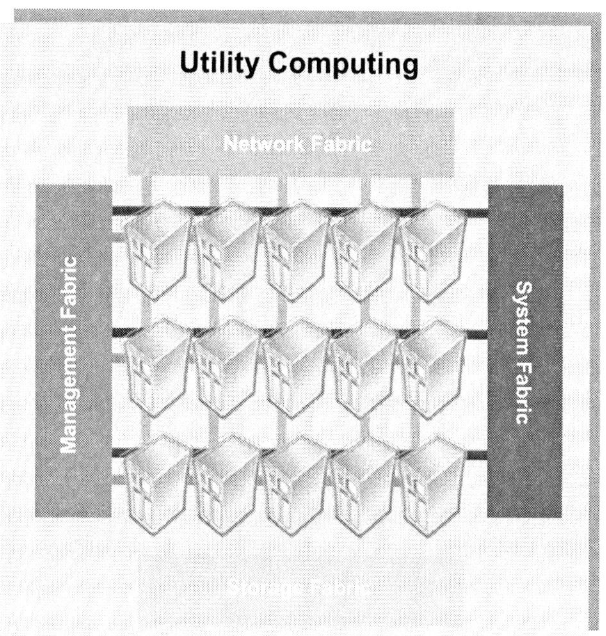

Figure 11-1. *Utility Computing Model.*

Utility computing provides compute resources and infrastructure management on an as-needed basis. By maximizing the efficient use of resources, utility computing seeks to minimize data center costs, improve operational agility and deliver predictable quality of service.

Information Technology as a Service

The other important side effect of a utility model is that it forces the business units to rationalize their computing infrastructure costs and apply those costs to projects and applications with a clear understanding of their return on investment.

Data centers continue to evolve toward a utility model where the importance of the application services delivered by an application computing infrastructure surpasses the importance of the underlying software and hardware environment. Part of the challenge comes from a fundamental shift in the operating system. Where organizations previously focused on Unix systems that relied on an expensive vertical scaling architectures, organizations have inadvertently moved into utility computing by expanding their use of IA-based systems along with the deployment of Linux.

Adopting an internal utility model has a subtle effect on the allocation of application computing resources by challenging established paradigms of IT-as-overhead and shifting the organization's model to IT-as-a-service. Linux and open source computing is providing this fundamental shift in the way we think of information technology.

The Utility Model

With a utility model, which allows organizations to easily associate specific costs to specific applications and services, technology organizations can make the transition from a supply-driven model to a demand-driven model. When business units have to justify the cost of technology as a specific line item on their budget, they must explicitly show the link between IT as a cost center and IT as a profit driver.

The utility model, however, does not have to be tied to a chargeback model where business units pay for resources directly. Even if the budget is not reimbursed, associating costs with specific line-of-business applications can lead to better allocation of scarce resources. Whether the market is used to drive competition among business units or just to align spending with business strategy, a Linux-based utility model ensures that technology resources are not wasted through misallocation.

In order for a data center to operate as a utility, the first step is adopting standardization. The economics of Linux allow datacenter managers to standardize their infrastructure on low-cost hardware. Once standardized on Linux-based hardware, the data center can leverage other technologies such as automation, virtualization, server-based computing, grid computing and blade technology. However, Linux is the first step in the transition toward utility computing.

The agile enterprise needs a technology framework that allows business logic to be rebuilt in real time as new opportunities arise. For businesses to remain competitive, organizations need an agile process and integration strategy between the business and the computing infrastructure. This dynamic infrastructure allows technology to automatically adapt to changing business needs. Linux has the necessary features, functions and controls that make it a better host for utility computing than other operating systems.

Virtual Machines

In the perfect data center, each Linux application runs on a virtual machine (VM). If the application's resources need to grow, the VM simply grows with it, sizing it perfectly according to its workload.

This idea of a virtual machine is not new. It's a technique that has been commonplace in large systems deployments for many decades. IBM developed the concept in 1964 for its mainframes. This was followed by DEC with the introduction of the PDP-8. In essence, virtualization technology separates the processes that manage CPU scheduling, memory management and data access from the actual physical hardware. The OS becomes a "guest" on the physical hardware — it no longer manages the underlying hardware, but instead runs on a virtualized system as presented by the VM monitor. (This term dates back to the 1970s with the development of the IBM mainframe.)

Virtualization provides benefits such as:

- Consolidating application workloads running on under-utilized servers (server consolidation); benefits are savings on hardware, environmental costs, management and administration of the server infrastructure
- Running legacy applications that might not run on newer hardware and/or operating systems; a VM can provide an execution environment for such applications by proving binary compatibility
- Creating operating systems, or execution environments, with resource limits, error containment and resource guarantees providing secure isolated application processing environments; VMs enable the dynamic creation of an execution environment for downloaded files from the Internet to ensure they are virus-free
- Providing the illusion of hardware, or a hardware configuration, that you do not have; virtualization can simulate networks of independent computers
- Running multiple operating systems simultaneously (i.e. different versions, or entirely different systems) which can be used for a hot standby processing environment
- Making software easier to migrate, thus aiding application and system mobility; allowing for application debugging and performance monitoring
- Treating application suites as "appliances" by running them in a VM

- Making tasks such as system migration, backup and recovery easier and more manageable

Virtualization via the utility computing model has the potential to dramatically change the way corporate computing is accomplished. Traditionally, applications are wedded to specific servers and storage devices. Virtualization technology allows applications and data to be shifted among a group of Linux systems, or within an individual Linux server, in ways that make the physical system perform more efficiently.

The performance improvements made with today's processor designs, including multi-core and multi-threaded chip designs, have now outpaced the performance requirements for many applications. While processing power is getting less expensive, space, power, installation, integration and administration are not, and they cost the same whether a server is heavily or lightly utilized. Since virtualization lets a single physical system behave like multiple virtual systems, VM demands less hardware resources for most applications due to this inherent overlap, or sharing, of resources.

The Tao of Virtualization

With virtualization approaches, the concept is to give up a little — either in performance or system resources or both — to gain a lot in terms of resource utilization flexibility. In this regard, the management capabilities of VM are every bit as important as their virtualization capabilities. That is, the ability to recognize an increasing workload and then move processes to faster systems or increase the resources available to those processes is more important than whether the virtualization technique exacts a slight performance penalty on the system.

By taking advantage of server virtualization, the efficiency of the Linux computing environment is improved. Because there are a lower number of physical servers, there is a big reduction in hardware acquisition and maintenance costs as well as an increase in overall system utilization

A big benefit of using virtualization with Linux systems is that applications are isolated from each other and are not impacted by typical application upgrades or underlying configuration changes. Applications running on a VM allow the deployment of multiple OS configurations and versions — known as the guest operating systems — used without any impact on application or system availability. Linux virtualization helps streamline and economize the development and testing processes of an organization since it provides realistic application testing and validation without acquiring a completely new hardware environment.

Other Virtualization Techniques

There are several server virtualization technologies: hardware virtualization, para-virtualization and operating system virtualization. Hardware virtualization provides a full virtualized hardware environment (hardware emulation) for the guest OS. This is accomplished either in a hosted or non-hosted configuration. (For example, VMware GSX is a hosted hardware emulation whereas VMware ESX is non-hosted.) Solutions such as VMWare, Microsoft Virtual PC and Bochs use this technique, allowing them to run multiple VMs, each capable of hosting its own guest OS.

IBM provides three levels of partitioning: physical partitioning, logical partitioning and software partitioning. With physical partitioning, the partitions are divided along hardware boundaries. Each partition might run a different version of the operating system (as in IBM xSeries and BladeCenter servers).

In logical partitioning, there is no affinity between the processor, memory and I/O, thereby making it possible to provision and re-provision the resources to the virtual servers independently. Both the iSeries and pSeries servers offer Micro Partitioning where the Power5 processors can be allocated to tenths of a processor among the partitions. In addition, both the iSeries and pSeries servers allow you to run multiple operating systems in different partitions, and allow processors, memory and I/O to be shifted among active partitions without requiring the operating system to be rebooted.

Software partitioning requires software to be installed either on the native OS (VMware GSX) or directly on top of the hardware (VMware ESX). In either case, multiple operating systems may be installed. It is very easy to migrate, change or consolidate any of the virtual machines.

However, this type of virtualization suffers from complicated administration. All of these methods run their own individual instance of the OS. Ultimately, you end up with a massive array of operating systems — and most likely all different versions and types — to separately manage and patch. You have limited ability to dynamically reallocate as needed. These techniques will claim to enable reallocation of resources without requiring a reboot but some applications (i.e. Oracle) will need the reboot.

Cost Considerations

One aspect to consider with VM technology is the cost for software versus the cost for another Linux server. For instance, in some cases the software

Creating Virtual Private Servers

Three other Linux virtualization techniques besides the Xen project are VMware, User Mode Linux (UML) and Linux-VServer. These solutions give your organization the ability to isolate incompatible application software running on the same systems. This greatly simplifies application change control and upgrade processes.

VMware

The VMware (http://www.vmware.com) product line is currently the market-leading commercial virtualization solution for IA-compatible hardware. VMware is built on two virtual machine technologies. ESX Server runs as the native operating system on server hardware in order to provide the guest operating systems, and GSX Server runs as an application on top of Linux (or Windows) to provide the guest operating systems.

GSX Server is primarily used as a development and test platform. ESX Server provides a more robust environment for production workloads; however, it is limited to the hardware environments it can support (unlike GSX Server which runs on anything that Linux can support). The VMware suite also includes VirtualCenter, which provides a comprehensive set of tools for creating, migrating and managing virtual machine instances among VMware systems.

User Mode Linux

UML (http://usermodelinux.org) is an open source solution that creates a virtual machine. UML allows you to run multiple instances of Linux on the same system at the same time. It provides a secure way of running Linux versions and Linux processes. UML provides a patch to the Linux kernel that allows Linux to create an OS partition that has its own virtual resources, including a root file system and swap space.

With UML, you can assign the virtual machine only the hardware access you want it to have, and even assign it with more hardware and software resources than the actual physical computer it is running on.

Linux VServer

Linux V-Server (http://linux-vserver.org) allows Linux to be run inside Linux; different Linux distributions can be run inside any distribution. Each virtual server has its own packages, its own services, its own users. As a result, virtual servers are running with the same kernel as the host, and the performance is exactly the same as a non-virtual server (unlike other VM solutions). There is no overhead since there are no special daemons running.

V-Server shares most of the binaries and libraries with the host but can be updated independently even if they share binaries. All administrative tools work inside a V-Server just as they do for the host OS but, more importantly, a V-Server is completely isolated from the host. (A jail mechanism is used to securely partition resources on the virtual partitions.)

licensing cost for VMware ESX server is greater than the cost for adding another two-way Linux system. As a result, a popular Linux technology that allows multiple copies of the Linux OS (as well as other operating systems) to run at the same time on the same server is Xen. Xen is a VM monitor integrated into the Linux kernel that can execute multiple virtual systems on a single Linux server. This technique is known as para-virtualization and it is being integrated into the Linux kernel.

Xen's para-virtualization modifies the underlying OS in order to leverage the native control it has with the hardware. It also provides a special driver to handle low-level VM management activities (such as managing privileged hardware instructions). However, by modifying the OS to facilitate virtualization, para-virtualization yields dramatically better performance over hardware emulation mentioned above, but it will fail to virtualize operating systems for which source code is unavailable. Fortunately, Intel and AMD are now providing hardware support to assist with Xen's para-virtualization implementation.

OS virtualization is a third approach. The OS provides a completely separate, isolated and secure computing environment able to host multiple application spaces. SWsoft's Virtuozzo, Sun Solaris Containers and User-Mode Linux are examples using this technique. The main limitation with OS virtualization is that it does not support different OSs on the same server.

Figure 11–2 illustrates these different virtualization approaches.

The best benefit of virtualization is helping enforce a common operating environment. Once a standard OS configuration has been developed, a VM can easily duplicate computing environments across other physical and virtual systems. This not only provides a consistent server configuration but greatly accelerates server and application deployments. Figure 11–3 illustrates this concept, known as server cloning.

Now and Xen

Xen has garnered so much attention that its authors (originally from the University of Cambridge) have formed a company, XenSource, to support it. Xen is backed by Hewlett-Packard, IBM, Sun Microsystems and others that want to standardize virtualization under Linux. As mentioned, AMD, IBM and Intel are even building virtualization hooks into their next-generation chips that Xen will be able to leverage.

Xen isn't unique in being able to run virtual hosts — Linux users can run virtual machines using User Mode Linux (UML), V-Server, Bochs, EMC's

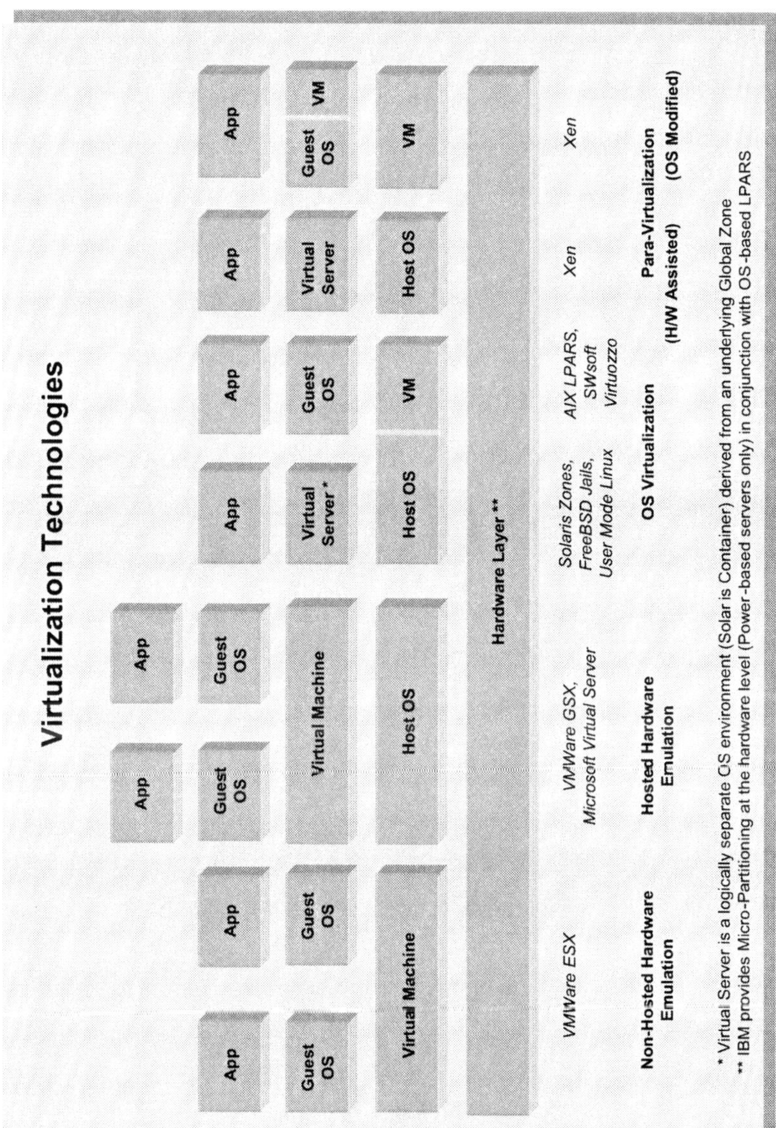

Figure 11-2. *Virtualization Approaches.*

VMware, SWsoft's Virtuozzo as well as via many other host-based virtualization solutions. Xen, however, operates differently than UML or VMware in that it requires the operating system to directly support its hypervisor technology rather than attempting to emulate an IA-based virtual machine, as VMware and Bochs do. As a result, the Xen approach has a performance edge over other virtualization technologies, plus applications do not require any certification or modification to run on a Xen-aware OS.

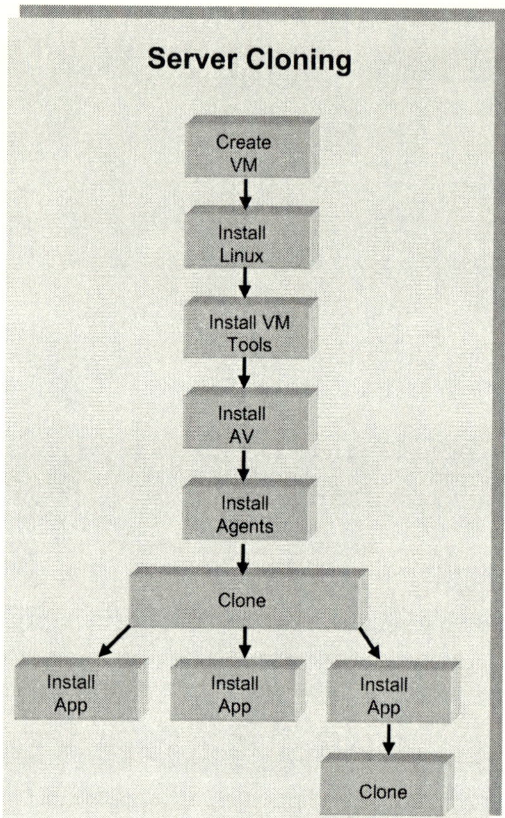

Figure 11-3. *Cloning Via Virtualization.*

Intel, AMD, Red Hat and Novell have promised support for Xen. As mentioned, Intel and AMD are supporting Xen via Vanderpool and Pacifica extensions, respectively, to support virtualization at the hardware level natively.

Service-Centric Approaches

Today's enterprises gain competitive advantage by quickly developing and deploying applications that provide unique business value and services. Quick application development along with easy deployment and simple management are key to an organization's success. Traditionally, business applications were tightly integrated with each other and, if an organization wanted to replace an application, oftentimes everything around it would fall apart. With utility computing, a different approach is to create a set of services that comprise the application service functionality. This is now known as building a service-oriented architecture (SOA).

A SOA not only enables a plug-and-play environment, but also allows new applications to be developed more quickly. Simple application services can be reused and orchestrated into a more complex service or business process, allowing business applications to be built out of existing application logic and data access patterns.

Linux on the Mainframe

If you are considering running Linux on your mainframe, be aware of these limitations:

- To run Linux on a mainframe, you'll need to run a separate Linux partition.
- Only three of the 265 available Linux versions today are specially designed for the mainframe. To date, these include special mainframe versions of Red Hat, SUSE and TurboLinux.
- If you currently have fewer than 20 Linux servers, consolidating on a mainframe will not provide a cost advantage.
- The mainframe does not work well with Unix and other server platforms.
- The initial entry costs and ongoing maintenance are expensive.
- Only about 250 Linux applications are supported on the mainframe versus thousands on the IA platform.

SOA has many benefits, but a primary goal is to increase reuse, which should drive down total cost of ownership and improve functional consistency. Loose coupling allows services to be integrated more easily and in a standard way. Once implemented, these services can be reused across your organization

With a SOA, applications can be built using a Web services architecture. Rather than the traditional monolithic approach of having all application functions run on a single application server, leveraging a Web-oriented architecture makes it possible for application functions to be hosted on dif-

Open Source SOA Projects

Below is a sampling of some of the SOA-related open source projects available.

Mule — Mule is an ESB messaging framework that provides a scalable object broker that handles interactions with services and applications using disparate transport and messaging technologies. For more information, visit http://mule.codehaus.org.

ServiceMix — ServiceMix is an open source ESB and SOA toolkit built on the semantics and APIs of the Java Business Integration (JBI) specification JSR 208. For more information, visit http://servicemix.org.

Celtix — Celtix A Java ESB runtime and set of extensible APIs to simplify the construction, integration and reuse of business components using a standards-based SOA. For more information, visit http://celtix.objectweb.org.

open-esb — Sponsored by Sun Microsystems, open-esb will be an ESB runtime based on Java Business Integration technology (JSR-208). For more information, visit http://open-esb.dev.java.net.

JEMS — JBoss Enterprise Middleware System (JEMS) is an extensible and scalable suite of products for creating and deploying e-business applications. For more information, visit http://www.jboss.org.

ActiveMQ — ActiveMQ is a fast Java Message Service (JMS) provider supporting clustering, peer networks, discovery, TCP, SSL, multicast, persistence, XA that integrates seamlessly into Java and J2EE containers. For more information, visit http://activemq.codehaus.org.

JORAM — JORAM provides access to MOM (Message Oriented Middleware). For more information, visit http://joram.objectweb.org.

OSMQ — Open Source Message Queue is a pure Java asynchronous messaging middleware framework with an interface that is less complex than JMS. For more information, visit http://www.bostonsg.com/osmq/index.html.

JBoss Messaging/JBossMQ — JBoss Messaging is a re-implementation of JBossMQ. JBossMQ, which evolved from SpyderMQ, is the current production-ready JBoss JMS provider. For more information, visit http://www.jboss.com/products/messaging.

Axis — Axis is a reliable and stable base on which to implement Java Web Services. For more information, visit http://ws.apache.org/axis.

Synapse — IONA Technologies, Sonic Software, Infravio, Blue Titan contribute to Synapse, a service mediation framework built on Web services specifications that will be supported by WS02. For more information, visit http://wiki.apache.org/incubator/SynapseProposal.

Sandesha — An implementation adhering to the WS-ReliableMessaging specification authored by BEA, IBM, Microsoft and TIBCO, Sandesha enables reliable communication between Web services and clients. For more information, visit http://ws.apache.org/sandesha.

RM4GS — RM4GS (Reliable Messaging for Grid Services) provides reliable messaging for Web services following the Web Services-Reliability specification supported by Fujitsu Limited, Hitachi Ltd and NEC Corporation. For more information, visit http://businessgrid.ipa.go.jp/rm4gs/index-en.html.

openadaptor — A Java/XML-based software platform that allows for rapid business system integration with little or no custom programming. For more information, visit http://www.openadaptor.org.

jUDDI — jUDDI (pronounced "Judy") is an open source Java implementation of the Universal Description, Discovery, and Integration (UDDI) specification for Web Services. For more information, visit http://ws.apache.org/juddi.

UDDI4J — UDDI4J is a Java class library that provides an API to interact with a UDDI registry contributed by IBM. For more information, visit http://uddi4j.sourceforge.net.

ferent systems, or for all functions to be hosted on a single system — it really doesn't matter.

Web services use Extensible Markup Language (XML), Simple Object Access Protocol (SOAP), Hypertext Transfer Protocol (HTTP) and other emerging application development standards. Clients for applications based on Web services are commonly written in Java or based upon Web browsers accessing portals. This approach makes the underlying client operating system completely transparent.

The open source community has several viable SOA solutions your organization can evaluate. And since open source solutions excel with building infrastructures that can be "glued" together, Linux is obviously the best bet with this opportunity.

Distributed Consolidation

The most prominent hardware innovation surrounding the notion of utility computing is the rise of blade technology. Blade technology provides an energy, space and cost-efficient hardware infrastructure for managing the scalability of Linux. Linux and blade computing have spawned the growth of a new computing platform with its innovative modular technology, density and availability features.

Blade servers are the basis of the scale-out rather than scale-up paradigm of system performance — a configuration of a large network of low-cost servers. Blade computing easily allows application performance to be flexibly scaled to meet end-user demand simply by increasing the number of blades. Blades are plugged into a common chassis containing a backplane that provides the networking, cabling and power.

As a result, blade servers are denser than rack-optimized servers because key components such as power and networking are not physically located on each individual server. And since blades comprise individual OS instances that are consolidated into a data center-friendly form factor, the emergence of "distributed consolidation" as a new computing architecture has arrived. This approach is ideal for utility computing.

Blade computing seeks to:

- Reduce complexity and administration costs
- Improve the functionality and ease the management of servers
- Reduce OS and application deployment time

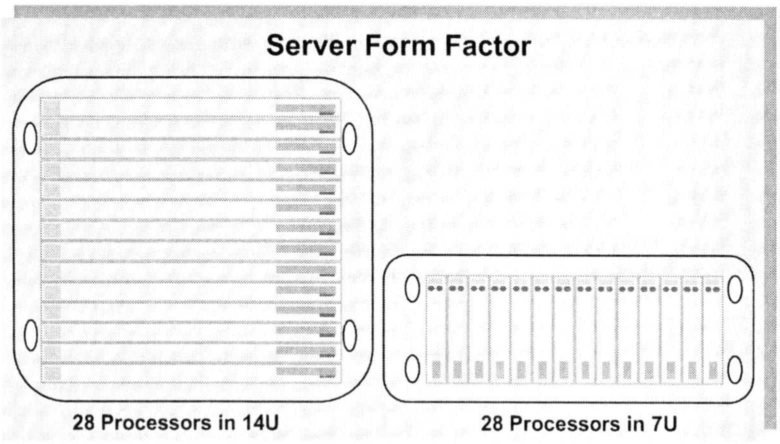

Figure 11-4. *Rack Optimized Servers Versus Blade Servers.*

- Automate administrative tasks
- Optimize server utilization
- Conserve data center floor space
- Streamline cabling
- Reduce operational costs

A blade system requires significantly less cabling than a rack-optimized server. It also consumes less power per server and, consequently, generates less heat. The most comparable independent rack-optimized server would be a 1U server (1U = 1.75 vertical inches). Blade servers offer twice the density of the thinnest rack optimized server. (A 7U blade server can host 14 independent servers whereas the equivalent number of rack-optimized servers would need 14U as illustrated in Figure 11–4.)

A major driver of blade adoption is the move toward enhanced, integrated systems management. Blade computers offer on-board management and provisioning systems that leverage more automation in their systems management and deployment processes. Vendors in the server blade space recognized the importance of integrated systems management as a means to combat the rising cost of single-server, single-application environments.

Because a blade chassis typically contains network switching options, users increasingly see the blade server platform as offering a layer of network consolidation. Network consolidation with blade servers is becoming increasingly more valuable as server vendors partner with leading networking vendors to deliver best-of-breed solutions within a single infrastructure.

The architecture of the blade server was specifically designed to be leveraged for economies of scale; whether with one blade in a chassis or 14, the number of cooling fans, power supplies, cabling and network connections remains the same. As a result, the cost per server is continuously reduced as more blades are installed.

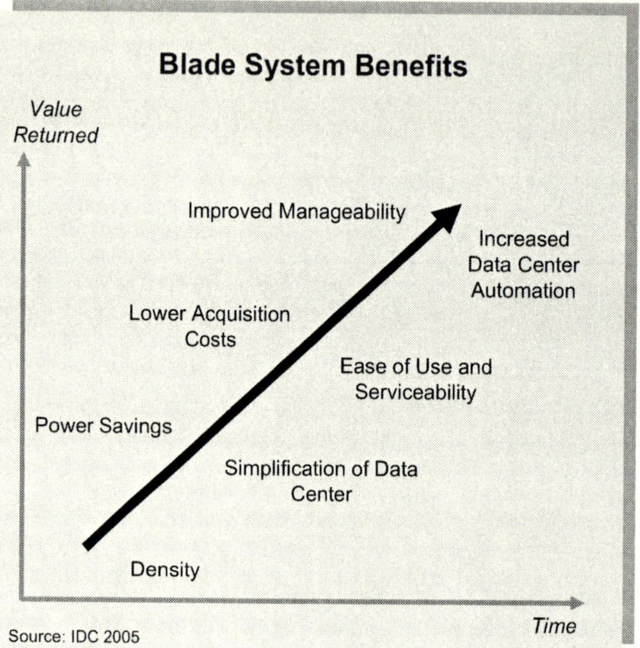

Figure 11-5. *Benefits With Blade Servers.*

Figure 11–5 shows the benefits this technology. Because of these benefits, the Server Blade Trade Association and industry researchers at IDC estimate that it is nearly a USD $4 billion market.

The ability of Linux to build and customize a flexible application computing architecture is unmatched by any other operating system. As a result, approximately 70 percent of the early blade server adopters in the U.S. are running Linux.

The Next-Generation Computing Fabric

Now imagine a data center comprised of blade servers that are clustered together. All of these servers have processors (no more than four) and memory that are all connected to disk storage farms and communication networks through a single, common networking fabric. And, by the way, this fabric is more powerful and capable than today's most expensive mainframe. Welcome the next-generation I/O fabric.

Deployment Decisions

Use Blades If...

- Need to deploy new servers frequently
- Need to frequently provision new operating systems, applications or patches across multiple servers
- Are involved in clustering, grids or service-oriented architectures
- Want field replaceable servers
- Need a more flexible architecture that you can easily build-as-you-grow

Use Servers If...

- Data center space is not limited
- Power consumption is not a concern
- You need large memory configurations
- You need multiple peripheral buses
- Cable consolidation is not a concern
- Not using clustered file systems
- Need more than four CPU sockets per server
- Require less than five servers (remote locations)

Figure 11-6. *Blades Versus Servers.*

InfiniBand (IB) and Advanced Switching Interconnect (ASI) represent a powerful new architecture designed to support I/O connectivity for the blade computing infrastructure. IB is supported by all major OEM server vendors as a means to create the next generation I/O interconnect standard in servers. With blade computing, IB delivers a potent combination of high bandwidth and low node-to-node latency. As a result, a blade computing cluster with the IB solution can deliver performance comparable to a large, high-end SMP server at significantly less cost.

Multi-processor architectures built around ASI silicon offer a more robust solution for systems featuring more than six processors and where interprocessor communications demand a low-latency environment. ASI adds features that provide peer-to-peer communications and shared I/O access mechanisms.

Blade computing with an IB or ASI fabric frees the CPUs on the blades from communication processing overhead. Using a protocol known as remote direct memory access (RDMA), each server can directly access the memory on another server without involving the CPU of the remote processor. The combination of high bandwidth and low latency greatly empowers distributed databases, such as IBM DB2 Parallel Edition or Oracle Real

Application Clusters (RAC), to deliver high scalability and availability from the use of low-cost computing blades. In so doing, a high-performance Linux application computing environment can easily be put together. Figure 11–6 shows typical differences between blade computers and rackable servers.

Key Takeaways

For Linux and open source to be successful in your organization, you must rethink your application processing environment, not simply re-implement your current computing infrastructure. It is important to leverage newer technologies such as virtualization, service-oriented architectures, blade technology and utility computing. Linux is about reducing the complexity and operational costs of your application environment by automating administrative tasks and optimizing server utilization. Rethinking your current computing architecture is critical with Linux-based infrastructures.

Business requirements do not speak to infrastructure requirements. Infrastructures running open source software on Linux platforms must leverage infrastructure trends such as utility computing, blade computing, virtualization, service-centric computing and intelligent networking fabrics. A Paradigm Shift occurs when the architecture provides an adaptable and flexible infrastructure.

Chapter 12

The Push Toward Commodity Technology

The net of these advantages is that Google does not have a search system; Google has a supercomputer that delivers applications.
— Stephen E. Arnold, The Google Legacy, 2005

There is a compelling price per performance value proposition deploying IA-based servers running Linux-based operating systems. Since Linux clustering solutions have matured, open source computing has set the price for companies to leverage this technology for business applications. At the hardware level, the IA instruction set provides a standard interface for processors that drive a commodity market supplied by Intel and AMD. The push toward using commodity technology is now a top priority for technology organizations.

Linux Clustering

Linux clusters brought commodity economics and the dynamic developments of the open source community into business-critical application architectures. A clustered system is a system that combines two or more computers into a processing group to improve an application's availability, performance or scalability. According to the latest Top500 directory of top supercomputers, most of the fastest supercomputers — such as the current leader, IBM's BlueGene/L — are actually Linux clusters.

Clusters can generally be classified as high-availability or failover clusters; load balancing clusters; or high-performance computing clusters. The boundaries between these types of clusters are somewhat indistinct, and often an actual cluster may have properties of each type. High-Availability and Load Optimization (HALO) clusters are a combination of HA clustering and load balancing. A HALO cluster leverages automatic failover in the event of node failure, but also provides load optimization by distributing traffic among multiple cluster nodes.

Oftentimes the best business case for Linux and open source is its ability to improve upon your current application availability. Architectures requiring high availability and redundancy will show the highest return on investment (ROI) when deployed on Linux. Clustering has been, and still is, the biggest advantage of Linux over its competitors in terms of price per performance and one that promotes a predictable ROI.

High Availability Clusters

High availability (HA) clusters are typically built with the intention of providing a fail-safe environment through redundancy. That is, they provide a computing environment in which the failure of one or more components (hardware, software, networking, application) does not affect the availability of the application.

During normal operation, the application environment executes on one system, while the other system is available to assume the workload in case any failure occurs on the primary application server. When a failure does occur, the standby system takes control of all necessary application computing, such as control and management of data access, networking and application processing, so that end-users don't even know that their application is now running on a different physical system.

The biggest disadvantage with HA clusters is the system administration required to maintain data synchronicity across the cluster. Since each server in a high-availability cluster maintains a separate and independent copy of its data, typical maintenance requires having to install applications and operating systems across all nodes in the cluster including applying patches to applications and the OS and changing configuration settings, as well as performing individual data backups for each system.

Linux HA clusters have greatly improved upon the traditional approach to providing application fault tolerance. A more efficient and economical approach is to have a single shared data store. Through the use of a clustered file system, a single system image can be provided across the cluster, reducing the overall operational costs of a traditional high-availability cluster environment. This is discussed in more detail in the next section.

Load Balancing Clusters

Load balancing clusters are a group of servers that have application access and requests distributed uniformly across them. When it is necessary to scale beyond more than one application server because of the application processing workload, load balancing clusters allow multiple servers to participate in providing the application service.

This creates what is known as a single virtual application service since the cluster transparently distributes user application requests among multiple servers. Load balancing clusters also provide redundancy and failover protection. If a Linux server becomes unavailable due to a failure, other systems in the cluster are available to continue the workload.

There are various methods of providing the load balancing algorithm in a cluster. The most common are:

- Round Robin DNS: Very simple load balancing that is implemented using properties of the DNS.
- Simple Randomization: This includes the ability to detect failed servers in order to avoid them as appropriate.
- Response Measurement: Algorithms are used to detect server response time and use those servers that are least busy.
- Content Type: These solutions allow balancing based upon content. For example, servers can be set up to exclusively deliver images, while others deliver dynamic content or handle streaming video. This allows servers to be optimized for the workload they support in order to provide better overall performance.
- Geography-based: Requests for servers can be redirected to the geographically closest server.

High-Performance Clusters

High-performance computing clusters are designed to use parallel computing in order to improve application performance. There are many examples of scientific computing environments using multiple Linux servers in parallel to perform high-performance computing (known as parallel processing).

High-performance clusters are typically made up of a large number of Linux systems. The design of high-performance clusters involves the need for concurrent access to the same file system(s) as well as a high-performance inter-process communication link between all the nodes in the cluster in order to coordinate the work that must be done in parallel. (See Infinity and Beyond for more information about interprocess communication links.)

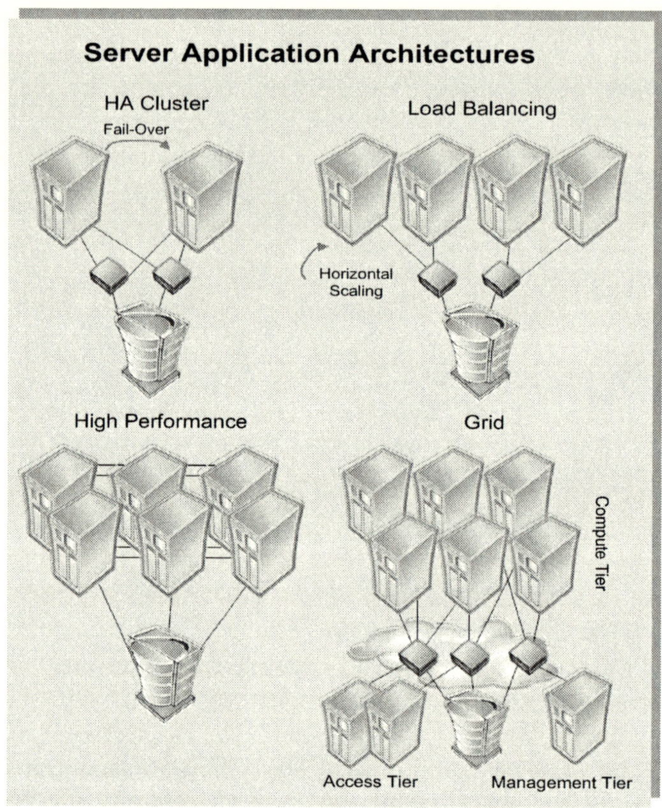

Figure 12-1. *Different Server Architectures.*

Developed by Donald Becker at NASA, a Beowulf cluster (http://www.beowulf.org) is a market-leading, high-performance Linux cluster technology. Based on open source development, Beowulf clusters provide scalable performance clusters based on Linux that run on commodity hardware and networking technology.

Figure 12–1 illustrates the architectures of these high availability solutions.

Clustered File Systems

A clustered file system (CFS) is a file system that has been optimized to be shared by multiple clustered servers over a storage area network (SAN) with standard POSIX file system semantics.

Much as network attached storage (NAS) allows multiple systems to concurrently access the same file system, a CFS uses a direct I/O channel to the storage device providing block-level access to data. In order to build a CFS, servers must be connected in a SAN that provides one or more data paths to shared storage pools providing each server with direct access to the data.

A CFS provides all servers within the cluster with the same OS image, binaries, application and configuration data. Administrative operations that would be required for each individual cluster server are eliminated. As the size of the cluster increases, there is no increase in its complexity or the likelihood of configuration errors, and no need for repetitive maintenance operations.

A CFS is either symmetrical or asymmetrical. It is asymmetrical when the cluster uses a centralized metadata server and lock manager to manage storage access. Each cluster node shares full access to disk storage, requiring that the nodes negotiate temporary ownership of any storage block to ensure consistency. Because of the centralized nature of arbitrating for ownership of resources, asymmetrical CFSs have distributed lock managers that employ sophisticated techniques to minimize the arbitration bottleneck. Unfortunately, inter-node negotiation over unallocated media is a common arbitration event, even with minimal data sharing. These metadata servers can become a bottleneck.

A CFS is symmetrical when it distributes metadata and file ownership responsibilities. Cluster nodes directly arbitrate for allocation and ownership decisions without needing centralized metadata servers.

Whether it is symmetrical or asymmetrical, a CFS enables all servers to access all the data on a SAN. Figure 12–2 shows why clustered file systems are becoming popular with Linux computing environments.

Advantages with Clustered File Systems

With a CFS, each server added to the cluster increases processing capacity. Applications can be scaled horizontally in an almost linear fashion. It is possible to dynamically allocate servers on the fly to support the application cluster and improve overall system utilization. A CFS provides continuous application availability as shown in Figure 12–3.

The ideal cluster configuration is a diskless shared root cluster where no server needs a local hard disk; each server boots directly from the SAN. Both application data and the operating system images are shared, allowing the root partition of each cluster node to access the same boot image.

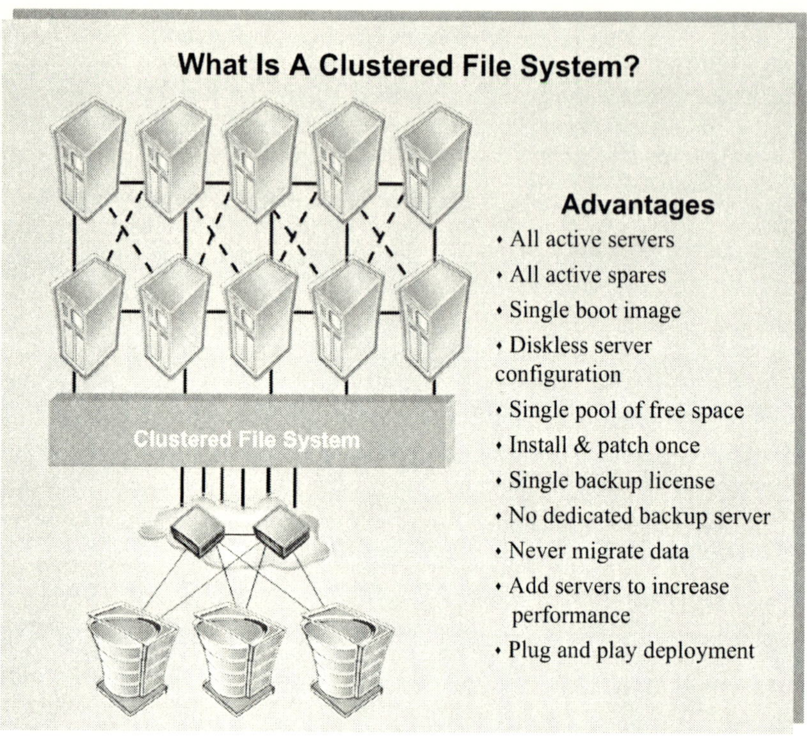

Figure 12-2. *Advantages With Clustered File Systems.*

Another benefit of deploying a CFS is the ability to re-purpose Linux servers. A server can be easily changed or provisioned by simply mounting a new file system and starting a new application service. No longer does an administrator have to physically install a new application on the Linux system.

It is also possible to convert an application server into a backup server. A data backup is normally done from backup client machines over the LAN to a dedicated backup server, or LAN-free from the application server directly to the backup device. Because every connected server using a CFS has access to all data and file systems, the backup server is able to complete a backup during ongoing operations without affecting the application service.

The Coming of Diskless Clusters

Diskless clusters are becoming increasingly popular with Linux environments. They are practical to build due to the convergence of several key technologies, such as clustered file systems and storage networking protocols.

Why eliminate hard drives from computer nodes? Removing storage hardware from cluster nodes reduces costs, noise, cooling requirements and

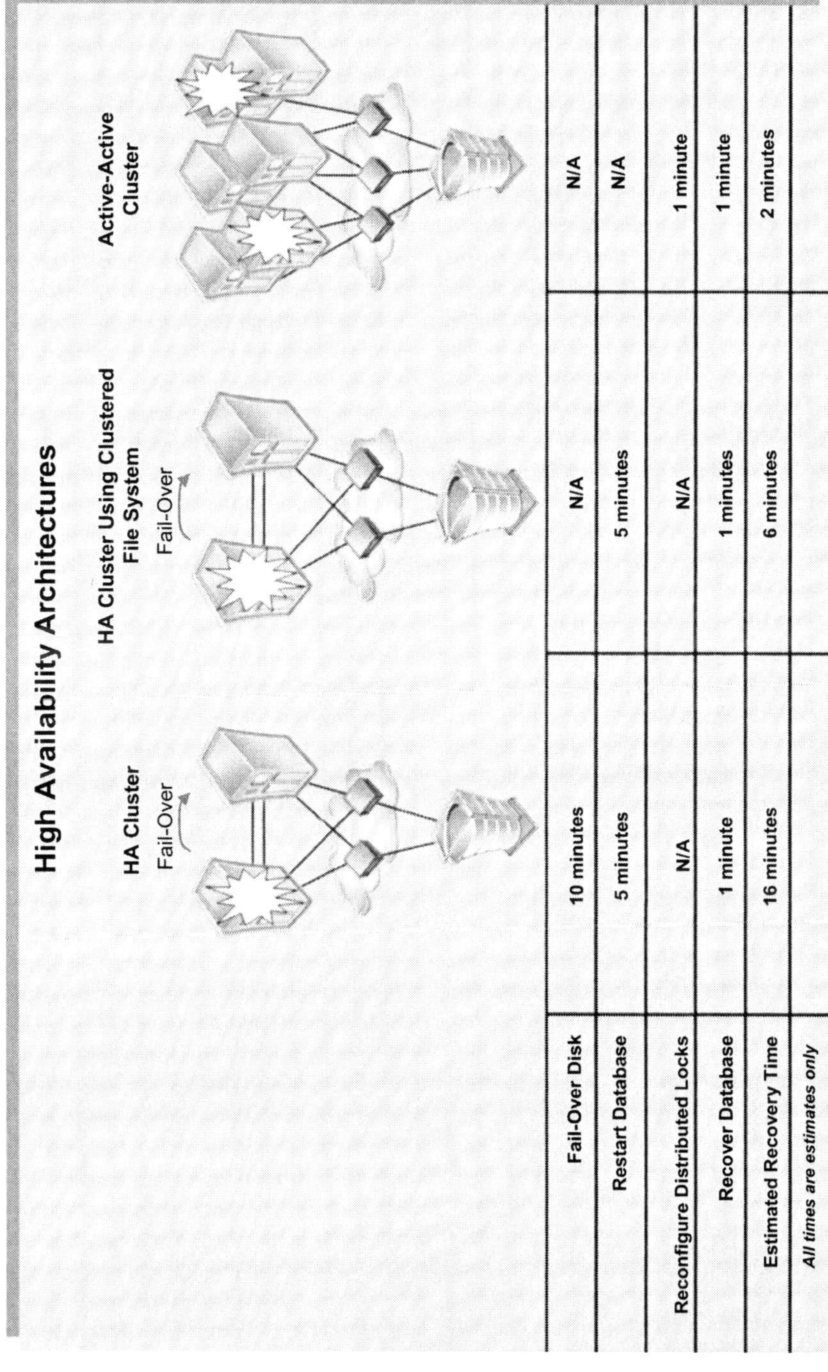

	HA Cluster	HA Cluster Using Clustered File System	Active-Active Cluster
Fail-Over Disk	10 minutes	N/A	N/A
Restart Database	5 minutes	5 minutes	N/A
Reconfigure Distributed Locks	N/A	N/A	1 minute
Recover Database	1 minute	1 minutes	1 minute
Estimated Recovery Time	16 minutes	6 minutes	2 minutes

All times are estimates only

Figure 12-3. *HA Architectures.*

power consumption, and improves the nodes' overall reliability. In the past, diskless clusters have used NFS as a storage system. For clusters that are not I/O intensive, NFS provides an acceptable solution. NFS can mount a remote, bootable OS image or have the OS image installed on a node's local RAM disk.

Lustre (http://www.lustre.org) is an object-oriented, highly scalable, parallel file system. Lustre breaks the file system into two components: metadata servers (MDS) and object storage targets (OST). File system metadata is distributed across multiple MDS systems and file data is distributed across multiple OST servers. Lustre supports various interconnects, including Ethernet, Myrinet and IB. While Lustre is open source, the newest version is only available from its commercial counterpart, Cluster File System (http://www.clusterfs.com).

The Parallel Virtual File System (PVFS2) is an open source parallel file system. Currently, PVFS2 (http://www.pvfs.org/pvfs2) supports TCP, IB and Myrinet interconnects and is built on top of an existing file system such as ext2, JFS, ReiserFS or XFS. PVFS2 stripes file data across multiple disks in different nodes in a cluster. For application clusters to take advantage of PVFS2, applications must be ported to use MPI-IO.

There are many other file systems available for Linux clusters. There are open source versions of AFS (Andrew File System) and DFS (Distributed File System) as well as commercially available solutions from IBRIX, SGI, PolyServe, Panasas, Red Hat and Symantec.

Grid Computing

Grid computing is a new way of building application clusters and a new way to think about information technology in general, as humorously shown in Figure 12–4. Grid computing enables the virtualization of distributed computing and data resources, such as processing, network bandwidth and storage capacity, to create a single system image. Grid computing is essentially clustering writ large. By letting a pool of servers on a grid perform the task of several applications rather than relying on just one server or one cluster, grid computing becomes an important first step toward the idea of utility computing and the Holy Grail of the real-time enterprise.

Research grids, for instance, typically give users from multiple organizations and security domains access to diverse computing resources. Fermi National Accelerator Laboratory, a national science laboratory of the Department of Energy, operates a grid of high-energy physics applications

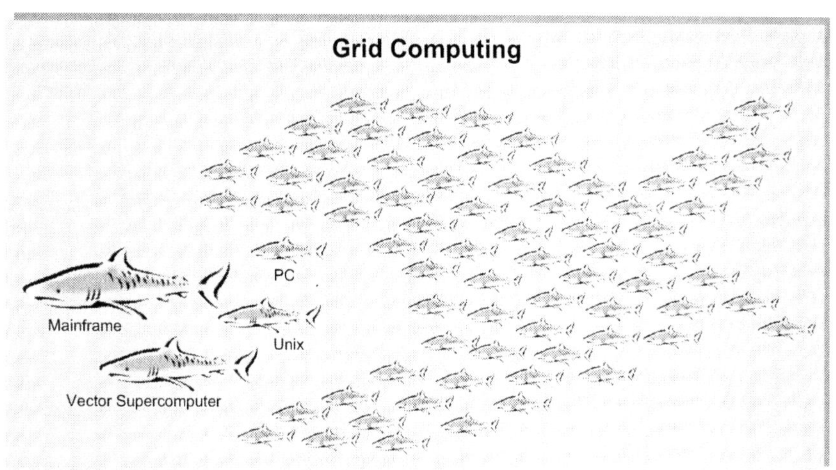

Figure 12-4. *Grid Humor.*

that's accessed by more than 5,000 users in more than 80 organizations. In contrast, a grid being run by a corporation typically will only provide its employees with access to resources owned by the organization.

The business case driving all of these efforts is the same: Provide customers with a utility model for their computing needs. Hewlett-Packard's Adaptive Enterprise, IBM's On Demand Business and Sun Microsystems' N1 have different takes on a grid central theme, but all are designed to provide low-cost computing power to customers. This commercial aspect to grids is relatively new.

Because Linux-based grids are so versatile, grids can be used for many functions outside of just ganging CPUs together. A Linux grid can be utilized for creating scalable storage pools, conducting backups or providing security functions. For example, a storage grid is a scalable virtual file server whose intended purpose is to export data to applications or databases.

Storage grids offer tremendous benefits, including being very cost-effective compared to proprietary storage arrays. A storage grid has no hotspots; there is no need to split data in order to optimize read-write performance; it offers vast scalability without complexity; it provides a global name space; it is highly available with built-in cluster management; and it is self-servicing since it can dynamically convert a storage node into a backup server that is capable of backing up the entire computing environment.

What Makes a Grid?

Grid computing is becoming a mainstream technology because of advancements such as simultaneous multi-threading, virtual machines and the adoption of Linux. A grid is designed differently than high-availability clusters. Heterogeneity, flexibility and reliability set grids apart from supercomputers, server farms and clustering technology. Grids are not as centralized or dedicated to specific workloads, but allow workload problems to find their needed computing resources. Rather than being built for specific configurations or application workloads, grids are balanced with attention to task priority rather than best-effort rules.

The New Frontier: Workload Rebalancing

A key benefit of a corporate enterprise grid is compute flexibility. Corporate grids provide the ability to change underlying physical resources with minimal disruption to the business applications and resources that depend on them. This type of infrastructure virtualization has been called a hinge technology — a technology that enables greater business agility by allowing companies to respond rapidly to changing business requirements and processes.

At its core, grid computing is based on open standards and protocols. The Globus Toolkit (http://www.globus.org) is an open source software toolkit used for building Linux grid systems and applications using the Open Grid Services Architecture (OGSA). OGSA allows organizations to optimize computing and data resources, pool them for large capacity workloads or share them across networks.

There are many factors to consider in grid-enabling an application. One must understand that not all applications can be transformed to run in parallel on a grid and achieve scalability. Furthermore, there are no practical tools for transforming arbitrary applications to exploit the parallel capabilities of a grid.

As organizations need to handle dynamically changing workloads and quickly provide computing power where it is needed most, the flexibility of grid computing is paramount. Linux-based grids are rapidly gaining momentum as organizations seek to gain benefits not available with traditional computing models. With grid computing, companies can harness their distributed computing resources, utilize them more efficiently and extract more usable power out of networked systems. Grids are highly scalable and can grow seamlessly over time — flexibly adding compute power when and where it is most needed, to better meet dynamically changing workloads.

A good place to start with building a Linux grid is with openMosix (http://www.openmosix.org). openMosix is a Linux kernel extension enabling one large Linux system image from multiple Linux computers.

Grid and Virtualization

A grid presents a virtual Web service metaphor to applications — that is, the grid looks no different than a stand-alone server to a Web service. In fact, the grid is the server of choice for any J2EE application server.

The grid makes it possible to build service-oriented architectures and is the basis for utility computing, but most business applications will need to be redesigned to fully leverage grid computing. Virtualization technology is very helpful in these situations by providing an abstraction between the underlying CPU resources and the applications that request them.

Application and business logic virtualization, such as Web services, allow application business logic to run on any type of underlying application server, including grids. Data and I/O virtualization are helpful for running application services on grids, allowing applications to connect to an abstract layer that then retrieves data from any repository. Operating system virtualization provides an application server platform that is separate from the grid hardware.

Other Clustering Technologies

NPACI Rocks. This open source project is led by the National Partnership for Advanced Computational Infrastructure (NPACI) at the San Diego Supercomputer Center and the University of California. Rocks is a hybrid software stack featuring a blend of open source software technologies and proprietary products. It provides turnkey software installation and update for Linux clusters. For more information, visit www.rocksclusters.org.

OSCAR. OSCAR (Open Source Cluster Application Resources) is the first project by the Open Cluster Group (http://www.openclustergroup.org), an informal group dedicated to making clusters practical for high-performance computing (HPC). It is a collection of methods for building, programming and using HPC clusters, consisting of an integrated software bundle to install, build, maintain and use a Linux cluster. For more information, visit http://oscar.openclustergroup.org.

Key Takeaways

An interesting fact is that the majority of all HPC cluster computers in the world run Linux. Five or so years ago, commodity cluster computers would appear, however briefly, in the TOP500 list of supercomputers. Now, Linux-based commodity clusters are theTOP500.

Linux, coupled with the open source model, contributes to real business innovation. It is about improving your application processing environment. It's all about getting more performance. And it's definitely about lowering your cost of computing. By implementing Linux-based technologies such as Linux application clusters, Linux clustered file systems, Linux diskless clusters and Linux grids, there is nothing you can't do with commodity hardware.

Chapter 13

Scaling Linux Environments

Man's mind, once stretched by new ideas, never regains its original dimensions.
—Oliver Wendell Holmes

Information technology is interesting in that it seems nothing happens for many years then all of a sudden there is a step change that has a big impact on the way we think about processing architectures and application development. We are at the beginning of another step change.

Scaling Linux application environments represents an opportunity to provide better price per performance. That is, by taking advantage of Linux computing architectures and programming models, it is possible to build a much more cost-effective application computing infrastructure.

With Linux and horizontal scaling, organizations can deploy lower-cost systems and achieve higher levels of application performance.

Vertical Scaling

Scaling is an architectural process to increase your computing capabilities. As your computer requirements expand, you can choose to expand your systems vertically or horizontally. Vertical scaling essentially means implementing larger systems. Horizontal scaling means deploying additional systems to handle the workload.

With vertical scaling, services are scaled within the system — resources such as CPUs, memory and I/O capacity are added incrementally as system performance needs to be increased. Vertical scaling involves servers that are based on SMP (symmetrical multi-processing) designs.

SMP is the processing of programs by multiple processors that share a common operating system and physical memory structure. Since there is only one instance of the operating system, the processors, memory and I/O components are shared over a system interconnect. This interconnect is commonly a backplane that provides a low-latency, very high-bandwidth data path for the system's resources.

In vertical systems, all memory is shared, meaning all processors and all I/O connections have equal access to all the physical memory in the system. Memory appears to the application as one large available resource. Resources are scaled, or added to the system, by installing additional system boards in the system's backplane.

Multiple SMP servers can be used to build large application clusters in an architecture known as Non-Uniform Memory Architecture (NUMA). Physically separate multiprocessor chassis are interconnected with a bus or interconnect. In large NUMA system designs, this interconnect is much slower than a SMP backplane. Since the NUMA interconnect has significantly more latency than the backplane of a SMP system, memory access times are very dependent on the actual memory location. Consequently, under NUMA, a processor can access its own local memory faster than non-local memory (hence the name non-uniform memory access).

Another method of vertical computing is massively parallel processing (MPP). MPP is the coordinated processing of a program by multiple processors that work on different parts of the program, each running its own OS instance. An MPP system is also known as "loosely coupled." There are few remaining MPP system vendors in business and most offer special-purpose systems.

Horizontal Scaling

Horizontal scaling involves more networking and clustering technologies than vertical scaling architectures. The networking components are typically standard network interconnects including Fast Ethernet, Gigabit Ethernet, Dolphinics'Scalable Coherent Interconnect (SCI), InfiniBand, Myricom's Myrinet and Quadrics' QsNet. These types of interconnects are slower (lower bandwidth and higher latency) than the backplane used in SMP systems, but all of these offer higher bandwidth, lower latency, and less CPU involvement in message transfer than TCP/IP over Gigabit Ethernet does — yet at a price.

Horizontal scaling clusters are used to provide a single interface to a set of resources that can arbitrarily grow or shrink over time. The most common example of this is a Web server farm. The goal of a Web server farm is to provide the image of a single system by managing, operating and coordinating a large number of individual Linux servers.

With horizontal scaling, each node has its own OS instance, processor and memory space. Resources are increased by adding more nodes, not by adding more resources within a node. Independent servers are interconnected on a high-speed network fabric that enables servers to be added as incremental compute resources. Clustered databases, such as Oracle RAC and IBM DB2, as well as clustered file systems, rely on horizontal scalability.

Since the memory in horizontal scaling architectures is distributed, any access to these resources by other nodes is via the external interconnect bus, which is orders of magnitude slower than access through a system's internal backplane. As a result, the development of faster, lower latency interconnects is seeing rapid innovation. Lower latency interconnects allow multiple nodes to be clustered into a single system image, building powerful horizontal scaling architectures. Figure 13–1 illustrates the idea of vertical and horizontal scaling attributes.

What Works Best?

When application requirements can be met with horizontal scaling systems, it provides a less-expensive deployment option over a vertical scaling architecture since the per-processor acquisition cost of horizontal systems is generally lower than that of vertical scaling system designs.

Because Linux nodes can be added at any time, it is not necessary to overprovision servers at the time of first deployment, eliminating the capital costs associated with such stranded capacity. More importantly, organizations tend to make better computing investments by deferring equipment purchases since technology decreases in cost but improves in capability over time. And with blade computing, horizontal computing is even more cost-effective.

However, the management and infrastructure costs may be higher for horizontal architectures. When deploying horizontal systems there will be many more instances of the OS as well as more instances of the application server software (unless a clustered file system is used). In general, the more instances of an OS or application, the more expensive the environment will

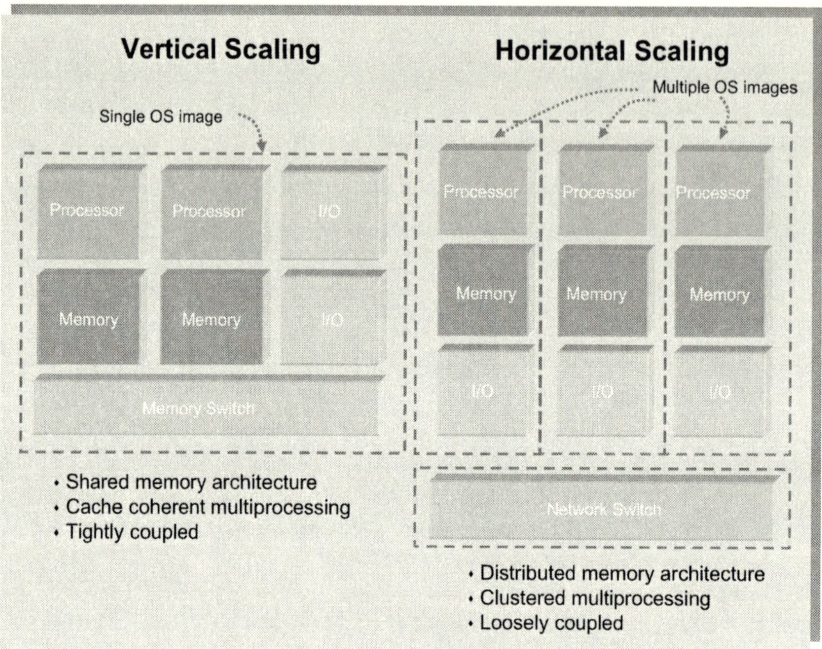

Figure 13-1. *Scaling Techniques.*

likely be to manage. Other management functions, such as backup and recovery, disaster recovery, software delivery and fault management are more decentralized and possibly more complex to manage and implement as well.

The general landscape for most application computing will involve the use of both vertical and horizontal scaling designs. However, many application workloads are being re-architected to support horizontal scaling when possible. Horizontal scaling offers much lower deployment and management costs for most workloads.

Following is a list of the most salient differences between vertical and horizontal scaling:

- Applications with execution threads that need to communicate with each other perform better with vertical scaling than with horizontal scaling. However, more applications are being designed to support horizontal scaling.
- High RAS (reliability, availability, serviceability) is a feature of the individual vertical system. In horizontal scaling, system availability is

achieved via massive replication (multiple nodes connected so the failure of a single node has little effect).

- Vertical scaling systems have a single OS instance covering the resources; some vertical systems can be further partitioned into smaller vertical servers (via virtual machines). Each system in a horizontal scaling environment has its own instance of the OS and applications.
- Vertical scaling systems are usually built with proprietary hardware components. Horizontal scaling systems can be built using commodity servers.
- Vertical scaling systems can be improved through the addition of more resources within the existing chassis, such as faster processors, more RAM and additional (or faster) I/O connections. Horizontal systems are enhanced by adding additional nodes or by replacing older nodes with faster nodes.
- Vertical scaling systems are almost all based on 64-bit computing. Horizontal systems are either 32-bit or 64-bit.
- Vertical scaling systems' interconnect speeds are usually much faster than horizontal scaling designs.

Identifying Bottlenecks

The most important task for those making architectural choices is to first understand the real bottlenecks in the computational workflow and the computational resources required to resolve them. In other words, what is the best way to size your computing hardware environment for your Linux processing requirements?

Capacity planning is at best an educated guess about what might happen. Benchmarks are arbitrary by definition and usually misleading across disparate hardware. There are three important principles to remember: statistics are voodoo, it's always a work–in progress and your results will vary.

There are a variety of methods that provide best-guess estimates of system processing performance. Generally, standard sizing models grossly overestimate the requirement for CPU and memory. The best way to determine the resources needed for a particular application is to build a real system and directly benchmark its performance (see Figure 13–2).

In its broadest perspective, a bottleneck is the step or process within every system that imposes a delay on the ultimate throughput of that system. All system designs contain bottlenecks. When a bottleneck is removed, another one appears or, worse, another one is actually created by improperly addressing the original bottleneck.

The Answer Is...It Depends

The difficulty is that system scaling has a different effect on performance in single-user versus multi-user environments, as well as non-threaded versus threaded applications. Today's traditional single-core processors can only process one thread at a time, spending a majority of time waiting for data from memory. In fact, as clock speeds have increased, so too has the relevance and impact of latency on overall chip performance. Software developers have used multithreading for years as a technique to speed throughput by enabling multiple streams of instructions to execute simultaneously.

Recent advances in chip fabrication have released CPU architectures based around multithreading known as chip multithreading (CMT), chip multiprocessing (CMP) and simultaneous multithreading (SMT). Typically, Unix and Windows systems utilize a form of symmetric multiprocessing (SMP). SMP is a computer architecture that combines multiple CPUs available to complete individual processes simultaneously (multiprocessing). It uses a single operating system and shares a common memory space. Figure 13–3 shows how hardware-level multithreading speeds overall system performance.

CMT, CMP and SMT

A newer and more cost-effective approach to SMP is using CMT technology, which diverges somewhat from the traditional SMP approach. A CMT processor implements multithreading using a variety of methods, such as having multiple cores on a single chip (CMP) and designing these core with the ability to execute multiple threads within a single core (SMT).

For example, some processors (such as the Sun Microsystems' UltraSPARC IV and AMD's dual-core Opteron) implement multithreading by incorporating multiple traditional processor cores in a single physical package (CMP). In some cases, one or more on-chip caches may be shared among the processor cores (allowing threads to constructively or destructively interfere with each other). Shared logic and data paths to cache, memory and memory controllers may exist, which can also cause some bandwidth issues.

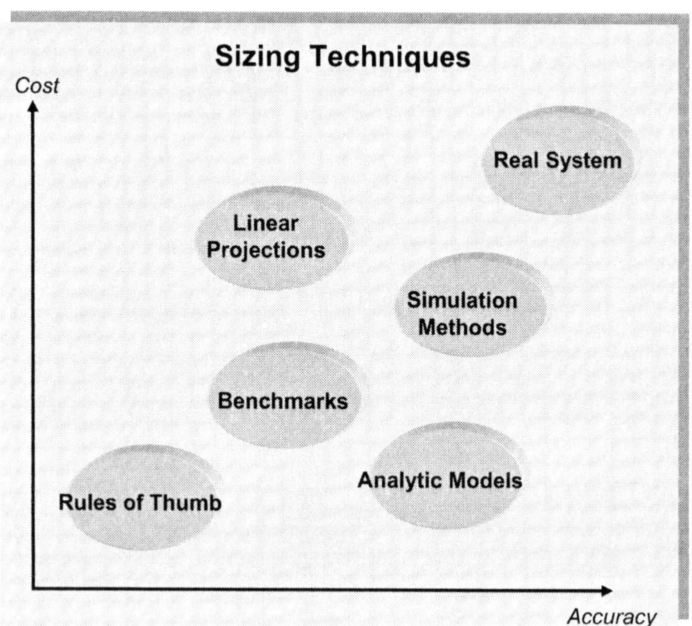

Figure 13-2. *Server Sizing Approaches.*

Dual-core chips generally give you about one-and-a-half times the speed of single-core processors.

Another approach is SMT, in which each core may present multiple logical CPUs. SMT is a processor design that combines hardware multithreading with superscalar processor technology to allow multiple threads to issue instructions each cycle. Examples include Intel's Hyper-Threaded P4/Xeon processors and Sun Microsystems' Niagara processor. (Niagara is a threaded CMP with four threads per core and up to eight cores per chip for a total of 32 logical processors—what Sun calls "symmetric multiprocessing on a chip.")

This architecture addresses chip latency by allowing the processor core to execute instructions from a different instruction stream (thread) if a given thread stalls. Threads executing on CPUs presented by a given core will typically share everything except a set of memory registers (necessary for maintaining the distinct thread state), so one thread's performance impact on another on the same core can be considerable.

It is important to understand your underlying application architecture. For example, many commercial applications such as ERP or Web services are highly threaded. The best system for this environment is one that can provide the processing power to run multiple threads at maximum perform-

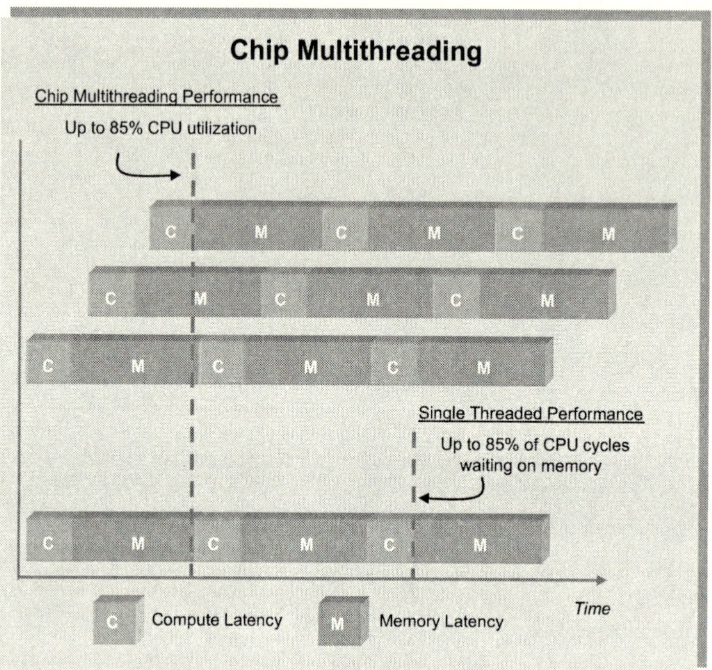

Figure 13-3. *Benefits With Multithreading.*

ance. Compute-centric workloads mainly utilize single-threaded applications but run that thread extremely fast. Figure 13–4 displays these scenarios.

Scaling Techniques

For existing environments, the first step is to identify all components and understand how they relate to each other. The most important task is to understand the requirements and flow of the existing applications—what can and cannot be modified. The application is critical to the scalability of any infrastructure.

At a minimum, your analysis must include a breakdown of transaction types and volumes as well as a graphic view of the components in each tier. As you analyze requirements for a new application, you have the opportunity to build scaling techniques into your infrastructure. As illustrated in Figure 13–5, it is not uncommon to incorporate both vertical and horizontal scaling techniques into application architectures. Using this tier approach with application architectures allows performance to be more easily scaled by separating architectural components according to their workload (see Figure 13–6).

To achieve proper scale, the application design must consider potential scaling effects. In the absence of known workload patterns, it is necessary to follow an iterative, incremental approach. When deploying new applications, this is a great opportunity to consider how best to leverage Linux scaling abilities.

A Processor by any Other Name

Linux performance is related to a number of factors. Generally, when you are trying to size a Linux server for an application workload, the first areas to consider are the number and types of processors being used in the system.

Comparing processor performance requires evaluating the following factors:

- CPU clock speed
- Processor cache size
- System bus capacity
- Addressable memory size
- Integer and floating point performance

To make matters difficult, there is no single absolute metric that can be used to compare various vendors' processors — or even processor product lines from the same vendor.

Although not a valid indicator of performance, CPU clock speed is still an important element of processing capacity. Holding everything else constant, comparing CPU clock speeds of two different processors from the same processor family will give a rough comparison of how much work the CPU itself can do. However, different chip architectures have varying levels of efficiency when converting rated CPU clock speed increases into processing improvements.

As a general rule, system performance increases by only 15 percent to 50 percent of the increase in processor speed. In fact, the more you increase the CPU clock speed, the less your performance will increase. And if the Linux application is not efficiently transferring data to and from the server processors, then there is little gain from increasing the processor clock. Other processor elements, such as a cache size, system bus capacity or addressable memory size, become more important.

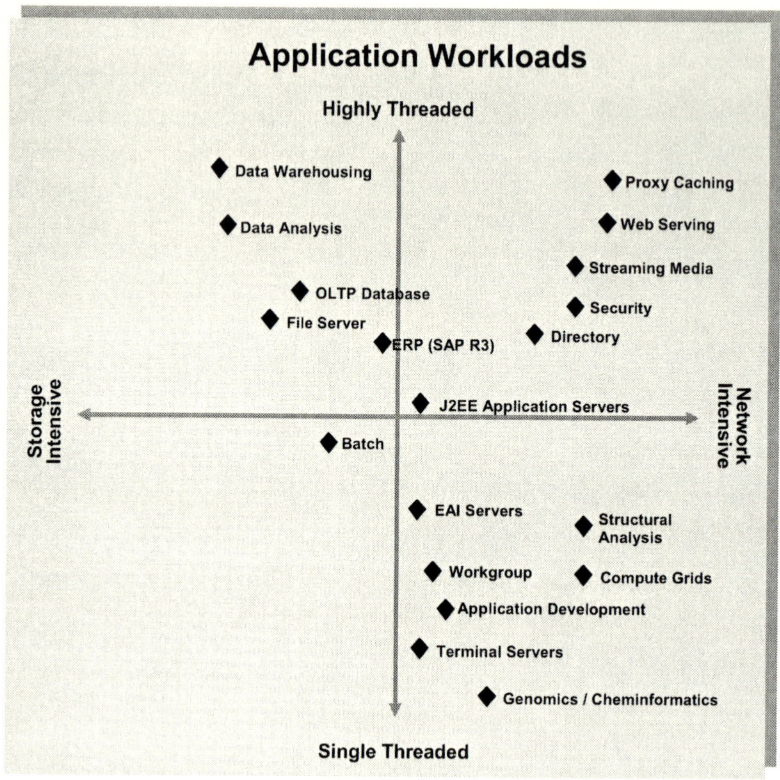

Figure 13-4. *Different Application Workloads.*

CPU-Level Cache

Typically, processors have several layers of processor cache. Level 1 (L1) cache is located inside the chip's execution core. Data and instructions that the execution pipeline will immediately process or have just processed are stored here. The L1 cache is itself fed by internal buses that obtain their data and instructions from the L2 cache. Data is moved to cache when it's needed immediately or when predictive mechanisms in the processor anticipate that it will be needed for upcoming instructions.

A three-tier cache design means that if an L2 cache miss occurs, the L3 cache is examined before a fetch to memory is initiated. L3 cache sizes are usually multiple megabytes, and chip performance can be greatly enhanced by the reduction of memory latencies provided by a multi-cache architecture. In fact, increasing CPU cache can have a substantial impact on processing performance for very memory-intensive applications such as Web and database servers. The addition of L3 cache is necessary to help narrow the ever-widening gap between processor speed and memory speed.

Typically, L1 and L2 are on the actual CPU core and L3 sits between processor and memory, but this is very much open to change in future designs.

The system bus capacity is also crucially important since the system bus is the main pathway for transporting data to and from the CPU. The system bus capacity is related both to the system bus speed as well as the size of the bus itself. Increasing either the system bus speed or size can have very important performance implications.

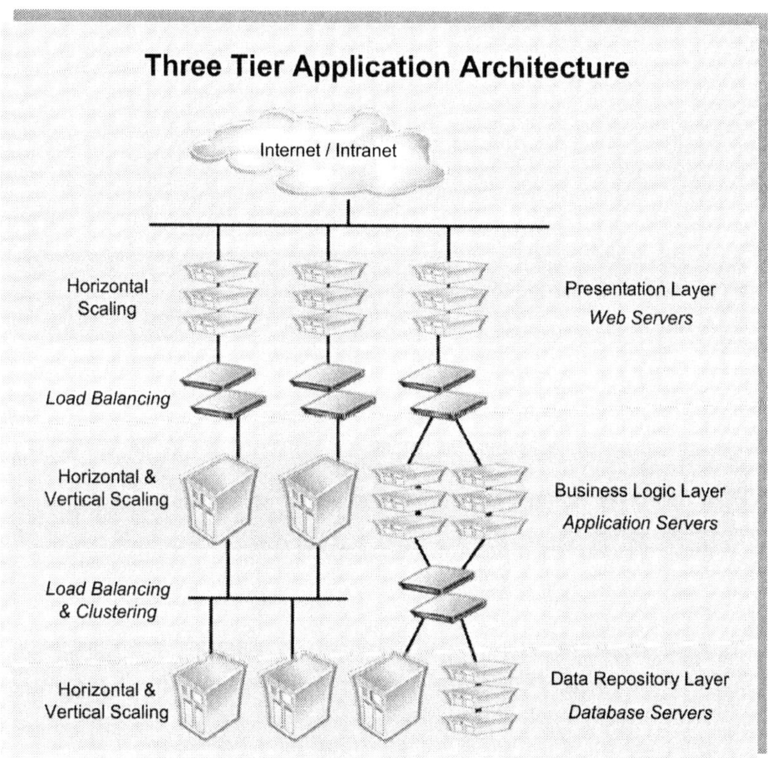

Figure 13-5. *Typical Three Tier Application Architecture.*

What Does This All Mean?

How do you translate all this into sizing a Linux server or Linux server environment? In order to size Linux servers correctly, you need to determine how CPU-intensive versus how I/O-intensive your Linux application is. Once the application characteristics are known, you can convert the

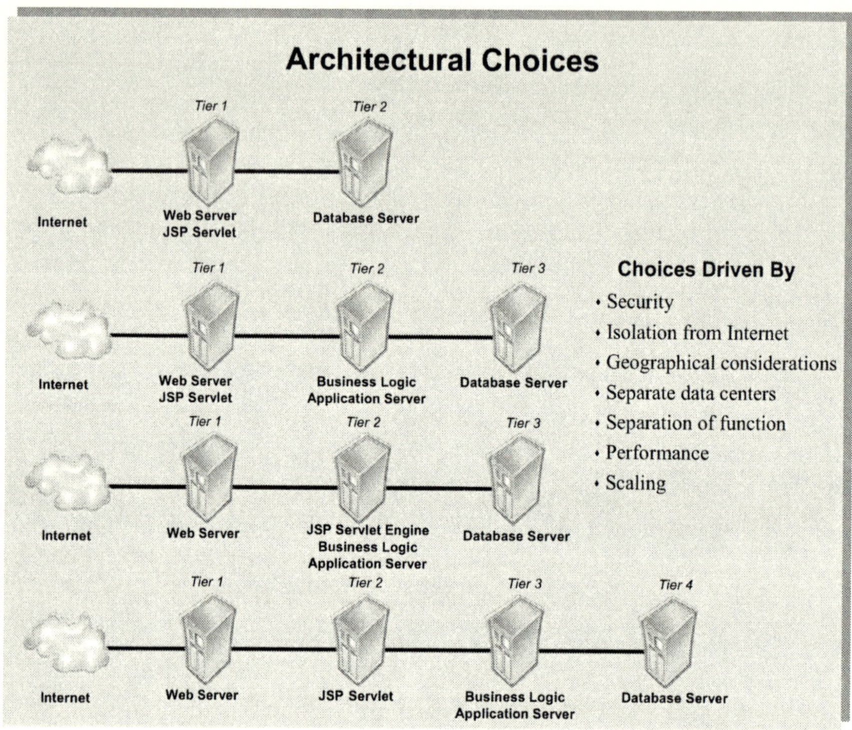

Figure 13-6. *Deploying Different Architectures.*

application requirements (e.g. number of concurrent users, transactions per second, Web page hits per second, etc.) into infrastructure requirements.

The discussion of CPU-intensive versus I/O-intensive can become a complicated and never-ending process. Most likely your Linux applications fall in a range of CPU-intense and I/O-intense workloads depending on the following questions:

- How autonomous are the transactions?
- How unstructured or non-uniform is the data?
- Is there application load balancing?
- How is data locking performed?
- How long is the CPU idle?
- How much data sharing exists?
- How sequential or serial are the transactions?

Knowing the characteristics of the workload you are going to deploy is essential. With this information, you can then identify where that workload falls on the serial-parallel continuum and consider how the Linux application will scale; and then be able to size the Linux compute environment accordingly.

If the workload is CPU-intensive, applications tend to favor faster CPUs (and more of them). If the workload is mixed with non-uniform usage patterns, applications favor greater internal bandwidth. Typical server farms are underutilized in terms of built-in processor capacity or headroom. With Linux workloads, this is alleviated with server virtualization by allowing CPUs, I/O, memory and devices to overlap across multiple applications. This overlap can improve performance in most cases — in most applications, the lion's share of cycles are wasted waiting on external I/O. And considering that the operating system files are the same, why not share them across multiple applications?

Proven Techniques

Manageability, security and availability are critical factors in all design decisions. Techniques that provide scalability but compromise any of these critical factors should not be considered.There are eight general scaling techniques you can use with Linux computing environments. Figure 13–7 illustrates the following concepts.

Faster CPUs

Faster processors can be leveraged by upgrading the hardware or software. However, the efficiency of the application software can greatly limit the hardware exploitation and vice versa.

Load Balancing

Server load balancing is the process of distributing service requests across a group of servers. Many content-intensive applications have scaled beyond the point where a single server can provide adequate processing power. Load balancing also provides redundancy and failover protection.

Improve Transactions Processing

The goal is to reduce the number of requests sent between requesters and responders (such as between tiers or processes) by allowing the requester to define new requests that combine multiple requests. The benefits of this technique arise from the reduced load on the responders by eliminating the

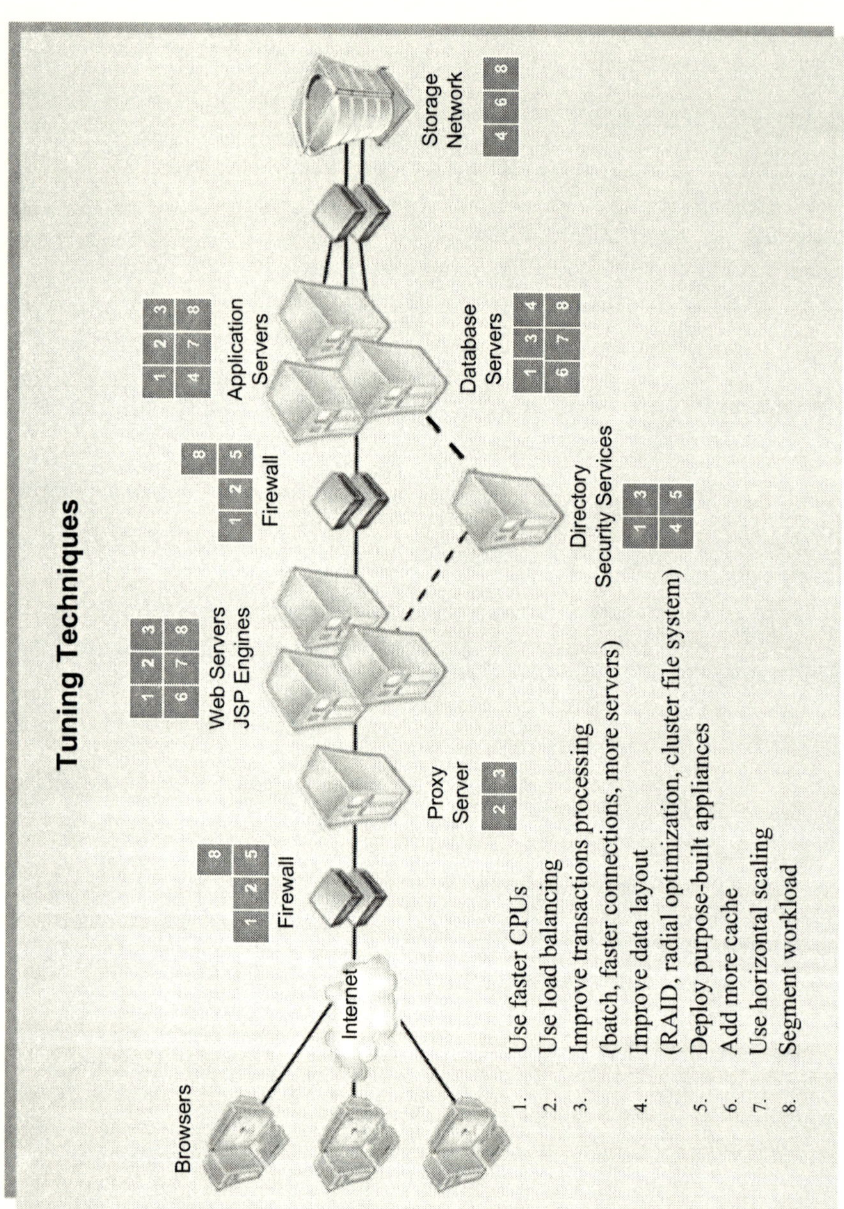

Figure 13-7. *Tuning Techniquies.*

overhead associated with multiple requests, which in turn reduces the latency experienced by the requester.

Improve Data Layout

Data layouts can use either horizontal or vertical striping techniques to make use of multiple controllers and attain parallel data access. Horizontal striping spreads I/O across controllers; vertical striping spreads I/O across disks. .

RAID technology has become almost irrelevant in terms of performance. Storage controller technology now utilizes special hardware and caching software that masks any performance penalty that RAID levels would introduce into the I/O path. Today's storage arrays can perform RAID-5 as efficiently as RAID-1. See Appendix for more details about RAID technology.

Deploy Purpose-Built Appliances

This technique applies to the edge servers, the Web presentation server, the directory and security servers, the network, and the Internet firewall. The goal is to improve the efficiency of a specific component using a special-purpose machine to perform the required action. These machines tend to be dedicated systems optimized for a specific function.

Some issues to consider regarding appliances are the sufficiency and stability of the functions and the potential benefits in relation to the added complexity and manageability challenges. It's worth noting, however, that the newer generation of devices is increasingly easy to deploy and manage; some are even self-managing.

Tuning Techniques

- Understand the application environment
- Categorize your workload
- Determine the components most impacted
- Select the scaling techniques to apply
- Apply the techniques
- Re-evaluate and repeat

Figure 13-8. *Rules of Thumb.*

Add More Cache

Caching is a key technique to improve application response time. Caching applies to the edge server, the Web presentation server, the Web application server, the network, the existing business applications and the database. The goal is to improve performance and scalability by reducing the length of the path traversed by a request and the resulting response.

Use Horizontal Scaling

This technique applies to the Web presentation server, the Web application server, and the directory, security and database servers. The primary goal is to service more application requests. Parallelism in machine clusters typically leads to improvements in response time. An individual request is not completed any quicker; it's just that more application requests can be serviced in the same time it takes to process a single request.

Segment the Workload

This technique applies to the Web presentation server, the Web application server, the database, the intranet firewall and the network. The goal is to split up the workload into manageable chunks, thereby obtaining more consistent and predictable response times. Combining segmentation with replication offers the added benefits of providing an easy mechanism to redistribute the application workload.

Figure 13–8 summarizes the basic processes to use with these performance-tuning techniques.

Key Takeaways

The computing infrastructure plays an increasingly important role in the success of any business. Market share, customer satisfaction and overall company image are now intertwined with the availability and performance of a company's Web site. The underlying computing infrastructure is expected to provide good performance, high availability, and a secure and scalable platform to support business applications all the time.

Scalability is a key success factor for business applications in a dynamic environment. There is clearly a cost- per-performance edge with Linux using horizontal scaling infrastructures and clustered file systems. With the proper application architecture, Linux-based computing can satisfy most business processing requirements. By using performance-tuning techniques, almost any application environment can have its overall performance improved.

Key #4

Finding the Right Project

An information-based Paradigm Shift begins by conducting an objective financial analysis in order to secure the proper executive-level sponsorship and commitment.

Key Overview

The organization must secure management commitment and sponsorship. Without proper management support, a Paradigm Shift cannot be achieved. Executive-level sponsorship is best obtained with an objective financial analysis ensuring proper validation and justification for the business-level objectives.

Chapter 14

Taking Costs Out (or TCO)

The decline in absolute dollars spent [on technology and content] during the three months and nine months ended September 30, 2001, in comparison to the corresponding periods in the prior year primarily reflect our migration to a Linux-based technology platform that utilizes a less costly technology infrastructure, as well as general price reductions for data and telecommunication services due to market overcapacity.
— Amazon.com 10-Q filing with the SEC, 2001

In the past, companies have made massive investments in data center infrastructures, enterprise computing systems and data management software with the best intentions of creating some type of business value.

Today, however, the relationship between the investment in information technology and the resulting value to the business needs to be very clear. The perceived business value must clearly show its direct relationship to the financial wellbeing of the company. The key business drivers are generally based on economic derivatives that directly lower cost, improve business revenue or increase organizational profitability (see Figure 14–1).

For most organizations, the business value is associated with some sort of cost savings. In fact, it has become a common denominator for all organizations — the need to contain and control costs. It has even come to the point where businesses are asking themselves hard questions about the real value of their IT investments. Technology organizations are under pressure to rationalize their computing infrastructures.

There are numerous case studies showing how Linux and open source deliver outstanding financial value. These benefits derive from greater deployment flexibility, improved reliability and security and use of open standards that do not create vendor lock-in. However, what most organizations need is their own case study indicating the "true" cost savings. It is

Today's IT Imperative

- Increasing use of IA-based systems as a way to take advantage of high volume microchip designs
- Reducing software costs, asset management complexity and licensing issues
- Providing greater levels of flexibility and vendor independence
- Creating highly customized, highly adaptable systems
- Building application infrastructures that are scalable and can be access anywhere at anytime

Figure 14-1. *IT Objectives.*

fairly straightforward to determine savings from acquisition costs but much more complex to quantify migration costs, disruption to the business, training and ongoing support for the new platform. As a result, it is necessary to build a financial model.

The Cost Challenge

There are numerous models that categorize the total cost of computing. Generally, it breaks down into the cost for hardware, software, maintenance, staffing, development and support. There are also many factors that can dramatically affect the financial calculations that may not be easily foreseen or controlled when breaking down these costs. For example, poor provisioning, management or server utilization could counter the reduced license, maintenance and capital costs of the hardware associated with a Linux deployment.

Ultimately, cost savings should only be considered in conjunction with business value, processing effectiveness or IT efficiency for the organization. Financial calculations should also include downtime costs and performance considerations. Many factors can skew a simple financial study, such as:

- Whether prices are being deeply discounted
- Whether new hardware was configured into the model
- The type of workload used in the financial analysis
- The software and applications used in the configuration

- Assumptions about administrative capabilities and efficiencies of the configuration
- The timeframe the model covers
- Whether support and service contracts were considered
- Whether there was adequate training given to the organization

You must factor any hidden costs into your financial model. Such hidden costs may include the skill level of the IT staff, the complexity of applications, cost to migrate to another environment or the complexity of the project. Also consider the fact that vendor discounting plays a major role in the financial analysis of a solution since deep price concessions can make a bad investment look rather favorable. In the end, the purchase price of hardware and software alone provides only a small indication of the total lifecycle cost for a Linux or open source solution.

The Financial Models

There are many ways to build a financial justification for your Linux initiative. The cost to support your Linux initiative is based on cost for its hardware environment, hardware maintenance and support contracts, software licenses and software maintenance agreements. Maintenance agreements will cost a percentage (generally 15 percent to 25 percent) of the initial acquisition costs of the equipment.

Most of the time, deploying or migrating to Linux requires purchasing a complete parallel computing environment including acquiring new hardware, software, storage and other infrastructure components. On a server platform basis, Linux is about equal to Windows. Research also indicates that Linux support-centric costs will not be much different than any Unix or Windows platform. Once these metrics are validated, it is easier — not to mention more credible — to construct the financial justification model.

There are many models to justify an open source project (balanced scorecard, real options analysis, business case analysis, portfolio management). A simple yet effective approach is to work through three simple financial models: feasibility study, total cost of ownership (TCO) and return on investment (ROI).

The first step in the financial analysis is conducting a quick feasibility test. Hardware and software costs are one-time charges, but maintenance fees are recurring. As illustrated in Figure 14–2, recurring maintenance fees are often a major reason why organizations are eager to replace their computing environment with new IA-compliant systems. For situations where this in not the case, it is probably better to leave your current environment alone. Most likely, however, you'll find there are many situations where this analysis shows extremely favorable results from buying new servers versus "keeping what you have."

CapEx and OpEx Perspectives

Feasibility studies provide a CapEx perspective to your project. However, most studies indicate that the acquisition costs represent only 15 percent of the true investment outlay. In spite of this, a feasibility study is a useful exercise for two reasons. First, the data collected for this model is needed for the TCO analysis and, second, the feasibility study provides a quick financial litmus test for your project.

The next step is to build upon the feasibility study and conduct a TCO analysis. A TCO study determines if a Linux migration effort makes financial sense for your organization from a balanced CapEx and OpEx perspective. The TCO accounts for the upfront capital expenses incurred in addition to the operational cost savings generated by your project. Studies indicate that for every dollar spent on hardware, more than 10 dollars is spent on the management of the hardware. TCO models attempt to capture this perspective by representing the sum of both CapEx and OpEx over the complete lifecycle of the investment. A TCO analysis is an effective way to sell your project to your sponsor or executive committee.

The TCO table shown in Figure 14–3 offers guidance for doing an objective TCO analysis. As illustrated, equipment costs have a prominent effect on the financial model. This is mainly because of their relatively short amortization period. Servers today do not last beyond three years because of the disparity in performance when compared to purchasing newer systems. As a result, a three-year cost of ownership model is usually adequate for a typical financial analysis.

However, with Microsoft environments, you do need to consider the fact that you are required to license not only their operating system, but also their e-mail server, database, office suite and development tools. In these cases, software licenses are often the bigger expense to the organization (see sidebar Software Pricing on the Rise).

It must be noted that no matter how honest a person or organization is, TCO assumptions can be made to be optimistic or pessimistic; an objective TCO is hard to come by.

Feasibility Study

	Year 1	Year 2	Year 3	Cummulative
Capital Expense				
Linux Servers	$ 107,545.00	$ 55,750.00	$ 25,750.00	
Server Upgrades	$ 40,940.00			
Software	$ 15,725.00	$ 12,000.00	$ -	
Network Upgrades	$ 12,750.00		$ 15,000.00	
Total Capital Expense	$ 176,960.00	$ 67,750.00	$ 40,750.00	$ 285,460.00
Depreciation Rate	$ 0.33	$ 0.44	$ 0.15	
Less Depreciation	$ (58,980.77)	$ (78,658.72)	$ (26,207.78)	
Net Capital Expense	$ 117,979.23	$ (10,908.72)	$ 14,542.22	$ 121,612.74
Maintenance & Support	$ 15,000.00			
Grand Total	$ 132,979.23	$ (10,908.72)	$ 14,542.22	**$ 136,612.74**
Capital Expense	$ -	$ -	$ -	
Total Capital Expense	$ -	$ -	$ -	$ -
Less Depreciation	$ -	$ -	$ -	$ -
Net Capital Expense	$ -	$ -	$ -	$ -
Maintenance & Support	$ 75,500.00	$ 95,750.00	$ 110,750.00	
Grand Total	$ 75,500.00	$ 95,750.00	$ 110,750.00	**$ 282,000.00**

Figure 14-2. *Multi-Year Feasibility Study.*

Why Linux and Open Source?

There are many reasons why Linux and open source provide a better CapEx and OpEx picture for your organization (see Figure 14–4) The most cited are its ability to allow your organization to:

- Use cheaper hardware
- Reduce (and even eliminate) licensing fees and maintenance contracts
- Use an internal development methodology
- Have less risk of failures from commercial vaporware/shelfware
- Create a more reliable computing platform
- Spread development costs through collaboration
- Quickly add new application functionality or fix problems rapidly
- Create reuseable and redeployable software code
- Have lower training costs

The Rising Cost of Software

Organizations should review their current business software usage and analyze future licensing and support costs. This information will be essential for any financial calculations. It is important to estimate these costs over the next three years.

There are four emerging trends in hardware that are changing the traditional pricing model that has been in use for the past 25 years in the software industry. Traditionally, companies such as IBM, Oracle and even Microsoft based their software licensing on hardware capacity, or the number of CPUs.

Recently, multi-core chip architectures have emerged to improve server performance. These multi-core chips have multiple processor cores in one socket. Based on the conventional software licensing schemes, dual cores equate to dual CPUs, which translates to twice the software licensing fee. It is estimated that single core systems will not be available beyond 2007.

Fortunately, most software vendors are not doubling their license fees for multi-core CPUs. Oracle, for example, looks at a dual core processor as 1.5 processors rather than two fully licensable CPUs.

Virtual machines will also attribute to an increase in software licensing costs. Virtual machines simulate hardware resources so that multiple operating systems can share or partition hardware resources. The benefit with VM technology is that it can dynamically scale computing resources across multiple operating environments.

This type of software partitioning will most likely result in higher software licensing fees because most software vendors will not recognize logical partitioning in their licensing models. Software vendors generally charge for the total potential capacity, irrespective of how much CPU capacity the software is using.

Another cause for consternation with software licensing is with rapid provisioning. With VM, rapid provisioning is the ability to shift computing resources according to application workloads. For instance, at month-end the financial systems may require more processing power than the order entry servers. How does the software licensing cost adjust for this temporary shift in processing power? Although this type of processing reduces overall hardware costs, software license charges have not been addressed.

At first blush, it might seem less expensive to run software on smaller CPU capacity servers. However, if you are scaling applications horizontally across multi-socket configurations, it might end up being more expensive than hosting it on a single multi-core server. Managing software licensing models can be challenging, but the cost savings can be significant.

Total Cost of Ownership

Capital Expenses	Year 1	Year 2	Year 3	Cummulative
Capital Expense				
Linux Servers	$ 107,545.00	$ 55,750.00	$ 25,750.00	
Server Upgrades	$ 40,940.00			
Software	$ 15,725.00	$ 12,000.00	$ -	
Network Upgrades	$ 12,750.00		$ 15,000.00	
Total Capital Expense	$ 176,960.00	$ 67,750.00	$ 40,750.00	$ 285,460.00
Depreciation Rate	$ 0.33	$ 0.44	$ 0.15	
Less Depreciation	$ (58,980.77)	$ (78,658.72)	$ (26,207.78)	
Net Capital Expense	$ 117,979.23	$ (10,908.72)	$ 14,542.22	$ 121,612.74
Maintenance & Support	$ 15,000.00			
Discounted Capital Expenses	$ 403,696.98	$ 22,297.58	$ 22,821.76	**$ 448,816.32**
Operating Expenses	**Year 1**	**Year 2**	**Year 3**	
Administration Expenses				
Desktop Support Reduction	$ (10,000.00)	$ (20,000.00)	$ (30,000.00)	
Headcount Increase Deferment	$ -	$ (50,000.00)	$ -	
Training & Education	$ 15,000.00	$ 10,000.00	$ 5,000.00	
Recurring Expenses				
Power & Cooling	$ 10,000.00	$ 12,000.00	$ 12,000.00	
Maintenance Costs Reduction	$ -	$ (45,000.00)	$ (55,000.00)	
Software Costs Reduction	$ (5,000.00)	$ (10,000.00)	$ (20,000.00)	
Data Recovery Improvement	$ -	$ (5,000.00)	$ (5,000.00)	
Discounted Operating Expenses	$ 9,433.96	$ (52,427.18)	$ (30,392.16)	**$ (73,385.38)**
TCO (Based on Three-Year NPV)				**$ 375,430.94**

Figure 14-3. *Multi-Year Cost of Ownership.*

While TCO plays an important role in the financial justification of your project, ROI is equally significant for the decision-making process. Using a TCO metric is a good way to measure costs but a bad way to analyze the full business value of the investment. While it may be useful to consider the overall total cost of ownership, the bottomline is this: Is it a good business investment?

Return on Investment

ROI can be more effective than TCO as a measure of business value, especially with new, emerging technologies. For this reason, there is a movement within the financial community toward a more comprehensive ROI justification, where TCO is just a portion of the overall analysis. In this view, ROI analysis is a higher-quality approach for making business decisions because it is more inclusive of the risks and returns of making new investments.

ROI provides a heavy OpEx perspective and, today, OpEx reduction is more important than CapEx expenditures. OpEx perspective in a ROI analysis should include factors such as outage time reduction, management and labor

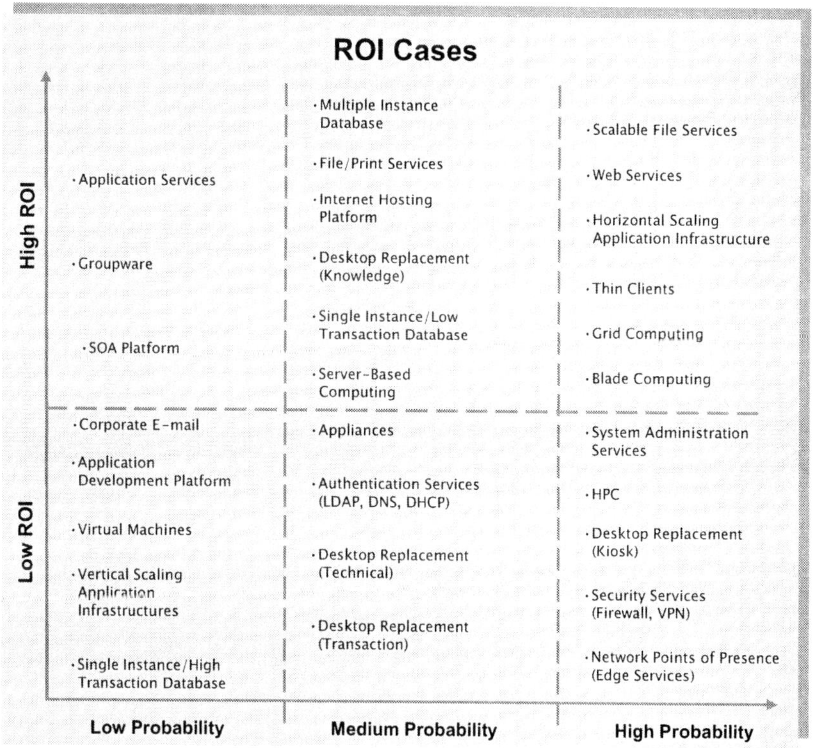

Figure 14-4. *Typical ROI Cases.*

effects, environmental costs, miscellaneous operations efficiency, code reuse and maintenance fees.

Hard and Soft Dollars

Figure 14–5 shows how soft and hard cost allocations are part of the ROI. Soft dollar savings are less tangible and more difficult to validate. These are often "feel good" numbers that executive management should understand and appreciate, recognizing that, normally, no tangible cost savings is recaptured. Typically, soft costs will involve intangible expenses such as productivity gains or losses, ease of application migration, ease of scalability, ease for building business continuance or improved employee morale.

Soft costs can comprise a significant piece of an overall Linux project and, at minimum, they should be documented if not assigned an absolute monetary value. For example, Windows owners are responsible for ensuring that they comply with Microsoft's licensing policies by maintaining inventories of software products installed. There is some value in not having to monitor this type of information. Because soft dollar savings typically represent the larger percentage of a given ROI and payback dollars, they should not be underestimated or disqualified from the analysis.

Hard dollar savings also emerge from the ROI analysis; these are real cost savings that could be removed from future budgets or operating cost structures. The total combination of both hard and soft dollar savings yield the payback picture for the Linux infrastructure.

Packaged software for Linux increasingly will be pre-integrated with the server hardware, thus reducing the need for tuning, optimization and development going forward. This will reduce the need for professional staffing for Linux software installation, configuration and application development. Of course, the inclusion of commercial third-party software may represent an increase in acquisition costs for a Linux solution.

The End Result

The goal should be to have enough information to make a go/no-go decision after calculating the financial analysis and constructing a project plan. To realize the full ROI potential of the Linux operating environment, companies should conduct a pilot study of the Linux project and collect the appropriate metrics from first-hand experience. Trying to keep track of what is necessary while at the same time comparing costs and carrying out "what-if?" analyses can be confusing.

The Cost of Power

Even without special, high-density packaging, power consumption and cooling issues are challenging and costly. A dual 3.2 GHz Xeon server draws about 437 watts of DC power under load, not counting the cost of any networking equipment or the power needed to cool the system.

With an efficiency of about 75 percent for a typical power supply, this translates into 580W of AC power per server, or roughly 10kW per computer rack (including cooling overhead). At 15 cents per kilowatt-hour, power and cooling costs are USD $1,500 per month per computer rack.

It is important to factor in the cost of electricity especially when dealing with computers running single application workloads. In fact, a better way to calculate energy costs is using the watts-per-thread metric. That is, calculate how many concurrent threads the system can handle and divide it by the total wattage of the system. What counts are watts per unit of performance, not watts alone.

The Business Case

Understanding the technology justification models can make the difference between anecdotal support and objective evidence of the business value of the investment. The purpose of the justification model is to convert the relationship between the investment and its anticipated payoff into logical or mathematical form, all the while accounting for other factors that might affect the measurement along the way.

A risk analysis is an essential part of the business case. A risk analysis provides the organization with a clear understanding of the risks involved and how you are planning to mitigate them. Make sure the business case has a post-implementation measurement process to ensure the benefits you have established in the business case are achieved.

There are many reasons why companies proceed with Linux migrations even though their cost-benefit analysis of the Linux rollout is less than posi-

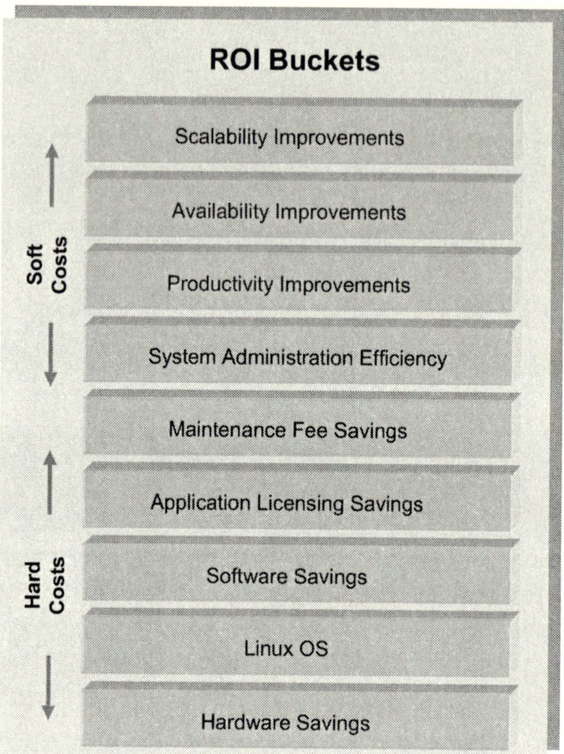

Figure 14-5. *Cost Allocation Budgets.*

tive. Nonetheless, it is important to get a financial picture of before and after the effort.

The objective of a justification model is to isolate the cost savings that can be attributed to the investment. Certain justification models may be more appropriate given various organizational imperatives such as upgrading existing technology, investing in infrastructure or acquiring new applications.

The business case must identify not only the most significant reasons for the migration, but also support and document the financial rationale behind the project. In building the business case, it is critical to examine the productivity enhancements that are provided with the new environment. This includes analyzing the:

- Acquisition and installation costs for hardware
- Annual hardware upgrade costs including maintenance contracts
- Acquisition and maintenance fees for the Linux OS
- Acquisition and maintenance fees for the Linux applications

- Cost of time and effort to port non-Linux applications
- Cost of additional infrastructure to support non-Linux applications
- Cost of time and effort to perform the application and data migration
- Cost of time and effort to train staff and end-users
- Cost of professional services required to support the migration
- Cost per hour of downtime for a given system
- Historical average downtime of each server due to intrusions or viral infections
- Historical average downtime of each server due to patch installation and system updates
- Productivity enhancements that may be delivered as a result of the migration effort

Figure 14–6 illustrates how the business case can be justified. It is also helpful to establish common terms and financial definitions (see Appendix D). Figure 14-7 illustrates a typical ROI financial model for a Linux or open source project.

Top Mistakes Made When Calculating ROI

Mistakes made when calculating a ROI can be disastrous for the organization. It is important to document and validate your findings extremely well. The following are the most common mistakes made when determining ROI on a Linux project.

Not knowing what proof is needed. Understanding what type of evidence is needed will greatly help the business case.

Not documenting well. Record evidence accurately in the business case, with clear notations concerning where it was found and when.

Not prioritizing the financial justification. Rank what is needed in order of importance to the credibility of the overall message of the business case.

Not asking people who are on the front lines. Engage all managers and employees who will be impacted.

Not putting vendors to work. Be clear that any feedback vendors provide must be specific, highly credible and nonbiased.

Not having multiple payoff areas. A business case will often have a single payoff area. If underlying assumptions behind that single theme calculation are rejected, the entire business case collapses.

To Achieve a Positive ROI

- Identify not only the return, but how it will be achieved
- Confirm there is a clear understanding of your company's business goals
- Make sure your company's software investment will support those objectives
- Outline the steps and associated cost in achieving these goals
- Establish quantifiable measurements for these goals

Figure 14-6. *Achieving a Positive ROI.*

Not applying due diligence. Once evidence and financial analysis are complete, ask tough questions about their relevance and authenticity.

Not flushing out key business themes as early as possible. The best scenario is one in which the decision team provides key theme candidates early in the project analysis. Keep an eye out for other themes that naturally emerge from the business case process itself.

Not deferring equipment purchases. Companies typically don't plan IT equipment purchases very well. By deferring computing costs by buying servers, storage, networks, applications, etc. only when they will be deployed (as opposed to buying everything all at once) organizations get more — that is, better technology, faster processors, newer versions — for the same amount of capital.

Key Takeaways

Organizations must be able to accurately model, measure and understand the cost, value and risk associated with all major technology investments. A critical step is establishing a quantitative link between key business processes, the computing services they depend on and the underlying infrastructure of platforms, applications and networks. It is the business rationale — not the technical features — that is the key factor in determining how effective Linux-based hardware and software investments will be.

Linux contributes to real business innovation. Organizations adopting Linux and open source are realizing a Paradigm Shift in the way organizations manage and control their technology spending.

Return on Investment				
Capital Expenses	Year 1	Year 2	Year 3	Cummulative
Capital Expense				
Linux Servers	$ 107,545.00	$ 55,750.00	$ 25,750.00	
Server Upgrades	$ 40,940.00			
Software	$ 15,725.00	$ 12,000.00	$ -	
Network Upgrades	$ 12,750.00		$ 15,000.00	
Total Capital Expense	$ 176,960.00	$ 67,750.00	$ 40,750.00	$ 285,460.00
Depreciation Rate	$ 0.33	$ 0.44	$ 0.15	
Less Depreciation	$ (58,980.77)	$ (78,658.72)	$ (26,207.78)	
Net Capital Expense	$ 117,979.23	$ (10,908.72)	$ 14,542.22	$ 121,612.74
Maintenance & Support	$ 15,000.00			
Discounted Capital Expenses	$ 403,696.98	$ 22,297.58	$ 22,821.76	**$ 448,816.32**

Operating Expenses	Year 1	Year 2	Year 3	
Administration Expenses				
Desktop Support Reduction	$ (10,000.00)	$ (20,000.00)	$ (30,000.00)	
Headcount Increase Deferment	$ -	$ (50,000.00)	$ -	
Training & Education	$ 15,000.00	$ 10,000.00	$ 5,000.00	
Recurring Expenses				
Power & Cooling	$ 10,000.00	$ 12,000.00	$ 12,000.00	
Maintenance Costs Reduction	$ -	$ (45,000.00)	$ (55,000.00)	
Software Costs Reduction	$ (5,000.00)	$ (10,000.00)	$ (20,000.00)	
Data Recovery Improvement	$ -	$ (5,000.00)	$ (5,000.00)	
Discounted Operating Expenses	$ 9,433.96	$ (52,427.18)	$ (30,392.16)	**$ (73,385.38)**

Figure 14-7. *Sample ROI Worksheet.*

	Year 1	Year 2	Year 3	
Help Desk Support Costs				
Virus Vulnerabilty Reduction	$ (10,000.00)	$ (15,000.00)	$ (20,000.00)	
Support Incident Reduction	$ (10,000.00)	$ (20,000.00)	$ (30,000.00)	
Headcount Increase Deferment	$ (50,000.00)	$ -	$ -	
Less IT Frustration	$ (1,000.00)	$ (2,000.00)	$ (3,000.00)	
Application Support Costs				
Lower Cost for High Availability	$ -	$ (20,000.00)	$ -	
Faster Desktop Deployment	$ (10,000.00)	$ (15,000.00)	$ (20,000.00)	
Lower Cost for DR Solutions	$ -	$ -	$ (20,000.00)	
Fewer Administrative Issues	$ (10,000.00)	$ (20,000.00)	$ (30,000.00)	
Microsoft Licensing Reduction	$ (5,000.00)	$ (10,000.00)	$ (20,000.00)	
PC Server Reduction	$ (10,000.00)	$ (15,000.00)	$ (20,000.00)	
Data Management Costs				
Backup Media Cost Reduction	$ (1,000.00)	$ (2,000.00)	$ (3,000.00)	
Backup Licensing Reduction	$ -	$ (5,000.00)	$ (10,000.00)	
Data Recovery Improvement	$ -	$ -	$ -	
Consolidated OS Management	$ (2,000.00)	$ (4,000.00)	$ (8,000.00)	
Expansion Costs				
Cost Per Megabyte Reduction	$ (10,000.00)	$ (20,000.00)	$ (30,000.00)	
Improved Resource Sharing	$ -	$ -	$ -	
Improved Storage Utilization	$ (5,000.00)	$ (10,000.00)	$ (15,000.00)	
Application License Reduction	$ (5,000.00)	$ (10,000.00)	$ (20,000.00)	
PC Replacement Reduction	$ (5,000.00)	$ (10,000.00)	$ (15,000.00)	
PC Maintenance Reduction	$ -	$ (15,000.00)	$ (20,000.00)	
	$ (126,415.09)	$ (93,689.32)	$ (92,810.46)	**$ (312,914.87)**
Net Present Value (Savings)				**$ 62,516.07**
ROI (Based on a Three-Year NPV)				**12%**

Figure 14-7 (continued)

Key #5

Ensuring Project Success

Steps must be taken to provide effective communication and training to the organization. The Paradigm Shift with Linux and open source begins with enlightening the organization in a practical and understandable manner.

Key Overview

The success of the migration rollout is dependent on the organization understanding the importance of Linux and open source. Organizations must conduct pilot studies and build interoperability labs that provide proper training, usability studies and technical validation.

If a migration project is going to be delayed or completely canceled, it is done during the pilot study. Pilot studies are an important key since they are the primary gating factor and fine-tuning process for achieving the Paradigm Shift.

Chapter 15

Integrating Linux and Open Source

All truths are easy to understand once they are discovered; the point is to discover them.

—Galileo Galilei (1564-1642)

Project planning is an essential element for Linux and open source efforts. In order to establish the administrative and procedural structures necessary to support an adoption of Linux and open source, a formal implementation plan must be developed.—

The biggest reason for project planning is providing the organization with details. These details should specifically outline the valid reasons for embracing Linux and open source as well as the process checklists for moving away from proprietary software to an open source licensing model. By mapping out the strategic business objectives associated with an open source project, the cost of individual project tasks can be spread out over several years.

A Linux migration effort must be in concurrence with the organization's goals and priorities. A successful project plan will provide the organization with a better understanding of how Linux and open source is in alignment with the future direction of the company.

The Project Management

It is critical that one or more individuals be given formal project management duties and the time to fully allocate to the project. Without strong advocacy and oversight from competent and dedicated project management staff, it is difficult if not impossible to proceed in an organized and efficient manner.

A person with a background in Unix, Linux and open source should be hired or promoted from within the organization. The ideal candidate for this position should have skills in project management and business processes, and should be able to effectively lead the migration team.

Good Project Planning

The first task of project management is to understand the project scope. To develop the project scope, the first step is to analyze the needs of the project. The project plan must document all components of the Linux migration, their time scheduling and required resources. This includes plotting the schedule and budget, identifying organizational roles and responsibilities during and after the migration project, and fully assessing any associated risks.

Finding resources for project managers, analysts, evaluation software, training and other costs will be necessary. Rather than place an additional burden on existing departmental budgets, it is worthwhile to create a specific budget line item for this purpose. This will improve the ability to account for the real costs of the implementation effort and minimize political friction.

A good project plan answers questions such as: Why is the Linux migration project being undertaken? Who are the project sponsors? What are the goals that must be achieved from this effort? How will these goals be accomplished (resources, costs, inconveniences)? What is the timeline for the project deliverable?

The project plan eventually becomes the project blueprint. It must adequately detail all point tasks required. At a minimum, the project plan should comprise scheduling for conducting project planning, building a pilot project, initiating the rollout process, performing the actual migration and finalizing acceptance.

Linux projects often will result in minor, and occasionally major, disruptions to an organization. With proper project planning and testing, these disruptions are extremely manageable and oftentimes completely avoidable. A typical project plan includes:

Project Planning

- Identify required hardware and software
- Write procedures for moving users and data to new environment

- Determine which infrastructure components can be switched over to Linux
- Determine which proprietary applications can be migrated to Linux
- Build a deployment schedule including contingency plans
- Deploy applications, utilities and tools in the new production environment
- Develop and document post-migration maintenance and management procedures
- Ensure backups and contingency plans are in place
- Test and validate new production environment

Pilot Project

- Determine status of third-party ISV applications
- Perform benchmark comparisons for performance and functionality
- Develop initial pass of a customized installation
- Document Linux deployment methodology
- Gain general working skills with Linux

Rollout Preparation

- Finish construction of deployment technology
- Build infrastructure needed to deploy Linux
- Finalize customized installation of Linux, including ISV components
- Deliver end-user documentation
- Perform final system QA

Production

- Begin rollout
- Prepare for second rollout with any necessary software patches

Acceptance

- Develop best practices document
- Obtain sponsorship sign-offs
- Finalize the financial analysis
- Document project failures and successes

Risk Mitigation

Obviously there is every intention for the migration to go as planned. However, the best-laid plans should always consider the unlikely chance that things don't go as planned. Admitting that things may go wrong and preparing for them makes good business sense. This should not be construed as taking a pessimistic view but rather just considering smart business contingencies.

There are several areas to consider when conducting a risk analysis. With Linux and open source projects, there is the potential for licensing risks, intellectual property risk, cost risk, project deadline completion risk, business performance risk, regulatory and compliance risk and security risk. There are critical business considerations surrounding the cost and complexity of IP management, strategic value of the software to the business, need to offload ongoing software development, and the vigor of the open source communities.

One area to take a hard look at is licensing risk. Organizations cannot simply ignore Linux and open source legal issues. The GPL and other GPL licensing derivatives contain reciprocity provisions that require any modifications made to the code be returned to the open source community in exchange for using open source.

It is therefore important to evaluate the risk of intermixing GPL licensed software with internally written code that would be subsequently redistributed. If the open source code is strictly used internally and never planned to be released to the public, then this is not a concern. The GPL and some GPL-derived licenses are restrictive only if the code is redistributed.

As a result, it is critical to include the management of open source licensing issues to a designated department or personnel. Software licenses as well as source code will need to be reviewed and managed according to their licensing terms.

It is also important to understand the future direction of any open source software that is being used. Although the open source project may align with the current direction of the business plan, its maintainer may have a different long-term course in mind. Bear in mind that it is up to the open source maintainer to determine the software release cycle. Features and enhancements may be at risk due of a release delay. Your organization should reassess Linux and open source risk quarterly.

Conducting a Pilot Project

Pilot projects provide a wonderful opportunity to explore and experiment with the new environment. They also provide the opportunity to explain to end-users the reasoning behind the migration and the effects it will have on them.

The sooner end-users become involved with Linux or the open source alternatives the better. This will ease the introduction of what may be a significant change to working practices. Figure 15–1 highlights a preparedness checklist.

Preparedness Checklist

- Re-evaluate current infrastructure for strengths and weaknesses
- Collect application matrix along with application physical and logical design topology
- Validate business level objectives, values drivers and goals for Linux and open source
- Conduct a feasibility study based on current and future hardware, software and deployment costs
- Validate application blueprint along with total cost of ownership model
- Develop migration plan including back-out scenario planning
- Ensure there is executive sponsorship and commitment for the migration project

Figure 15-1. *Project Checklist.*

Conducting a pilot project involves:

- Building the new Linux or open source environment. This might include deploying separate LDAP servers, building installation servers, providing file and print servers, and having end-user workstations for debugging and testing purposes.
- Having a dedicated development and training facility equipped with an adequate number of systems to be used for training. The initial purpose of this facility is to validate and fine-tune the "golden" configuration. It is also useful to generate enthusiasm for the project and to gather valuable feedback, such as validating the quality of the training and documentation.
- Having a fully automated installation process so systems can be set up with minimal human involvement. It is important that target systems be

installed in exactly the same way during the main rollout phase in order to verify this process. This testing will reduce, but not completely eliminate, some of the issues that will arise during the real rollout process. It might be necessary to reset configurations changed during training so that everyone starts with a known environment.

- Building a production parallel testing environment to conduct operational testing in a risk-free manner. If the rollout tactic includes using a dual image environment, then each application must be tested and verified it does not adversely affect other applications. A parallel testing environment is a must for accomplishing migrations with minimum risk to production installations.

- Getting customer acceptance for the new environment. An operational review ensures that new procedures are adequate, including a support plan and training plans for users. This is also an opportunity to document "lessons learned," which provides valuable input for future migrations and platform upgrades.

During the pilot study, your organization's Linux core image is finalized. Known as the COE (Common Operating Environment), the core image not only comprises software binaries, scripts, libraries and a secure operating configuration, but also a package manifest. The package manifest is the master index of your software stack. It is common for a streamlined core image to have nearly 300 packages.

Core Image Best Practices

It is important that the COE follow the Corporate Information Security standards baseline. The OS should be hardened such that it has:

- Userid/password controls
- Root-level access restrictions (sudo)
- Secured services (unused services removed)
- Virus scanning (ClamAV)
- Security baseline audit and reporting (ESM)
- Real-time intrusion detection
- Secure platform access (OpenSSH)

Most organizations use a separate development core image but generally the core image should be used as the standard platform, with the installation of applications, databases and developer tools handled on an exception basis. The objective should be to build all servers to the COE standard with zero percent variance.

A successful COE will be the single image used within your entire organization. It supports all hardware platforms, meets 90 percent of your application and database software requisites and runs securely in all your environments.

The management of the COE image is a critical process. This process should verify:

- Core image manifest
- Hardware interoperability
- Compliance with security audits
- Correct operation of all software components (smoke test)
- Interoperability with support infrastructure (KickStart, etc.)
- Interoperability with network infrastructure (DNS, DHCP, NTP, etc.)

The pilot study provides a good test bed for monitoring and validating that the core image is maintained across the network. Checking servers periodically for core image manifest consistency is a best practice your organization should permanently adopt.

Managing COEs can be a challenging task. Successful Linux adoption comes from establishing a consistent process for building and maintaining the COE. A COE should be automatically generated using a security hardened package manager (e.g. RPM) that gets installed at build time. It is important that your team reassess Linux and open source security baselines annually with security and systems platform audits conducted at least once per quarter.

Key Project Activities

The easiest way to guarantee success is through good project management fundamentals. Creating a new Linux architecture is not a one-time banquet, but a long-term process that needs constant attention.

Develop a high-level policy of support by formally declaring the intention of the company to move toward Linux and open source. This way the organization will clearly understand the intent and purpose behind any noted changes that occur with day-to-day activities.

A detailed inventory of the current applications, tools, scripts and hardware in the current environment must be clearly documented and continuously updated. Applications generally have dependencies that require careful scheduling. It is a best practice to uncover dependencies early through the careful assessment of critical architecture and design points to facilitate the project planning.

The project should be managed in short iterative cycles that provide incremental project information to the team members and stakeholders. A good way to ensure the organization is taking this project seriously is to create a written plan outlining the goals, standards and policies and update it frequently. These documents help communicate and sell the plan to the people most impacted by the project. These documents are useful later as a guide to help the organization with future technology decisions and procurement.

Linux adoption often reveals hidden design flaws in the original application environment. Make sure the project plan considers opportunities to improve on the current operating environment. A general rule with Linux and open source projects is to do the hardest and most important project tasks first to prove the architecture. Then ensure the project plan allows enough time for a thorough and complete quality assurance testing.

The project plan should review all leases, subscriptions and license fees for opportunities to upgrade, and eliminate or replace the respective assets before they are deployed in the new environment. This is a good opportunity to replace any computing asset that has become expensive to maintain and support. Use this opportunity to repurpose hardware or replace expensive proprietary hardware with less-expensive Linux compatible systems.

Ensuring Success

One of the most effective ways to achieve a technological agenda is to put strict controls on the purchasing process. Specifically, organizations should include purchasing provisions that require all hardware and software purchases to consider Linux and open source. In the case of hardware, it is advisable to require hardware that is compatible with common Linux distributions and that comes from a company with a stated goal of supporting Linux and open source.

All outgoing Requests for Proposals (RFPs) should be formally required to solicit and consider bids from companies that embrace Linux and open source. While not all purchases can (or should) favor Linux and open source, any decision that does not consider or ultimately select such a product should be justified in writing.

Ideally, a permanent testing environment should be set up and maintained throughout the project. This testing facility can be used for future training, testing or product evaluations. The pilot testing should include a test migration plan to prove that the tool set and migration strategy that will be used are valid and correct. The pilot environment must meet the current production hardware and software standards.

It is important to disseminate to the organization the business-level objectives and procedures behind the project. It is also important to provide supplementary information that explains or supports the Linux and open source initiative. Related and non-essential information is helpful and should be posted to a self-service portal so the organization can become more familiar with the importance of this effort.

Organizations have a wealth of technological and business experience in existing staff. A formal task force or SWAT team should continue the analysis of Linux and open source. This task force should not only include advocates of Linux and open source, but also those who have the greatest objections to it. While individual employees should not have the power to derail the implementation and business goals established by management, their perspectives on the risks and problems of implementing Linux and open source will be essential to ensuring the success of the process.

Finally, risk analysis and risk mitigation plans should be continually reviewed. This may uncover additional risks associated with configurations, incompatibilities, scheduling and resource conflicts.

Project Planning Best Practices

Effective planning for Linux and open source deployments is based on setting goals and then mapping out how to accomplish those goals. It is important to take a long-term view of the organization's overall business goals with the Linux initiative and map plans of actions, instead of cramming Linux objectives into several months or a single year's budget.

There are many critical success factors involved with project planning as shown in Figure 15–2. The following six best practices are helpful with the project planning effort.

Educate. Training is key, but it is frequently rushed during the project. A completely new application environment will require additional time for end-user training. Build a Web-based training package to facilitate the training process. Use Moodle, an open source course management solution (http://www.moodle.org), to develop the course instruction and presentation materials.

Critical Success Factors

- Don't underestimate migration costs
- Start with the backend support infrastructure first
- Engage at the business level and update the project with costs savings
- Require a business champion for the duration of the project
- Identify critical business target processes and ensure they can be satisfied
- Clearly identify service support levels for each application and user
- Standardize internal application development process to support desktop deployment
- Standardize on open source file formats
- Ensure adequate training is conducted

Figure 15-2. *Important Considerations.*

Another best practice is to use open source in your test environment. This provides your staff education and experience with open source software projects without introducing risk into your production environments.

Support. It is important that those directly responsible for the day-to-day Linux effort are visible and approachable. Each person involved in the project needs to understand that customer service is paramount to the success of the project. Additionally, it is also necessary to establish what software and hardware environment will be supported. The development and standardization of your organization's COE will help.

Depending on the open source software that your organization is using, there might be multiple vendors with a range of support offerings available. Major projects have competing suppliers of enterprise-grade support. Developing the ability to self-support may be a way to significantly reduce costs.

Automate. Many porting tasks are repetitive and time-consuming. Use automation whenever possible to minimize both human error and the time it takes to complete the task. Automating system and network configuration functions minimize human intervention as well as provide a more secure environment by minimizing the mistakes caused from human error.

Test, Test, Test. Regardless of the rollout tactic, the migration to a new computing environment is always fraught with unseen difficulties and surprises. It is important to allow plenty of time for performance and recovery testing. The testing should be focused on all operational characteristics, including application performance, security, availability and scalability.

Testing against multiple platforms will reduce the cost of change downstream, and the only cost for this activity is the time spent testing. If your tests are automated (as mentioned above), this should be a reasonable activity to support. Pilot studies provide an opportunity to learn and prepare for these difficulties and will eliminate any surprises.

Analyze. To take full advantage of asset utilization, analyze the current inventory. Consider upcoming upgrades in order to avoid any conflicts with ISV release schedules. Review hardware equipment lists for lease expirations as well as resource availability.

Review. The final implementation provides hard data on the actual resources and effort that were required to perform the project. This provides a good opportunity to review and verify the whole project from start to finish.

Encourage open source community participation within the scope of your employment and confidentiality guidelines. Linux and open source development communities welcome knowledgeable participation and by participating your organization can influence future features and direction. Even casual participation in the community is good training and will improve your open source project evaluations and experience.

Training

Technical training should begin as soon as possible in the project plan. End-user training can be schedule later, but should be scheduled to align with the project completion. Training end-users too early can be self-defeating if the students don't get a chance to practice what they've learned.

Certified training professional programs can jumpstart the education process. Many programs have sprung up to meet growing interest in Linux certification to validate technical skills. Among them are Computer Technology Industry Association (CompTIA) and Linux Professionals

Learning Linux

Organization	Certification	Focus	Prerequisite
Computer Technology Industry Association (CompTIA)	Linux+ Certification	Any Linux administrator	Six months of Linux experience
Linux Professional Institute	LPICI	Installing Linux PCs, attaching them to LAN	None
	LPIC2	Installing small Linux networks	LPC1 and two years of Linux experience
	LPIC3	Installing multi-site networks	LPC2
Novell	Certified Linux Professional	Manage Linux administrative tasks	None
	Certified Linux Engineer	Networking in a heterogeneous environment	Knowledge of Linux administration
Red Hat	Red Hat Certified Technician (RHCT)	Installing Linux PCs, attaching them to LAN	None
	Red Hat Certified Engineer (RHCE)	Linux server, networking and security	RHCT or equivalent
Systems Administrator's Guild (SAGE)	cSAGE	Systems administration	Experienced system administrator with mentor
	mSAGE	OS and network administration, programming proficiency	SAGE certification

Table 15-1. *Vendor Training Resources.*

Institute. Novell and Red Hat offer many courses, certifications and tests based on their individual distributions of Linux. Additionally, the Systems Administrators Guild, a group of Usenix network professionals, offers basic networking exams and specialized Linux modules.

The hiring of new employees should consider, if not favor, skills and experience with Linux and open source development. This will not only help to establish organizational momentum, but will reduce the cost and burden of training and retraining employees. As with software purchasing, a written justification for the selections made should be documented and a manager with authority should approve all employee hires. Table 15–1 outlines various Linux certifications.

Key Takeaways

It is important to consider every project not as an isolated activity but an integral part of the organization. Invest the time and resources to understand the business, service delivery and operational needs and involve all affected parties at the inception of each project, including business units, financial experts, and infrastructure, development and support staff.

It is critical for your organization to continuously look for ways to integrate open source into your commercial software environment. However, this activity must include establishing assurances that open source code will not be subject to intellectual property lawsuits. You will need established procedures to avoid violating licensing terms that are different from what you're used to.

While many customers choose to partner with a vendor for Linux-related software and support, most have the expertise in-house to customize or troubleshoot the operating system. Most organizations train their IT staff to meet the demands of Linux service and support.

Key #6

Performing the Great Escape

Creating a Paradigm Shift with open source Linux software involves more than just transitioning to the new hardware and software environment; it requires automation and business service management.

Key Overview

As with any new computing environment, performing a controlled and well managed rollout is critical to the success of the project. Linux and open source adoption requires forethought on how to manage logistics such as scheduling servers and data to be migrated, notifying users of planned outages, responding to user inquiries and having processes to resolve reported software problems and errors. It is imperative that the organization adopt business service management functions that provide support functions and guarantee the established service levels.

Chapter 16

The Great Escape

Theorem: A simple and well-designed infrastructure may never require extensive management tools.
Corollary: Management tools will never simplify a poorly designed infrastructure.
— *Teter's Golden Rule*

Rolling out Linux and open source applications is a journey — not a destination. As outlined in Chapter 7, this journey begins by assessing business-level objectives, understanding the user segments and being particularly aware of specific line-of-business priorities.

While a migration to Linux and open source arguably provides the best financial alternative for business enterprise infrastructures, the move must be executed in an effective manner to realize the full advantage. A Linux migration project requires forethought on how to manage logistics such as scheduling servers to be migrated, notifying users of planned outages, responding to user inquiries and resolving reported software problems and errors. Figure 16–1 shows how this can be accomplished.

Although the costs associated with transitioning from the embedded environment can seem too significant, migrating systems does provide a great opportunity to re-design and re-engineer the infrastructure. This becomes a chance to build better processing efficiencies and capabilities into the infrastructure.

Rollout Tactics

The key to delivering cost savings to your organization lies not only in aligning technology with your business strategy but in the efficiency of the

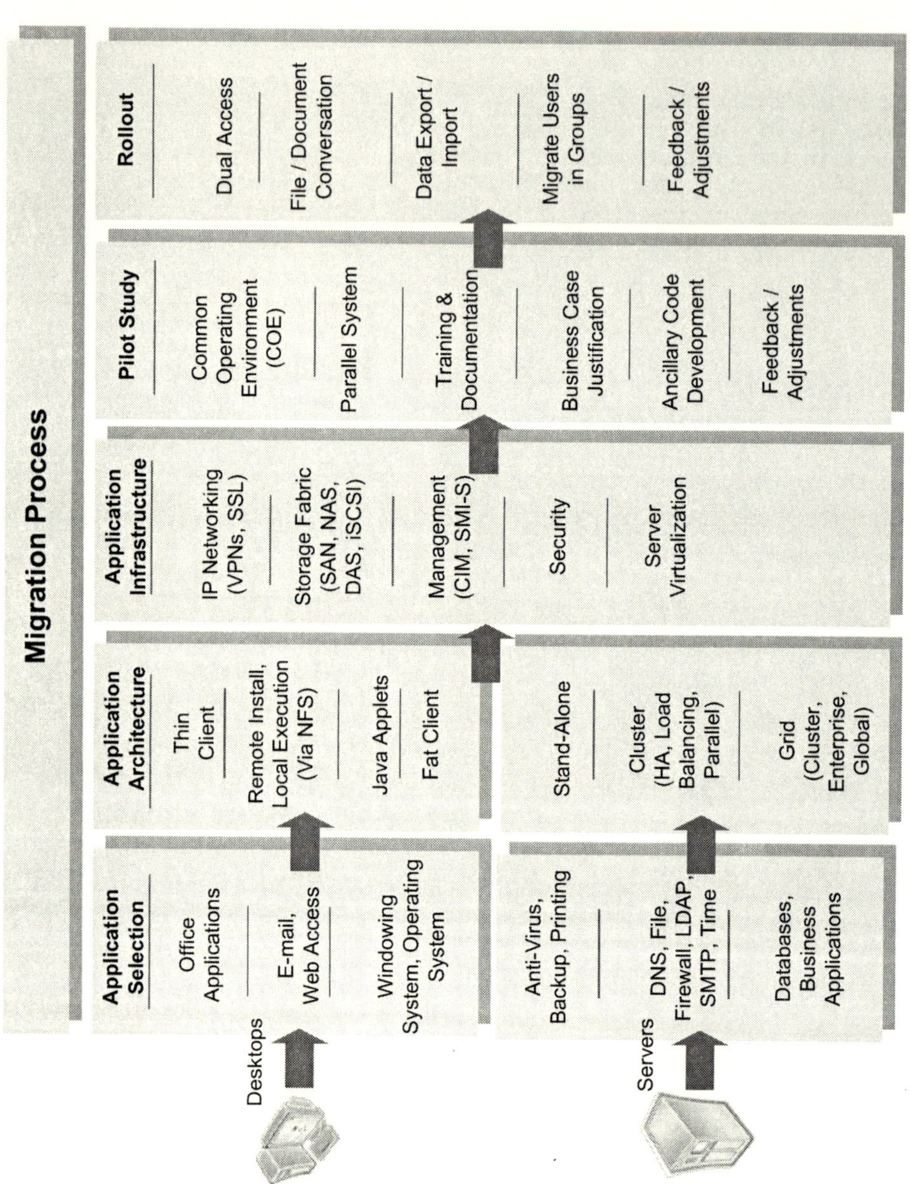

Figure 16-1. *Desktop and Server Migration Process.*

project execution. The migration process must provide a fast and efficient transition to Linux.

The migration process should be designed to reduce the manual effort required for server installation and patching by automating as many of the steps as possible. Automation not only accelerates the project implementation schedule but also facilitates the process of standardizing on a single OS configuration, thereby simplifying system administration and eventually improving overall service levels. Figure 16–2 illustrates the automated management process.

Deploying a standard Linux configuration or common operating environment, across all servers in the computing environment facilitates a quick implementation. Using a golden boot process along with automated installation programs will minimize system administration efforts as well as create a consistent environment (see Appendix E). Generally, the migration effort

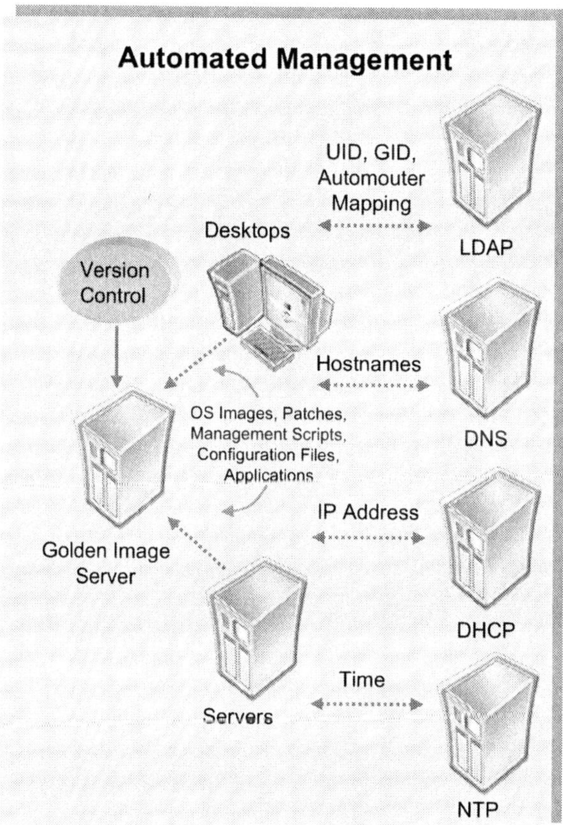

Figure 16-2. *Automating System Management.*

comprises building the new environment, testing the new environment and managing the new environment.

If There's a Will, There is a Way

Other approaches include providing a dual-processing environment, whereby both the old and new systems are run in parallel. However, having

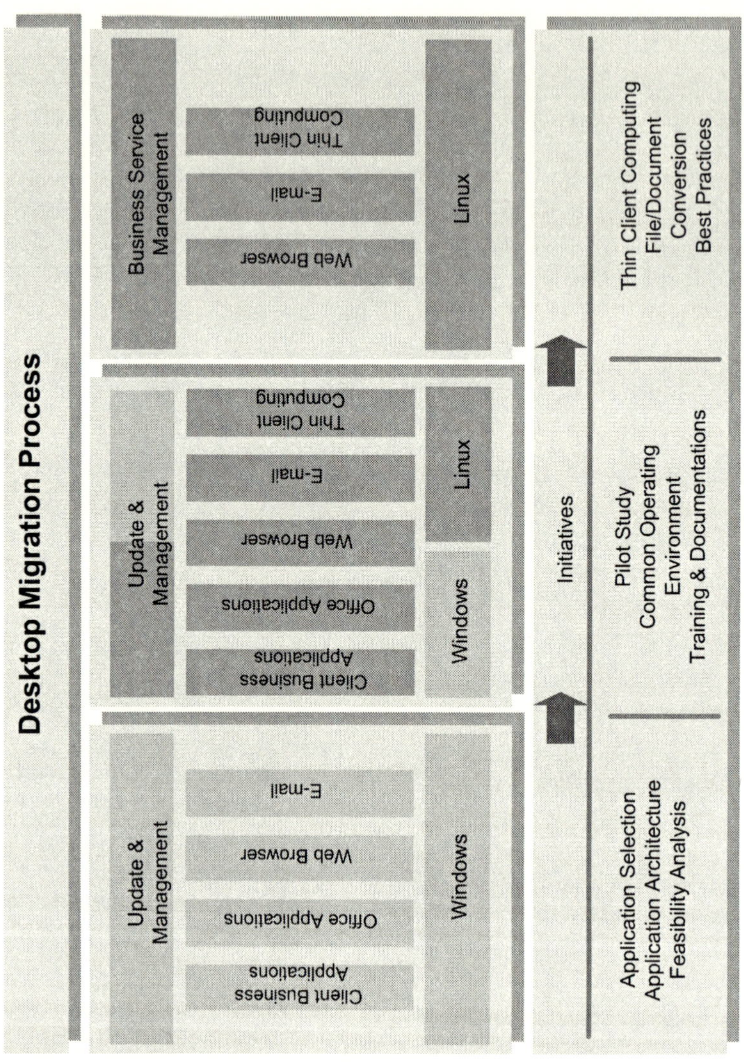

Figure 16-3. *Steps in Desktop Migrations.*

a parallel system infrastructure does make cooperation between users using non-Linux systems and those using Linux more difficult. There might even be minor restrictions with regard to authentication between the heterogeneous system environments. Co-existence between the previous operating system and the new platform may be necessary and needs to be taken into account in testing the operational readiness of the new platform.

Replacing the existing system and its packaged applications with a new Linux computing environment with the same packaged applications is perhaps the easiest method of moving from one system to another while providing equivalent functionality. For instance, OpenOffice.org, Mozilla or

Apache provide an easy replacement for MS Office, Internet Explorer and IIS respectively. Risks can also be contained and resources managed by transitioning users in reasonable group sizes.

Many organizations find that Linux and open source solutions are best rolled out to fixed, single-function applications first. This might include using low-end Linux servers and open source solutions for directory services, security appliances, management systems or terminal servers. This greatly simplifies administration and management controls and lowers the cost for support, operation and maintenance. Single-function solutions are often deemed preferable for infrastructure services over adding software to general-purpose servers.

Figures 16–3 and 16–4 demonstrate how desktop and data center migrations can be accomplished.

Data Migration

As with most Linux projects, data migration is an essential component of the project plan. The process will depend on whether the data migration is for the desktop or data center environment, with each presenting unique challenges. Desktop migrations have been greatly simplified with the support of file conversion utilities. For instance, StarOffice has a macro and document converter that can reformat MS Office files with a 90 percent success rate for simple documents. However, documents with complex formatting generally require individual attention.

Data center data migrations typically require a migration assessment that specifically analyzes the business processes associated with the data that will be migrated. And since data can be stored in various formats, this assessment must consider if the source data needs to be reformatted. By default, features and functionality provided by database vendors are generally platform generic, so there is no issue when migrating platforms. For instance, a standard full database export-import procedure provides a very straightforward data migration process for the migration of an Oracle database across platforms.

Key factors influencing a data migration are costs (i.e. new software licenses, new hardware or professional services), complexity, impact on business operations and the degree of data availability during the migration process. The range of factors that need to be considered include:

- Criticality of the business data

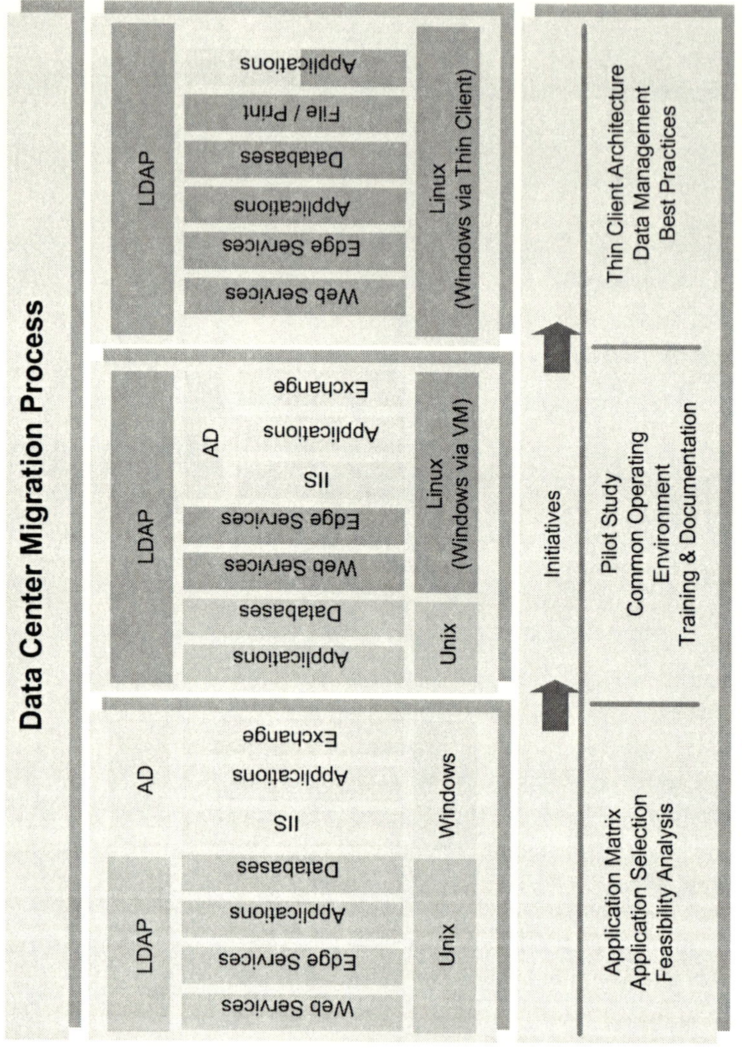

Figure 16-4. *Steps Data Center Migrations.*

- Criticality of availability of the data and related business processes
- Business processes and interdependencies between the business processes
- Server (and operating system) platforms that data is being migrated from
- Storage array subsystems that are part of the migration
- Data security and data availability requirements
- Size of data volumes to be migrated and expected growth of those volumes
- Time-critical factors such as application downtime

Data Classification

It is important to identify which data is critical to the business and which data can be classified as legacy data and possibly excluded from the migration process. By looking at the business processes along with their interdependencies and uptime requirements, the sequence by which the data needs to be migrated from the old environment to the new environment can be better identified. Pay special attention to data controlled by any regulatory requirements.

Another critical aspect of data migration is ensuring the target infrastructure meets the data availability and application performance requirements. This can cause problems when an organization discovers after the data migration is complete that the underlying data infrastructure is inadequate for the application environment.

Data Movement Options

Data migration projects should validate the existing backup and restore processes in order to define the strategy for handling backups during the data migration effort. In fact, backup and restore procedures provide a simple tactic for migrating application and end-user data.

A faster solution is to leverage the network to copy data to the target environment. If the data is available via a network file system, this technique can provide a straightforward data migration process. Both data migration methods just mentioned have the advantage of not requiring any additional software, hardware or skills.

Another data migration strategy is leveraging data replication. Data replication can either be accomplished using replication, cloning or mirroring techniques. Symantec Volume Manager has a unique solution known as Portable Data Containers (PDC) to migrate and convert data for Linux. PDC is built into Symantec Volume Manager, which provides a virtual file system to the target Linux host environment.

By wrapping the data with the appropriate meta-information, PDC lets data be accessible from any operating system. Using this metadata approach, the time it takes to perform the migration is independent of the amount of the source data.

Figure 16–5 illustrates the basic idea behind data migration tactics.

Critical Success Factors

Linux and open source computing provide the great escape from the high cost of proprietary software environments. However, open source computing requires attention to detail and process controls. This includes:

Timing for the Project

The timing of the Linux and open source migration decision is one of the critical factors that affects the success or failure of a project.

Managing Unrealistic Expectations

Executive management must have realistic expectations. A cross-functional team provides a balanced outlook and serves to temper expectations.

Establishing Explicit Payoff Metrics

Since the failure of Linux or open source projects is often from unrealistic expectations, establishing pre-launch metrics and business-level goals is critical.

Building the Right Infrastructure

Linux and open source computing depend on an underlying hardware infrastructure that provides a reliable, scalable and high-performance environment. It is important to ensure that the hardware environment has been adequately tested and validated for the new environment.

Providing a Self-Service Portal

Providing information on demand for the supporting services of a new computing environment needs to be addressed. Self-service portals provide a great way to reach employees and streamline corporate information access.

Conducting Training

Linux and open source solutions will fail if the organization does not know how to use, manage and operate the application environment. Organizations must schedule and conduct training as part of the project plan.

Using Automated Management Tools

Automating software and configuration management is a top priority. Define users and groups with adequate privileges and class separation to leverage automation processes. Use the management system's reporting features to report any variances.

Adopting Industry Standards

Industry standards maximize an organization's ability to choose. Open standards create a fair, competitive market that does not lock a business to a particular vendor or application. By embracing industry standards, companies are free to implement solutions with no hidden fees or obligations. Obtaining the advantages of open standards begins by declaring it a high priority and including it in your planning and processes.

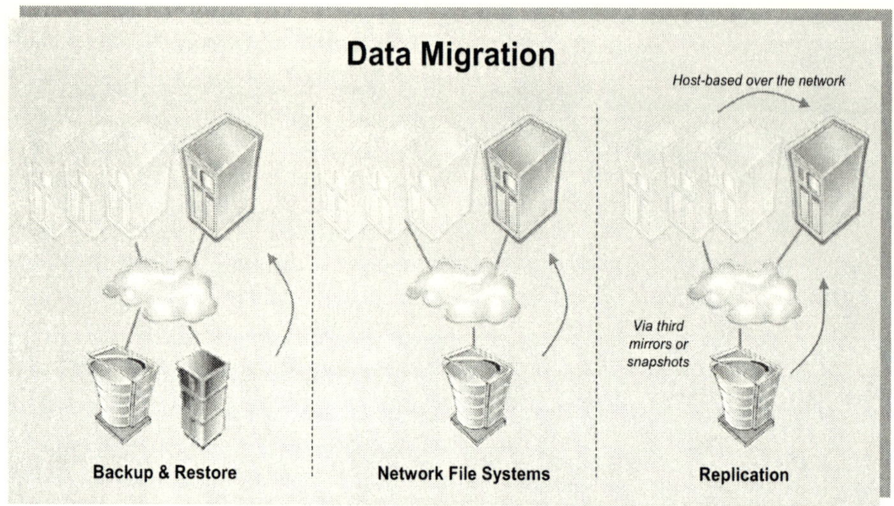

Figure 16-5. *Ways to Migrate Data.*

Risk Management

The highest priority in a data migration project must be given to ensuring data integrity and identifying appropriate risk mitigation strategies. It is also important to take into consideration the time required to migrate the data. In the case of a very large database, it may be beneficial to create a number of smaller export files from the original database, by schema owner or even object, and then perform multiple imports into the target database in parallel.

You can use empirical data to estimate the time needed to migrate. The transfer rate can be verified during pre-migration testing. Knowing the transfer rate and the amount of data to be migrated will enable the project team to fine-tune the migration schedule.

Volume is not only the amount of data; it is also the number of files. Block-level copying of data can take longer if there are many small files, as is often the case with unstructured data.

Even using an offline migration process, experience has shown that it can take up to twice as long as the estimated transfer rate. If hardware mirroring is used as the migration method, end-user access will prolong the migration as well as cause application performance degradation.

Data Migration Testing

Migration testing should include both storage and applications. If the migration is completed offline, the testing should include a comparison of pre- and post-migration volumes, number of files, number of database records, etc. It is helpful to perform a migration in phases by dividing the volumes to be migrated into a series of smaller, sequential migrations.

It is recommended to allow a few days between the pre-migration shutdown and the migration to allow for troubleshooting. This waiting period helps systems to stabilize and provides you with the time to resolve any issues that arise as a result of the hardware or software upgrades before the actual migration.

Having a back-out plan is also highly recommended. A back-out plan provides multiple go/no-go decision points where you can determine if the migration effort should proceed and, if not, execute the back-out plan. The go/no-go juncture may occur at the completion of the migration, the storage-related testing or the application testing.

A post-project review is helpful in identifying areas that can be improved to reduce risk, improve the user experience or reduce the cost of the migration effort for future projects. Figure 16–6 highlights migration best practices.

Change Control

It's no surprise that interdependencies among application components are so critical that changes made to the production environment are the leading cause of system failures. Generally, these failures are caused by changes made by personnel. Now consider the impacts and system changes a Linux or open source movement within the organization might cause.

Adopting Linux within your organization only increases the need for standardized change control practices. Due to the nature of open source, software versioning and code management are part of managing the application. Processes used to manage these changes must be systematic and repeatable. Each change request must be categorized, assessed for risks, communicated and scheduled with other dependent change requests.

By coordinating and automating Linux and open source activities, you can simultaneously improve both responsiveness and application service quality. Through process automation and proper change control mechanisms, organizations can increase their responsiveness to change and better control the new environment to reduce potential failures.

Migration No-No's

- Trying to standardize everything at once
- Confusing the concept of a business architecture as just another technology project
- Choosing a technologist to lead the project
- Using the technical architecture as an excuse to always say no to new requests from the business
- Making financial ROI the top goal instead of focusing on a specific competitive advantage

Figure 16-6. *Things Not to Do.*

Key Takeaways

Regardless of what rollout tactics are chosen, it is imperative that the transition methodology start with a clear understanding of which business services are dependent on the applications that are about to be changed. The migration process should be designed to reduce manual effort for deployment and maintenance by automating as many of the steps as possible.

It is important to identify the data that is critical to the business and which data can be classified as legacy and possibly excluded from the migration process. Change control is absolutely critical to open source projects. In an effort to minimize change control efforts, automation is paramount in keeping the Linux and open source environment standardized. After the migration project, a post-project review will identify how to reduce the cost of future migration efforts.

Chapter 17

Automating the Process

Don't say you don't have enough time. You have exactly the same number of hours per day that were given to Helen Keller, Pasteur, Michelangelo, Mother Teresa, Leonardo da Vinci, Thomas Jefferson and Albert Einstein.
— H. Jackson Brown

One of the largest costs that organizations face is dealing with hardware and software inconsistencies. Organizations continuously face problems with their server environment — in particular with their configurations — varying from server to server and location to location.

To mitigate these unnecessary support issues, the migration process should include the ability to:

- Install a standard operating system image, creating a consistent server image
- Automatically configure the hardware, data storage and user roles
- Automatically install the applications and appropriate configuration policies
- Automatically deploy systems management tools such as backup and monitoring software
- Perform quality assurance tests

By using an automated process, systems are deployed and configured consistently. This in turn reduces conflicts and issues on the network. Not only is system support simplified and efficient but configuration across multiple systems is easily managed and controlled. Figure 17–1 illustrates in a humorous way why an automated, controlled process is imperative for your organization.

The Reality Is…

What You Say	What Your Boss Hears
• Application failure…	• Bad process
• Scaling issues…	• Bad management
• Hardware failures…	• Bad management
• OS consistency issues…	• Bad process
• Data corruption…	• Bad management

Figure 17-1. *Perception Is Reality.*

Automated Installation

Using automated tools to deploy new systems enables the organization to create a structured environment that is built on a set of standards and processes. The most important element in creating a highly available, flexible and efficient processing environment is to first create a consistent and structured system build process.

Since open source software is fixed, patched and updated frequently, it can easily become an ad-hoc acquisition process. It is important for your organization to develop a software acquisition procedure that is based on a repeatable, sustainable and supportable process.

A structured build process will not only reduce the complexity and provide the basis for a repeatable process, but will generally have lower error rates and better predictability and ultimately be easier to support.

It is recommended that infrastructure servers not use a unique installation process, but use the standardized installation and configuration process that all other workstations, desktops and servers use. By instilling this consistency within the installation process, any system can be easily replaced if and when it fails. It is important, however, to recognize the difference between mastering the system and mastering the data on which the system depends.

Most packages require not only particular files to be updated, but numerous contingent tools and libraries. Resolving these dependencies is a time-consuming and error-prone process. As a result, there are several update programs available for Linux to assist with the installation and update process.

There are many commercial Linux products, such as Red Hat Network, Novell ZENworks and Altiris Server Management Suite, that offer system and configuration management tools. These tools are extremely useful — especially when your organization doesn't mind paying their license fees.

Most distributions also provide free tools, such as KickStart, Red Hat-based up2date, SUSE-based AutoYaST, Mandriva-based urpmi, Debian-based APT-RPM or YUM (which is currently maintained by Duke University).

There are many open source alternatives for system management functions and controls (see Figure 17–2). Even if you use commercial tools, open source alternatives can be customized easily to provide very effective network-, system- and device-level management.

Critical business applications demand a self-monitoring management solution. It is important to monitor and validate the core image across the network. Checking servers against their COE manifest should be done at least quarterly.

Collectively, open source management tools provide an application management framework to deploy, configure and manage your business applications. By leveraging the breadth of management functionality developed in the open source community, IT organizations are fully capable of designing management functionality on top of an open source solution and toolkits. Appendix F provides a reference point for discovering the broad range of open source network and system management solutions.

Business Service Management

Linking network and infrastructure performance with corporate business processes provides both technology and business management with much more visibility into the computing infrastructure. Known as business service management (BSM), this insight shows how unavailable or poorly performing services are affecting end-users as well as other application services.

In order to be proactive, it is imperative to align the business priorities with a top-down view of the business services, not just by looking into network availability but by monitoring Linux application performance.

Performance management tools are the lifeline of an enterprise. They provide deep insight into the problems that degrade the quality of end-user services. These tools can isolate performance degradation problems emanat-

Open Source Management Tools

Big Sister — network monitoring
Cacti — systems performance
Cfegine — network configuration
JFFNMS — network monitoring
Kismet — wireless network detection
MRTG — network traffic monitoring
Nagios — system monitoring
NeDi — network discovery
Nessus — security scanning
Netdisco — network management
Nmap — network discovery
Ntop — network traffic analysis
OpenNMS — network monitoring
RRDtool — analytical graphing
Snort — network intrusion detection
Syslog-ng — log file analysis
Webmin — system administration
Zabbix — network monitoring

Figure 17-2. *Management Solutions.*

ing from elements like database servers, Web servers or network and infrastructure components.

The most fundamental performance information is end-user response times for any given application. This can be generated by sampling traffic patterns, usage behavior and application response times. The optimal position is having the system properly instrumented to isolate and identify specific conditions that lead to performance degradation.

The purpose of BSM is to track data end-to-end from an application's point of view. Thus it is necessary to capture performance data at the client, network, Web server, application server, database server, OS and storage array levels. This data should be collected continuously, such as every 15 minutes every day of the year. Performance data can then be plotted onto graphs and published onto portals and dashboards.

Security and vulnerability auditing is essential to BSM. Linux and open source provides a vast collection of auditing and security applications, including many that are built into most Linux distributions. For auditing there are tools such as syslogd, klogd, auditd and SNARE. Open source security and vulnerability testing programs include nmap, bsign, Nessus, SARA and John the Ripper.

This may still seem reactive but over time this BSM data provides a very predictive baseline of your Linux environment and becomes proactive when alarms can be set to notify administrators when the data falls outside normal limits.

In addition to monitoring your infrastructure, it is also necessary to watch for publicly released security alerts. Vendors and package maintainers release security updates through notifications from Bugtraq, CERT, SANS and CVE.

BSM data provides critical information the enables organizations to more quickly and accurately assign potential problems for remediation. It provides information about the nature of a problem since it tracks a detailed history of metrics prior to the actual fault or failure occurring.

Key Takeaways

It is important to focus on infrastructure simplicity, consistency and manageability. These considerations should become an integral part of Linux and open source deployments. Business and technology decision makers must work together to define clear standards and justify exceptions based on cost breakdowns and the business value that is expected to be delivered.

By emphasizing manageability, systems will be deployed and configured consistently. This in turn, reduces conflicts and issues, and simplifies system support and configuration management across multiple systems. And although the costs associated with transitioning away from the existing computing environment can seem too significant, it is important to remember that this is providing an opportunity to build better processing efficiencies and management capabilities into the application infrastructure.

Linux and open source software are constantly changing. A software management process is required to manage and monitor these changes. The process must accommodate removal of stale packages, addition of new security policies, controls and fixes, and revision of internal software standards.

Security and vulnerability auditing is essential to BSM. Linux and open source provide a vast collection of auditing and security applications. There are also many publicly available Web sites dedicated to information secu-

rity. Consequently, it is important for someone in your organization to be responsible for the delivery of BSM.

Key #7

Practicing Continuous Process Improvement

Effective standardization and the enforcement of consistent management and operational processes institute a Paradigm Shift.

Key Overview

It is important to identify process improvements, consistent management and operational processes. The business and technology organization must take all reasonable steps to use established methods of success, accurate financial analysis and the use of process improvement and controls. Effective standardization and enforcement of best practices sets in operation the new Linux and open source computing paradigm.

Chapter 18

Continuous Process Improvement

The thinking that got us into this situation is different than the thinking that will get us out.
— Albert Einstein

Linux and open source are poised to take the next step in their evolutionary growth. However, this step requires that Linux-based systems — which would include not just Linux, the operating system, but also the supporting software and hardware infrastructure, middleware, application packages, management tools and services — offer a level of availability, scalability and reliability on a parity with the current legacy systems in place.

The necessary functionality and support for enterprise deployments are available for Linux systems. These capabilities include scalable hardware architectures, ISV-supported business application software, advanced and clustered file systems, enterprise-class database technology, virtual processing software, and monitoring and provisioning tools as well as a secure and reliable operating environment. Organizations now have more choices and attractive new options for future system deployments because, of course, Linux and open source are all about choice.

Success Requires a Process

While the specific drivers of change are always evolving, the reasons that organizations need to continuously improve are relatively constant. This includes addressing flaws and failures that were discovered through the migration as well as those that were brought to the attention of the organization through employee feedback.

Sometimes events that appear to be the cause of a migration effort are actually a symptom of a larger problem, so it is important that organizations ensure they have found the true source of the problem when designing process improvements. It is important to continually look at how to improve upon the Linux computing environment. In particular, this should be done in the context of:

- Changing business focus. Adapting new business strategies might require a change in the approach to Linux usage. Mergers, acquisitions and other organizational changes cause disruptions to standard operating procedures.
- Changing technology. Business-level objectives might need updating based on new technologies and solutions that are required for day-to-day business.
- Changing best practices. Best practices are constantly changing in every industry to account for changing market and technology conditions and other factors, and this must be reflected in the Linux and open source environment.
- Strategies for Success. There are a number of change management strategies that organizations can implement to increase success with Linux and open source.

Figure 18–1 provides important critical success factors to consider.

Change Management

Change management is an important aspect of continuous improvement because, at its core, change management seeks to address the people aspect of any project. The goal of change management is to ensure the success of program changes by assessing and addressing the impact of those changes on the organization.

Characteristics of unsuccessful projects often include one or more of the following:

- Lack of project alignment with overall business strategy
- Poor business requirements identification
- Insufficient buy-in and support from senior management
- Incomplete understanding of how the changes will affect key stakeholder groups
- Poor communication about the change within the organization, including impacts and benefits

- Failure to budget sufficient resources to address process, communication and training requirements

Critical Success Factors

- Focus on initial deployment costs (both hardware and software)
- Focus on ensuring application stability
- Avoid exotic hardware configurations
- Avoid software bloat (select only the applications absolutely required)
- Assess all compatibility issues (consider use of Terminal Services for native Microsoft application access)
- Provide training and workshops
- Continually highlight long-term benefits to the organization

Figure 18-1. *Critical Factors for Deployments.*

Fifty Proven Best Practices

What follows is a list of approaches and techniques that have proven to promote successful Linux projects. Over time, best practices are merely derived from discovering what works and what doesn't. Often these pearls of wisdom are the result of having to address recurring problems — best practices are merely the methods implemented to alleviate and circumvent them. Figure 18–2 highlights the salient best practices for Linux and open source projects. The following list is a look at these practices in more detail.

1. Make use of the Linux community when you need help, through newsgroups and e-mail lists. The community has a well-deserved reputation for helpfulness. Changes occur in the world of Linux very rapidly. It is important to task someone in the organization with tracking relevant developments.

2. Start the deployment of Linux slowly, where it is most feasible. This step will start the adoption of Linux by building experience, confidence and internal support. Continually look for projects that are

Best Practices

- Compare your IT spending profile against industry norms
- Emphasize manageability with new IT investments
- Deploy manageable platforms based on open industry protocols and APIs
- Limit the number of hardware configurations and software images in your environment
- Communicate expectations to users
- Review in-place standards before the environment gets changed
- Walk through the migration in a lab environment
- Thoroughly test and validate results before going live
- Start with a small, low risk domain first

Figure 18-2. *Continuous Best Practices.*

appropriate for Linux (such as when you are required to upgrade application software), then make a business case for it. When projects are proposed, consider whether Linux is appropriate and, if so, whether Linux can improve upon the current processing environment.

3. The most important aspect of architecture is documentation. Make sure you document it properly and integrate the documentation into your project planning, communicating it to all involved parties.

4. The success of a Linux rollout is dependent on the organization's understanding of the need for the conversion. The future outcome and success from the project are dependent on the business objectives behind the migration effort. Tying the value drivers and goals to the migration process is critical for the success of the project. A failure to adequately fund a Linux migration program will not only contribute to its demise, but will also send the message that the organization does not take it seriously.

5. Test, test and test again to make sure your new implementation strategy and your migration methodology work properly. Detail these results and make required adjustments to your strategy. The key to this test plan is to document everything. Interview users, administrators and help desk personnel to get their input on what is working and what is not.

6. Begin with a proof of concept — a sample implementation of the target infrastructure with a minimal number of users — to find out if the approach is appropriate. One of the best ways to do this is to use virtual machine technologies such as VMware or Win4Lin to create a virtual infrastructure.

7. Plan the pilot study with key users, involving as many high-level decision makers as you can in your pilot. Their usage of the new infrastructure will help foster better acceptance of the new technologies.

8. Motivate your organization to make the move to Linux. Begin by providing both business and technical drivers for the migration. Clearly articulate any new services as well as employees who will be supporting the new environment.

9. Once the pilot project is complete, take the time to gather input from users on the migration process to make sure you review and improve it as required before proceeding to full deployment. Once you begin full deployment, make sure you communicate successes to the user base to continue to foster excitement about the project. Once the project is complete, you should perform a project post mortem to capture migration best practices.

10. Restrict other application development where possible. The key is to avoid trying to do everything at once to minimize risk.

11. Gradually start prototyping and conducting limited rollouts of experimental open source alternatives, building technical and user expertise. Analyze existing user groups, identifying any self-contained business pockets.

12. Identify a portable development platform for internal future application development. In order to promote the ability to migrate to other platforms, it is helpful to identify and standardize on a development platform and language such as C, C++, Java, Python, Perl or PHP. The current reliance on Win32 application development is particularly dangerous, because it is difficult to port to Linux. An alternative development platform such as Java would ease the transition between plat-

forms. Organization should minimize the use of Windows-specific API calls, regardless of the development platform.

13. Make the help desk and the administrative team part of the pilot project to get them up to speed on new features. Migrate the Linux project team first, and then migrate key support personnel. Have standard help desk responses for potential user migration issues prepared ahead of time to facilitate the support process.

14. Use the Pareto Principle — 80 percent of the users access 20 percent of the available functionality. Identify what the other 80 percent of functionality costs the organization. Is it absolutely imperative for average users to have the same desktop configuration as the power users?

15. Begin with a pilot program targeting key users, usually up to 10 percent of your user population. This will let you burn in your migration process, testing all user communications, training programs and support strategies. Track any user or technical issues and adjust your migration strategy as needed.

16. Determine the feasible scope of the migration. If a wholesale switch to Linux across all or most of the organization is possible, determine the phases of the migration. Clearly identify the easiest targets first.

17. Identify and qualify potential targets for deployment and document all application dependencies, access methods and management controls. Closely examine business-critical applications, making sure all key features are still available under a Linux-based environment. Start with non-critical systems, ensuring that each step in the migration is manageable.

18. The cost of cross-training and supporting users is likely to be the main obstacle of a Linux migration. Various business groups have different functionality needs. Some may actually remain with Microsoft as an essential operational requirement. Consider obtaining supplemental support for open source packages (from companies such as Covalent).

19. Establish a cross-functional team to define and monitor business processes. At the same time, monitor the Linux and open source technical roadmap. Together, these activities will help establish your organization's open source adoption roadmap.

20. Give one executive responsibility for the project and make sure that leaders from the technology organization and all related business units are involved.

21. Provide time and incentives for IT employees to explore open source alternatives and provide training for new technologies particularly within any support teams. Objective and informed compatibility decisions can then be made on any proposed transition process. Do not force anybody into the role, but understand that identifying the correct people is a key element in the transition.

22. Linux demands intimate knowledge of your application computing environment. In particular, it requires more knowledge about the business objectives of your applications as well as the systems and networks that support them. It is critical to conduct an assessment (e.g. develop an Application Matrix) of your application computing environment.

23. Ensure that the highest levels of management are committed to the project; experience has shown that this is the No. 1 priority for migrations. Without this commitment the best-laid plans can be jeopardized.

24. Identify various domain experts within the organization. These individuals will become key players within the planning and implementation phases.

25. Establish buy-in and leverage "change champions." Change champions play a critical role both in the migration planning and approval process. During the approval process you should identify, for each key stakeholder, respected individuals with whom you can review the overall business case and expected impacts. Try to find individuals who can be used as references in support of the program.

26. Think about the vision of the Linux migration. How would individuals and groups need to change their work habits? What efficiencies/cost savings/cost avoidance would result? Areas to consider include new procedures and processes, new tools and systems, and additional or new training.

27. Organizations should prepare by closely evaluating and understanding their exact business usage, server requirements and desktop interoperability needs. The expense and impact of continuing to use proprietary software should be calculated and justified. Regardless of the underlying computing infrastructure, business application requirements remain the same.

28. Once implementation begins, it's critical to directly involve representatives from the key stakeholder groups. Try to draw upon these individuals when gaining support for your business case. Prior to identifying

these champions, make sure you can set expectations around their roles and responsibilities.

29. Create a comprehensive communication plan. Communicate and communicate again. That being said, communicating smartly and targeting your message requires thoughtful planning and analysis. Don't forget to have a feedback mechanism as part of the plan.

30. Once the project has been completed, aggressively focus on benefits realized. Monitor the success metrics established in the business case and make sure that you are achieving the promised benefits. Do not let minor disruptions or complaints damage the overall success of the migration project. Use your plans and persistence to overcome these post-implementation obstacles and to make your Linux migration a long-term success.

31. Organizations should seek informed advice and help from experienced Linux users and experts. Monitor other enterprise migrations by establishing employee contacts wherever possible.

32. Remember that a Linux migration is a gradual and evolving process that needs careful planning, controls and management sponsorship.

33. Break down the overall business into its components. Examine the business as discrete functions and processes (i.e. what is actually being done) instead of looking at the organization from product line families, corporate departments or geographical divisions.

34. Instead of focusing on big monolithic applications made up of millions of lines of code, start to think about discrete modular elements of application functionality that can be modified more easily as the needs of the business change.

35. By increasing the flexibility and componentization in your business design, the infrastructure can evolve from silos of complex, over-provisioned, proprietary hardware and software to a standards-based infrastructure in which capacity can be optimized across your entire organization.

36. Aggressively retire out-of-date platforms and operating systems. Take advantage of today's automated management tools and services, but be aware that technology alone is not a solution. People and processes are equally important in turning IT assets into strategic advantages.

37. Move toward centralization, standardization and automation for all key processes, including asset management, deployment and migration, configuration management and fault management.

38. Manage all systems — both desktops and servers — in a similar fashion. (LDAP and DNS and other special infrastructure servers would be the only variations to this standard process.)

39. Optimize relationships between business units and technology departments, and work to improve communication among all those who support or depend on the infrastructure. Work with business units to understand end-user needs, and to provide better access to accurate, real-time information when and where it is needed most.

40. Consider outsourcing desktop fleet management to an experienced vendor. High quality consultants have optimized tools and methods that can often deliver better results at lower costs.

41. Look to partner with vendors and solution providers that have specific experience and skill sets.

42. Keep your support contacts up-to-date. You are responsible for complying with all operating system and application vendors' license agreements. Make sure that the support e-mail address is always correct. It will be used to notify users of the availability of patches, upgrades and any newly discovered security issues.

43. The organization needs to make explicit a Linux and open source policy. The policy at a minimum should address:

    - What software licenses are allowed within the organization?
    - How is Linux and open source software managed and controlled?
    - What are the rules and guidelines for working with software under an open source license?

44. Use ISO files rather than physical CD-ROMs (although ISO files do not take the place of golden masters) for operating system and application installation. Disk access is faster than CD-ROM access, especially when more than one person is accessing the files at the same time. This also eliminates the need to physically handle CD-ROMs and encourages consistent use of the network images.

45. Keep all important data, such as home directories, on network file servers.

46. Insist on the use of open standard file formats, such as Postscript, PDF or XML. Do not use proprietary file formats for files that are only intended to be read, not edited. This is a good practice in general because editable file formats are a common way of spreading computer viruses.

47. All future application development should be based on a three-tier computing model where application code is independent of the application interface and data access. Monolithic client applications are notoriously difficult to manage and scale.

48. Insist all new application development is accomplished using portable languages such as C, C++, Java, Python or Perl. Enforce the use of cross-platform libraries and GUI toolkits such as wxWindows (http://www.wxwindows.org) or the FOX toolkit (http://www.fox-toolkit.org). Avoid building applications that require proprietary APIs.

49. An intranet site must be established to provide support and how-to information along with tips on getting the most from the new environment. You should provide a Wiki format that allows users to add content as in an Internet forum. From that one source of information the organization can get training, downloads, project status and communications. It is important that the users feel included in this effort. A help desk portal should be provided to help end-users with any problems they are experiencing.

50. Create a dedicated project team assigned to manage incidents and track down root causes of errors reported by users. This team can address user errors or process problems immediately, resulting in fast troubleshooting response. Assign a dedicated support staff to follow Linux kernel improvements (http://www.lwn.net is a good site to monitor frequently).

Key Takeaways

The way business applications are deployed and managed plays a key role in technology cost and complexity. When every application is optimized as an isolated software entity with no regard for consistency, the result is a patchwork of hardware, management consoles, back-end databases, processes and skill sets.

The solution is to promote cross-organizational communication and to establish enterprise-wide standards for business applications, infrastructure and processes. Clear standards provide development teams with a menu of optimized design patterns, hardware and software platforms, configurations, architectures, tools and services. Not only does this improve the reliability and manageability of your Linux environment, it also provides a simpler and more consistent environment for consolidating systems, management tools and processes.

Ask, don't reinvent — that is, leverage the work of others. Interview industry peer groups and vendors; participate in community-based organizations such as OSDL; conduct online research. Successful Linux initiatives are about using developed standards, streamlining and automating processes and, more importantly, participating in the open source community.

Chapter 19

Looking Ahead

A hero is someone who understands the responsibility that comes with his freedom.
— Bob Dylan

Summary

Restoring the balance of power between customers and vendors, along with gaining greater flexibility, transparency and freedom of choice have been key drivers for Linux adoption and the open source movement, creating one of the biggest disruptive shifts in the industry. The advantages that Linux offers — reliability, security, price per performance and freedom from proprietary vendor lock-in — to your business application environment strike at the very heart of the issues plaguing IT organizations today.

If there is one overarching message that readers should take away from this book, it is that Linux and open source computing requires a process. It is a journey — not a destination. And although it may seem that transitioning away from your current computing environment can seem too daunting, this truly is an opportunity to build a better application infrastructure for your organization.

Transitioning to a Linux-based computing environment offers significant cost savings and performance improvements. Linux and open source computing provides a viable enterprise computing platform, however it is important that your organization wisely choose its projects for open source alternatives and Linux-based computing. While most Linux and open source projects will migrate smoothly, the use of the Seven Keys will greatly ensure success.

Your organization can provide a more reliable and predictive Linux-based infrastructure environment. It is important to remember that Linux and open source will not magically create a self-governing computing infrastructure. It is up to the organization to make every effort to enforce management controls and processes to allow open source computing to thrive.

Adopting industry standards increase your ability to take advantage of future innovations. By using industry standards as a basis of selection for the best solution of your environment, you will find that those solutions will provide the right balance between cutting edge innovation and proven industry approaches and strategies. Fortunately, Linux and open source are built on widely accepted industry standards.

The more your organization uses and deploys solutions based on open standards, the greater is its vendor independence. This decreases the cost for organizations changing application solutions and solution vendors by decreasing the cost associated with changing an embedded business application.

One thing IT professionals believe about open source software: It provides more opportunity for innovation than commercial or proprietary software. Most organizations contend that open source spurs more opportunities for technical innovation with a significant majority endorsing it because it encourages business innovation.

While this book attempted to outline what is necessary for successful Linux and open source adoption, there is no substitute for using qualified and experienced Linux professionals. Also, it is important to remember that Linux and open source adoption is not an “all or nothing” proposition. In fact, if there is anything that the reader should take away from this book is that open source adoption is about IT optimization.

The goal is to optimize your computing infrastructure in the most economic way possible providing the most “bang for the buck” for your organization. And this might mean having a mix of Linux and non-Linux solutions. Organizations now have more choices and attractive new options for future system deployments, because of course, Linux and open source are all about having a choice.

Appendix A

Application Matrix

Web Transaction Portal		Web Servers	WebLogic Servers	DB Server	DSS Cube Server	eContent Servers
Physical Configuration						
Application	Application Name	IBM x235	IBM x365	IBM x445	IBM x445	Sun E420R
	Version					
	Support Personnel	8 to 15	10	2	2	1
	Personnel Contact Number	2x450Mhz	12x400Mhz	16x400Mhz	4x450Mhz	4x450Mhz
	Number of Users	1 GB	12 GB	16 GB	4 GB	4 GB
	Access Outside of Intranet	NFS	NFS	FC	FC	FC
	Physical Location	Corp	Corp	Corp	Corp	Corp
Hardware	Server Type	IBM x235	IBM x365	IBM x445	IBM x445	Sun x4100
	Serial Number					
	Number of Servers	8 to 15	10	2	2	1
	CPU	2x900Mhz	12x900Mhz	16x900Mhz	4x1.2Ghz	4x1.2Ghz
	Memory	1 GB	12 GB	16 GB	4 GB	4 GB
	Disk Interface	NFS	NFS	FC	FC	FC
	Disk I/O Channels	2	2	4	4	2
	Network Interface	Gigabit Ethernet	Gigabit Ethernet	Gigabit Ethernet	Gigabit Ethernet	Gigabit Ethernet
	Number Free Slots	0	0	1	2	2
	Network I/O Channels	4	4	4	4	4
	I/O Capacity	2 PCI	2 PCI slots across 2 I/O boards	5 PCI slots across 3 I/O boards	4 PCI	4 PCI
Software	OS Version	Red Hat 3.1	Red Hat 3.1	Red Hat 3.1	Red Hat 3.1	Red Hat 3.1
	Application	Apache/WebLogic	BEA WebLogic	Oracle	Oracle	Vignette eContent
	Version	1.3.14	5.2	8.1.7	8.1.7	4.0.3
	Latest Version	No	Yes	No	No	Yes
	Virtualized Server	No	No	Yes	Yes	No
	Load Balanced	Yes	Yes	No	No	No
	Clustered	No	No	Yes	Yes	Clustered w/ eNotify
Disk	Internal (GB)	<10	<10	<10	<10	<10
	External (GB)	1	1	300	100	10
	Mirrors (GB)	0	0	300	100	0
	LUNs (target ID)					

Application Matrix (continued)

Availability Requirements						
	Availability (1-5)	5	5	5	4	5
	Hours of Operation	7x24	7x24	7x24	5x8	7x24
	Meeting SLA	Yes	Yes	No	No	Yes
Performance Requirements						
	Simultaneous Connections	10,000	10,000	350	15	25
	Requests Per Second					
	Data Throughput (MB/s)	175	155	175	225	175
	Level of Performance (1-5)	5	4	5	5	4
	I/O Characteristics	High percentage of reads and shared space desirable	Shared storage desirable for ease of management Shares data with eContent	Random read/write	Massive number of indexed reads. Large number of scattered writes	Random read/write
	Meeting SLA	Yes	Yes	No	No	Yes
Scalability Requirements						
	Growth Projections	Extreme	High	High	Medium	Medium
	Expandable	Good	Good	Medium	Medium	Excellent
	Meeting SLA	Yes	Yes	Yes	Yes	Yes
Accounting Information						
	Owner / Admistrator	Mark Teter	Mark Teter	Mark Teter	Mark Teter	Mark Teter
	Initial Hardware Cost					
	Initial Software Cost					
	Depreciated Value					
	Maintenance Cost					
	Years in Service	1	1	2	2	3
	Capacity Cost ($/MB)	$0.10	$0.10	$0.10	$0.15	$0.08
	Operating Status	Good	Good	Excellent	Excellent	Excellent

Appendix B

Integrating Windows Applications into a Linux Environment

Below is a listing of the most popular methods of integrating Windows applications into a Linux-based computing environment.

rdesktop

The rdesktop is an open source client for Windows Terminal Servers. Rdesktop natively supports RDP (RDP is based on Citrix technology and was licensed from Citrix in 1997) in order to present a Microsoft environment to a Linux desktop. Unlike Citrix ICA, rdesktop does not require any server extensions. For more information, visit http://www.rdesktop.org.

HOBLink JWT

HOBLink JWT is a Java technology for accessing Windows Terminal Servers using RDP. For more information, visit http://www.hobsoft.com.

GraphOn GO-Global

GO-Global for Windows eliminates the need for additional infrastructure such as Windows Terminal Services (WTS) or Citrix MetaFrame. For more information, visit http://www.graphon.com.

Citrix MetaFrame

Citrix MetaFrame is an application publishing product built on the Independent Computing Architecture (ICA). Unlike traditional frame buffered protocols like VNC, ICA transmits high-level window display information, much like the X11 protocol, as opposed to purely graphical information. For more information, visit http://www.citrix.com.

Wine

The Wine project started in 1993 as a way to support running Windows 3.1 programs on Linux. It is an open source implementation of the Windows API on top of the X Window System. Wine does not require a Windows operating system (unlike solutions that support RDP or ICA). Wine does not emulate an X86 processor so applications that do not make system calls will run just as fast with Wine as they do with Windows. For more information, visit http://www.winehq.com.

CodeWeavers CrossOver Office

CrossOver Office is a commercial implementation of the Wine project. CrossOver Office Server Edition allows Windows applications to be executed under Linux without requiring a Windows license. For more information, visit http://www.codeweavers.com.

NeTraverse Win4Lin Terminal Server

Win4Lin uses the Linux file system instead of creating a virtual file system like VMWare. As a result, there can be only one version of Windows installed on a Win4Lin machine. (By contrast, VMware can have multiple Windows installations installed and running at the same time.) For more information, visit http://www.win4lin.com.

Sun Microsystems Java Desktop System

Sun Ray technology utilizes a smart card to "hot desk" — allowing end-users to move their desktop with them as they move from Sun Ray client to Sun Ray client.

The Java Desktop System provides fully integrated desktop software, mostly based on open source. It includes GNOME; office productivity tools featuring the StarOffice suite; fully-integrated e-mail and calendar; Web browser; instant messaging; Adobe Acrobat, Macromedia Flash, RealNetworks RealPlayer and Java technology. For more information, visit http://www.sun.com/software/javadesktopsystem.

VMware VirtualCenter

Perhaps the most popular virtual machine in the industry, VMWare is a wholly owned subsidiary of EMC Corporation. VMWare provides virtual machines for X86 hardware including the ability to migrate a running virtual machine to a different physical server with no application service disruption. For more information, visit http://www.vmware.com.

Appendix C

Storage Networks for Linux

Storage networks are solving many IT infrastructure problems that have arisen over the last several years. These problems are the result of managing continuous application availability and ever-increasing amounts of application data. And Linux is right in the middle of this.

There are essentially two approaches to storage networks: network attached (NAS) or channel-based fabrics known as storage area networks (SAN). NAS is oftentimes seen as an alternative to using SAN technology. It is simply a storage system that provides file services. That is, storage is accessed is through host-based file system device drivers (a.k.a. file I/O operations).

A SAN on the other hand, is a direct extension of the Linux kernel; it provides an I/O channel from the server to its storage. Typically this I/O channel is based on an ANSI-approved standard known as Fibre Channel that provides a high-speed serial connection to deliver SCSI packets (a.k.a. direct I/O). The truth is NAS and SAN are complementary technologies that both improve application data availability and manageability.

For large-scale storage environments, both NAS and SAN technologies hold the greatest promise for providing a more stress-free storage model versus the alternative of direct attached storage (DAS). DAS is storage that is embedded in the Linux servers much like today's desktop PCs. The trouble with DAS is that all storage management activities must involve the host it's connected to. Whether you need to expand the storage pool, or replace a failed disk drive or backup the data volumes, the Linux host is impacted.

SAN and NAS both provide ease of storage management since the storage is decoupled from the server. Ultimately, this provides better asset utilization, non-disruptive data management activities, ability to separate the storage buying decision from the server acquisition and a lower management cost through storage centralization and consolidation.

The major differences between SAN and NAS are:

- SAN creates private networks for storage pools whereas NAS creates shared storage networks
- SAN uses utility storage protocols (Fibre Channel) whereas NAS uses network protocols (NFS)
- SAN requires special purpose host adapters (HBAs) whereas NAS leverages general purpose network cards (NICs)
- SAN is a direct extension to the kernel whereas NAS is not 100-percent POSIX compliant.

RAID Technology

RAID (redundant array of independent disks) provides I/O reliability when storing data. Commonly, RAID is either RAID-1, RAID-0+1 or RAID-5. A RAID-1 array group consists of a pair of disk drives in a mirrored configuration that duplicates all writes to each disk. Read requests can be satisfied by whichever disk in the pair is able to satisfy the request first, improving overall read performance — a single read is not performed any faster, but multiple reads have better performance because they are performed simultaneously. RAID-1 issues write I/O sequentially to disk drives and then the physical writes are performed in parallel. As a result, host-based RAID-1 is nearly as fast as controller-based RAID-1.

RAID-0+1 configurations improve on RAID-1 by layering mirroring on top of striping. Most mirroring implementations use striping to improve sequential and random read performance through the advantages of striping across multiple controllers and disk spindles. RAID-1+0 configuration is when two drives are mirrored together and then the mirrors are striped. In both cases (0+1 or 1+0), the loss of a single drive does not cause failure. However, if you lose one more drive from either the primary or mirror, RAID-0+1 will fail. In RAID-1+0, there can be single disk failures from all mirror pairs and the RAID group still remains online. RAID-1+0 greatly improves overall availability as well as performance with sequential reads. RAID-0+1 or 1+0 provide good performance with large scans as well as random reads due to the round-robin effect with the mirrored side of the volume.

RAID-5 stripes data and parity across all disks in the stripe set. RAID-5 performance is good for read-intensive environments due to the effects of striping across multiple spindles. However, write-intensive environments suffer due to the read-modify-write process for parity calculations. This is especially true with host-based RAID; however, most advanced disk arrays provide controller-based RAID-5 that uses cache and special hardware to offset the performance penalty from parity calculations.

Storage Networking Basics

The goal of a Linux storage environment is achieving lower costs through high utilization of its capacity, lower costs through efficient data management and lower costs through its high-availability. Both SAN and NAS provides Linux computing environments with many benefits, such as the ability for:

- Server and storage consolidation
- Non-disruptive scalability for growth
- Improved backup and recovery
- Tape sharing and pooling
- Better I/O performance
- High-availability server clustering
- Improved disaster tolerance
- Ease of data migration
- Reduced total costs of ownership
- Consistent and centralized management
- Tiered storage architectures to match the value of the data to the cost of the storage

When deploying a SAN with a Linux file system (i.e. ext3), each server mounts and accesses its disk partitions individually. As a result, concurrent access from multiple Linux servers is not possible without the use of a clustered file system.

Deploying a clustered file system on SAN-connected Linux servers allows full concurrent access to all file system data. Clustered file systems are common in grid-based Linux servers as well as when deploying a horizontal scaling compute architecture.

NAS, on the other hand, allows multiple Linux servers to share a mounted file system. Since NAS storage systems utilize the NFS protocol, Linux servers are provided with a locking mechanism to arbitrate among multiple hosts trying to write to the same volume concurrently.

NAS will generally offer lower performance than a Fibre Channel (FC) SAN environments primarily because NAS uses a Layer 3 IP networking protocol versus a Layer 2 FC channeling protocol. One strategy is to combine the performance and scalability characteristics of a SAN storage environment with the cost effectiveness of a NAS environment. A topology that achieves this goal uses SAN technology to provide the back-end disk storage, and then uses IP networking and NFS protocol to share the disk capacity.

IP Storage

Another approach to building a storage network for Linux servers is using iSCSI (Internet Small Computer System Interconnect). iSCSI, developed by the Internet Engineering Task Force (IETF), is a technology that encapsulates SCSI packets on an IP network. It offers block-level access like to disk capacity like FC, but uses an IP transport to create what is known as an IP SAN or IP Storage.

It is important to understand that since IP SANs provide block-level access, data access can not be shared concurrently among multiple Linux servers. Each Linux server individually mounts and accesses the disk partitions just like with a FC SAN, albeit over an IP network.

iSCSI can be supported over any physical media that supports TCP/IP as a transport, but typically iSCSI implementations use Gigabit Ethernet (GbE) networks. The iSCSI protocol can be supported via a Linux software driver or can be optimized in hardware for better performance using an iSCSI HBA.

With Linux systems, iSCSI provides a number of advantages. Applications such as remote backup, disaster recovery and storage virtualization can be deployed very cost-effectively since iSCSI can leverage common Ethernet technology. Ethernet has a very low cost of deployment due to the commodity nature of NICs, cabling and switches.

Ultimately, an IP SAN offers the same benefits as a FC SAN, but at a lower cost of deployment. And since iSCSI is based on standards defined by the IETF, the eventual transition to 10GigE networking will not require any modification to Linux servers.

In an effort to improve the I/O network processing on Linux systems, special hardware adapters are available known as TCP offload engines (TOE). A TOE performs a variety of basic networking functions for the operating system on the NIC adapter itself. They have a special-purpose CPU placed on the hardware-accelerated NIC adapter to pre-process packets instead of the OS having to perform these functions.

The purpose of a TOE is to reduce the high performance cost of processing IP and TCP packets. Using a TOE card, functions such as checksums and packet segmentation control are now handled by the NIC without involving the Linux host. This reduces both the Linux CPU overhead as well as reduces traffic on its memory bus.

A TOE is effectively invisible to the network — it doesn't require any special implementation or configuration within the network. However, it does require special drivers. In an effort to simplify the process of improving network processing, Intel has announced I/OAT (I/O Acceleration Technology), offering it as an alternative to TOE adapters.

This storage acceleration capability will provide faster throughput as well as increased reliability for data by assisting the storage controller's ability to perform RAID-6. (The details of RAID-6 are outside the scope of this book, but essentially it provides better data reliability protecting against a double disk failure within a RAID-5 set.)

Unlike NIC-centric solutions like a TOE, Intel I/OAT is a system-wide solution that addresses all packet and payload processing bottlenecks throughout the server platform. It is a server platform, network I/O acceleration technology addressing all segments of the server I/O bottleneck problem.

Appendix D

Financial Lingua Franca

CapEx (Capital Expenses)

CapEx are expenditures used by a company to acquire or upgrade physical assets such as equipment, property and industrial buildings. In accounting, a capital expenditure is added to an asset account (i.e. capitalized), thus increasing the asset's basis.

Internal Rate of Return (IRR)

IRR is the rate of return that makes equivalent the positive cash flow from savings with the negative cash flow created by the investment itself. IRR is the rate at which the cash inflows are exactly equal to the cash outflows.

Stated in financial terms, IRR is the discount rate at which the present value of cash inflows equals the present value of cash outflows. Hence, IRR is where the combined discounted cash flow (DCF) equals zero.

Small projects can have high IRRs, but may not necessarily be fairly compared with much larger projects with the same IRR. Even though it is not the best measurement of investment potential, the IRR is an effective yield on the project; that is, the discount rate that causes the net present value to be equal to zero. Its disadvantage is that it might give an incorrect viewpoint when deciding among mutually exclusive projects.

Net Present Value (NPV)

NPV is the value today of a future amount of cash invested at a specified discount, rate. In its simplest form, NPV is the value today of cash received at a future date given a discount rate (cost of capital). For example, the present value of $110 received a year from now, assuming 10 percent interest, is $100.

Net present value is defined as the present value of all future cash flows at a given interest rate. When NPV is positive, there is potential for earnings in excess of the standard. NPV limitations include its reliance on cash flow projections and is related to inherently subjective quantitative forecasts. It does not flush out any "cushion" that might be built into the numbers.

Financial managers want to see all of the future net cash flows associated with a technology initiative, discounted by an appropriate interest rate so they can determine present value of the future cash flows, and compare this with other potential investments.

OpEx (Operating Expenses)

Expenses that are purchased in order for a company to operate and maintain its business.

For example, the payment of employee wages is an operating expense. Operating expenses are the bulk of most total cost of ownership models since they generally outweigh capital costs. They include rental expenses, leasing costs, maintenance and management fees and administration costs.

Payback Period (PP)

PP is the period of time needed to recover the investment being evaluated. It is often called the breakeven point. While PP is relatively easy to calculate, it presents some difficulties when applied. It does not address the issue of how much "return" is being made from the investment. It only addresses when the initial investment is recovered. It assumes that the benefits and costs are relatively equal during the period measured.

The PP is where the net benefits equal the costs associated with the technology initiative. The payback period is a good measure of risk, letting the organization know how long it is going to take to recoup the investment outlay.

Return on Investment (ROI)

As a generic term, ROI means an investment analysis typically identified as a business case. As a specific term, ROI is a method of calculation related to the net financial impact of a set of costs and benefits. In the context of financial analysis, a common formula used for ROI calculation is the average of all net benefits over the life of the project divided by the initial cost of the project. ROI ignores the economic life of the investment.

ROI is the cumulative net benefits (benefits minus direct costs of benefits such as applying a profit margin to total revenue influenced) derived from a technology initiative, divided by cumulative costs of the enabling technology investment and associated deployment and ongoing costs.

ROI is the number one way financial managers are making technology purchase decisions. They are using this metric to control technology purchases and to make smarter technology buying decisions. It allows them to quickly cut through the technology hype to determine the true economic worth to the organization.

Total Cost of Ownership (TCO)

TCO is where most companies begin to scrutinize the costs of a potential technology solution. TCO seeks to measure all of the expenses, both human and technical, behind a given technology initiative. It includes all costs related to the technology lifecycle, including procurement, deployment, maintenance and support.

A TCO analysis can be very good for budgeting purposes, or choosing between alternative courses for technology initiatives. It is not recommended to evaluate potential technology initiatives based on TCO alone.

Key cost areas to be considered in the TCO analysis include software (including maintenance and upgrades), hardware and other infrastructure-related costs, personnel, consulting and training.

Appendix E

Maintaining Golden Images

It is important to remember that infrastructure management is essentially a long-term development process. A challenge to installing and maintaining a manageable collection of servers is having a system for consistent and reproducible operating system installations. There are various strategies for producing consistent operating system installations.

The golden image server provides an automatic and unattended way to distribute Linux install images, patches, management scripts and configuration files. The strongest contributor to a high total cost of ownership is *ad hoc*, manual changes made to individual machines, regardless of operating system. This is true of every operating system available, not just with Linux.

All Linux workstations, desktops and servers should periodically contact the gold server to obtain updates. Rather than push changes out to servers and desktops, each individual system needs to be responsible for polling the gold server at boot, and periodically afterwards, to maintain its own revision level accurately mirroring all types of files, including sources, binaries and hard and symbolic links.

Boot-time configurations are done on a repeatable basis, keyed by host name or class-of-server variables in the boot-time configuration scripts. A single golden image server is highly recommended in order to achieve simplicity and reliability across the Linux environment. Consequently, all software that is mastered from the gold server must be controlled by standard version control processes. In fact, software version controls and practices are the first steps with a Linux migration effort.

It is important to keep the Linux operating environment as generic as possible. This translates to identical Linux configurations across both desktop and server classifications. The primary reason for this requirement is to provide a simple disaster recovery process. As a result, maintenance and management are greatly reduced, and in the event of machine failure, recovery is simple and fast.

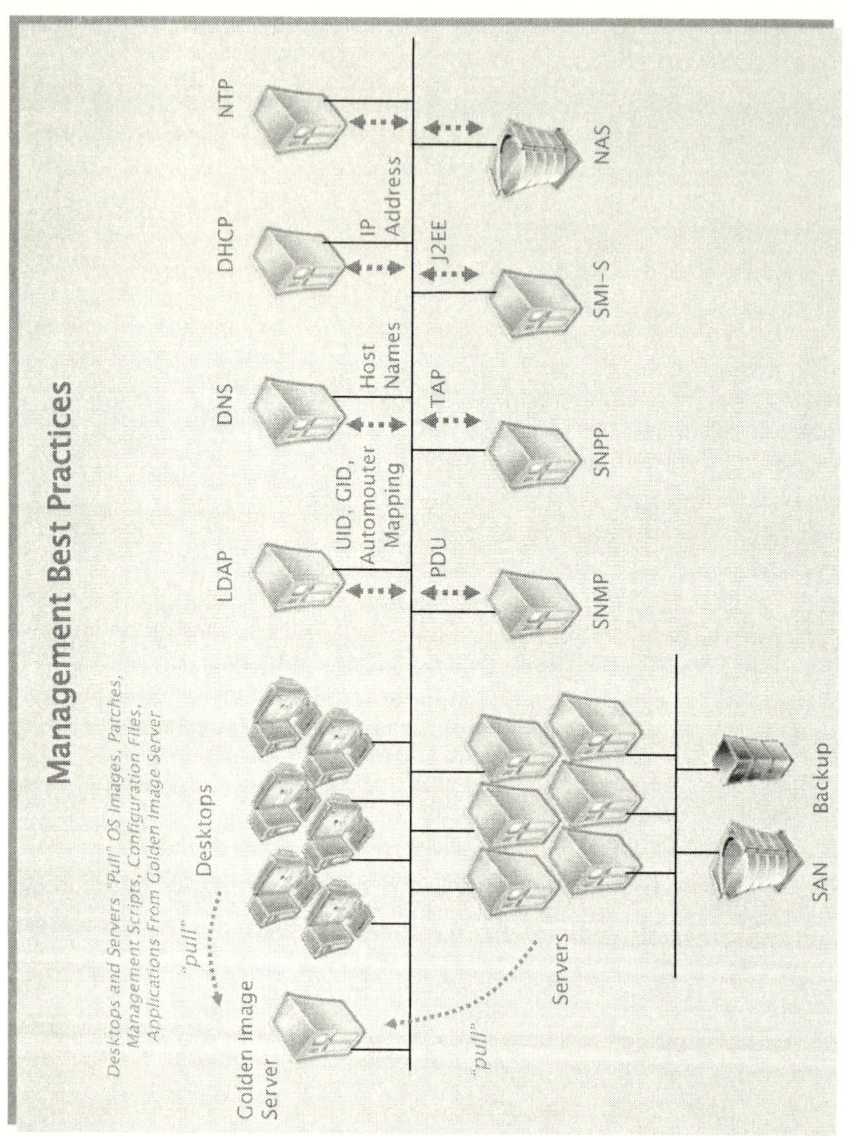

Figure E-1. *Network Management Best Practices.*

The use of environment variables is an elegant way to manage custom patches and configuration changes on Linux machines. By having environment variables set in /etc/environment or the equivalent, configuration changes can be easily managed across the complete Linux network of systems. Even making simple changes, such as configuring a client to use a multi-headed display, can be easily scripted. This strict discipline provides the ability to exactly and quickly re-create a machine in case of disaster.

Setting up a time server and having clients set their clocks against a time server is an important and often overlooked function. The Kerberos authentication protocol relies on accurate time of day clocks. In addition, many applications rely on synchronized clocks between the client and server, especially for file locking.

In a sense, there are very few time servers. Rather, most "time servers" are actually time clients of another time server which is a reliable source. The most accurate time servers are called stratum 1. When a client sets its clock against a certain stratum time server, the client becomes a stratum n+1 client. It is common practice for a single server in an organization to set its clock against a stratum 1 or stratum 2 time server, thus becoming a stratum 2 or stratum 3 time server. Then many clients in the enterprise can set their clocks against this local time server.

Localization

The initial boot strap process should only require a system to be plugged in, turned on and left unattended. This is usually accomplished by bootp entries on the install or gold image server. The bootp entries will point to diskless boot images for the bare metal Linux systems. This process should format the hard drive and set the hostname, domain name, and all other unique attributes.

In a nutshell, Linux system configuration is all about localization. This includes everything that makes a system unique, or that makes a Linux node a participant of a particular group or domain. For example, hostname and IP addresses must be different on every Linux host, but the contents of /etc/resolv.conf should be similar, if not identical, on hosts that occupy the same subnet. Automounter maps that deliver users' home directories must be the same for every host in an authentication domain. The entries in client crontabs need to be mastered from the gold server.

Kickstart is Red Hat's automated installation software. It installs Red Hat distributions from CD-ROM, hard disk or network, and boots from network, CD or floppy disk. The open source Anaconda installer offers text or graphical interfaces, and can be interactive or fully automated by a configuration file.

PXE (Preboot Execution Environment) is an Intel BIOS technology that provides a mechanism to download and run a native IA binary from the network before an operating system is booted. The services that make up a PXE boot network install environment include:

- BOOTP (boot) server
- Trivial File Transfer Protocol (TFTP) server
- Network File System (NFS) server for the second stage of the install, Kickstart
- Domain name system (DNS), which is helpful but not mandatory

The chain of events in PXE boot is as follows:

- The system BIOS uses the BOOTP protocol to download the pxeboot application
- TFTP protocol is then used to download a configuration file that points to a Linux kernel and specifies kernel boot parameters.
- The kernel is executed with the boot flags specified in the PXE configuration file.
- Automatic OS installation programs can then be launched (i.e. Red Hat Kickstart) for automating a network or CD-ROM installation of the Linux OS

Appendix F

Management Solutions

The following is a list of open source management solutions. It is very limited but a good place to begin looking for the right mix of tools to automate the management process.

Amanda

Amanda is a backup scheduler, originally developed at the University of Maryland. Amanda performs compression using standard Linux utilities such as gzip and bzip. If network utilization is high, the compression can be done on the client to reduce the network load as well as backup times. For more information, visit http://www.amanda.org.

Bacula

Bacula is a set of programs that provide backup, recovery and verification of data across a network. It is based on a client-server architecture that is efficient and easy to use while offering many advanced storage management features that make it easy to recover data. For more information, visit http://www.bacula.org.

ClusterSSH

ClusterSSH is based on open source utility ssh, the standard for creating a remote and secure shell environment. To manage multiple servers, ClusterSSH allows the creation of multiple connections where keystrokes from one console can be repeated across all the servers simultaneously, allowing the ability to edit multiple files, restart services and configuring identical Linux system configurations. For more information, visit http://clusterssh.sourceforge.net.

Cfengine

Cfengine is a set of tools that automatically administers and configures Linux servers via a high-level language. Cfengine can copy files from a central repository as well as automatically execute shell scripts based on pre-described conditions. If any Linux server managed by cfengine diverges from its optimal configured state, cfengine will make the necessary corrective actions to put it back into compliance. For more information, visit http://www.cfengine.org.

Cricket

Cricket is a network monitoring system that provides time-series data trending. Cricket was expressly developed to help network managers visualize and understand the traffic on their networks. Cricket has two components, a collector and a grapher. The grapher leverages the RRD Tool, which takes care of storing, normalizing and graphing the data after the collector gathers it. For more information, visit http://cricket.sourceforge.net.

GroundWork

GroundWork's functionally is comparable to most popular commercial tools, including OpenView, Patrol, Tivoli and Unicenter. Based on open source software including Nagios, RRDTool and MySQL, GroundWork provides a complete network management solution. GroundWork aggregates device and network data into management-level reports and dashboards. For more information, visit http://www.itgroundwork.com.

mon

mon (Service Monitoring Daemon) is a general-purpose systems management and monitoring tool. It is easily extensible allowing any application to be monitored. The mon package contains 37 pre-built monitor scripts and there are many more available on the Internet. For more information, visit http://www.kernel.org/software/mon.

MRTG

MRTG (Multi Router Traffic Grapher) is a network traffic monitor used to collect and display network traffic data. MRTG uses SNMP to collect the data and produces Web pages to display the results. Where SNORT examines network traffic for security breaches, MRTG monitors and displays network utilization. For more information, visit http://freshmeat.net/projects/mrtg.

Nagios

Nagios is a host and service monitor designed for network fault notification. Nagios probes hosts and network services, and provides exception-based external notifications via e-mail, instant message or SMS. Current status information, historical logs and reports can all be accessed via a Web browser. Nagios is very extensible, making it a very powerful monitoring solution. For more information, visit http://www.nagios.org.

NetDisco

Netdisco is an open source Web-based network management tool. With Netdisco you can locate the switch port of an end-user system by IP or MAC address. It uses router ARP tables and Layer 2 switch MAC forwarding tables to locate nodes on physical ports and track them by their IP addresses. For each node, a time stamped history of the ports it has visited and the IP addresses it has used is maintained. For more information, visit http://netdisco.org.

ntop

ntop is a network traffic probe that shows network utilization. Based on the libpcap library, ntop provides information such as:

- Network traffic and statistics for each protocol
- Host OS and host name of each node in the network
- Analysis of IP traffic according to the source and destination (who's talking to whom)
- RMON-like network traffic statistics

For more information, visit http://www.ntop.org.

OpenNMS

OpenNMS is a highly customizable management platform. It provides three main functional systems: service polling, data collection and notification management. The service polling component tracks the availability of managed processes and services; the data collection component collects, stores and reports on network information (including managing their thresholds); and the notification management component takes care of receiving all internal and external network events as well as provides an escalation facility. For more information, visit http://www.opennms.org.

RRD Tool

RRD Tool (Round Robin Database) is a utility to graph time-series data. Created by the author of MRTG, RRD Tool stores its data in a very compact format that does not expand over time. It can be used via simple shell scripts or as a Perl module. For more information, visit http://freshmeat.net/projects/rrdtool.

Snort

Snort is a network intrusion prevention system that can perform protocol analysis, content searching and matching. It detects a variety of attacks and probes such as stealth port scans, CGI-based attacks, Address Resolution Protocol (ARP) spoofing, buffer overflows, attacks on daemons with known weaknesses and OS fingerprinting attempts. Snort utilizes descriptive rules to determine what traffic it should monitor and a modularly designed detection engine to pinpoint attacks in real time. For more information, visit http://www.snort.org.

rsync

rsync is a powerful open source utility that is used for incremental file transfers. rsysnc synchronizes local and remote file directories by only transferring the differences between two files. It can update whole directory trees and file systems, preserving symbolic links, hard links, file ownership and permissions. This is a great way to non-disruptively keep multiple configuration files up –to date. For more information, visit http://www.samba.org/rsync.

Webmin

Webmin is a Web-based interface for system administration. It can set up user accounts, Apache, DNS and file sharing. For more information, visit http://www.webmin.com.

Acronyms

ALU: Arithmetic Logic Unit
ASF: Apache Software Foundation
ASI: Advanced Switching Interconnect
BSD: Berkeley Software Distribution
CapEx: Capital Expenses
CD: Compact Disc
CDDL: Common Development and Distribution License
CFS: Clustered File System
COE: Common Operating Environment
CPU: Central Processing Unit
CRM: Customer Resource Management
DCL: Data Center Linux
DCL-WG: Data Center Linux Working Group
DNS: Domain Name System
DOIP: Display over IP
ELC: Embedded Linux Consortium
FC: Fibre Channel
FDIC: Federal Deposit Insurance Corporation
FHS: Filesystem Hierarchy Standard
FPU: Floating Point Unit
FSF: Free Software Foundation
FSG: Free Standards Group
GPL: General Public License
GUI: Graphical User Interface
HA: High Availability
HBA: Host Bus Adapter
HTML: Hyper Text Markup Language
HTTP: Hyper Text Transport Protocol
IA: Intel Architecture
IB: Infiniband
ICA: Independent Computing Architecture
IDC: International Data Corporation
IDE: Integrated Development Environment
IEEE: Institute for Electrical and Electronic Engineers
IETF: Internet Engineering Task Force
I/O: Input/Output
ISV: Independent Software Vendor
IT: Information Technology

J2EE: Java 2 Platform, Enterprise Edition
JDS: Java Desktop System
JRL: Java Research License
LDAP: Lightweight Directory Access Protocol
LSB: Linux Standard Base
LUN: Logical Unit Number
MPL: Mozilla Public License
MPP: Massively Parallel Processing
MTBF: Mean Time Between Failures
NAS: Network Attached Storage
NFS: Network File System
NIC: Network Interface Card
NPV: Net Present Value
NUMA: Non-Uniform Memory Access
OFE: OpenForum Europe
OGSA: Open Grid Services Architecture
OLTP: Online Transaction Processing
OpEx: Operating Expenses
OS: Operating System
OSDL: Open Source Development Lab
OSI: Open Source Initiative
PC: Personal Computer
PDA: Personal Digital Assistant
PICMG: PCI Industrial Computer Manufacturers Group
PIM: Personal Information Manager
POSIX: Portable Operating System Interface
RAC: Real Application Cluster
RAID: Redundant Arrays of Independent Disk
RAS: Reliability, Availability, Serviceability
RDBMS: Relational Database Management System
RDP: Remote Desktop Protocol
RFC: Request for Comments
ROI: Return on Investment
SAN: Storage Area Network
SCSL: Sun Community Source License
SLA: Service Level Agreement
SMP: Symmetric Multi-Processor
SNMP: Simple Network Management Protocol
SOAP: Simple Object Access Protocol
SQL: Structured Query Language
SSL: Secure Sockets Layer
TCO: Total cost of Ownership
TCP: Transmission Control Protocol

TLB: Translation Look-Aside Buffer
TLS: Transport Layer Security
UML: User Mode Linux
USB: Universal Serial Bus
VM: Virtual Machine
VNC: Virtual Network Computing
VPN: Virtual Private Network
W: Watts
XML: Extensible Markup Language

Index

A

adaptive computing, 178

ADTI, 72

AES, 6

Amanda, 321

Andrew Tanenbaum, 5, 25

Apache, 95, 126

Apache License, 59

Apple Public Source License, 59

application matrix, 121, 301

application middleware, 130

application selection, 122

APT-RPM, 279

Artistic License, 61

ASI, 196

Asianux, 88

AT&T Bell Labs, 23

automated installation, 278

AutoYaST, 279

Axis, 126

B

Bacula, 321

Beowulf cluster, 200

Berkeley Systems Distribution, 23

best practices, 287

blade computing, 193

blade servers, 193

Bochs, 187

BOOTP, 320

Boston Consulting Group, 27

BSD, 23, 25, 33, 36

BSD License, 52

business case, 172, 239

business service management, 279

C

CapEx, 232, 313

CentOS, 88

Cfengine, 322

CFS, 201

Chandler, 12

change champions, 291

change control, 275

change management, 286

Citrix MetaFrame, 303

Clam AV, 144

clustered file systems, 201

ClusterSSH, 321

CMT, 215

CodeWeaver, 304

Common Development and Distribution License, 59

Common Operating Environment, 254

complete fair queuing, 80

computing fabric, 195

Computing on Demand, 178

Consumer Electronics Linux Forum, 10

copylefting, 50

core image, 254

cost of power, 239

cost of software, 234

Courier, 144

CPU-level cache, 220

Cricket, 322

critical success factors, 272

CrossOver Office, 304

CUPS, 126

D

DAS, 307

data classification, 271

data migration, 269

database alternatives, 130

Debian, 88

desktop migrations, 269

desktop usage models, 149

DHCP, 127

diskless clusters, 204

Display over IP, 167

distributed consolidation, 192

DNS, 127, 320

dual licensing, 55

E

Electronic Frontier Foundation, 70

Embedded Linux Consortium, 11

EnterpriseDB, 133

Eric Raymond, 23

F

Federal Deposit Insurance Corporation, 69

FHS, 10

Filesystem Hierarchy Standard, 10

financial models, 231

Firebird, 134

forking, 54

FOSS, 47, 48, 51

free software, 30

Free Standards Group, 9, 10, 11

Freedesktop.org, 9, 10

freeware, 64

FSG, 10

FUSE, 85

G

GDI, 151

General Public License, 48, 50, 64

Geronimo, 127

Globus Toolkit, 206

GNOME, 11, 12, 13

GNU, 24, 25, 26, 34, 35, 43

GNU SQL Server, 135

golden images, 317

Google, 107

GPL, 252

gpl-violations.org, 68

GraphOn GO-Global, 303

grid computing, 204

GroundWork, 322

H

high availability, 198

HALO, 197

hard and soft dollars, 238

HBA, 310

high availability clusters, 198

high-performance clusters, 199

HOBLink JWT, 303

horizontal scaling, 211

hot desking, 167

Hurd, 24

hyper-threading, 79

I

Intel Architecture, 107, 108

IBM, 23, 25, 29, 32, 33, 34, 37

IDC, 5, 16

identifying bottlenecks, 214

Independent Computing Architecture, 165

industry standards, 298

InfiniBand, 211

infrastructure blueprint, 177

Ingres, 134

Intel I/OAT, 311

Interbase, 134

internal rate of return, 313

IP storage, 310

iSCSI, 310

ISO files, 293

J

Jabber, 127

Java Desktop System, 304

Java Research License, 60

JBoss, 127

Jetspeed, 128

JFS, 81

K

Kenneth Brown, 72

kernel locks, 78

KickStart, 279, 319

KNOPPIX, 89

L

L2 cache, 221

Lars Wirzenius, 25

Lesser GPL, 52

LI18NUX, 11

Linus Torvalds, 5, 25, 75

Linux 2.6, 76

Linux databases, 131

Linux desktop, 151

Linux distributions, 85

Linux e-mail, 141

Linux instances, 83

Linux migration, 97

Linux on the mainframe, 189

Linux Standard Base, 10, 11

Linux Virtual Server, 128

Linux VServer, 185

load balancing, 199

load balancing clusters, 199

localization, 319

LSB, 11, 85

LTSP, 128

Lustre, 204

M

Mac OS, 151

Mandriva, 89

MDA, 138

Microsoft, 73

migration process, 266

Minix, 5, 25

MIT License, 53

MMU, 83

Modified BSD License, 60

mon, 322

MontaVista, 90

Mozilla Public License, 61

MPP, 210

MRTG, 322

MS Office alternatives, 152

MTA, 138

MUA, 138

Myrinet, 211

MySQL, 134

N

N1, 178

Nagios, 323

NAS, 201, 307

net present value, 313

Netcraft, 33

NetDisco, 323

NeTraverse, 304

Netscape Public License, 61

Network Time Protocol, 128

NFS, 128, 320

NIC, 310

no-install Linux, 82

Nokia, 770 13

NPACI Rocks, 207

NTFS, 81

ntop, 323

NUMA, 76

O

O(1), 78

OIN, 74

open source databases, 133

open source development Lab, 11

open source initiative, 47, 48

open source software categories, 132

open source strategy, 125

PowerPC, 92

OpenForum Europe, 11

OpenLDAP, 128

openMosix, 206

OpenNMS, 323

OpenPrinting, 11

OpEx, 232, 314

Oracle Real Application Cluster, 133

OS scheduler, 78

OSCAR, 207

OSDL, 9, 11

OSRM, 74

P

parallel virtual file system, 204

Pareto principle, 290

payback period, 314

pilot project, 251

portable data containers, 271

Postfix, 144

PostgreSQL, 134

preboot execution environment (PXE), 320

preemptable kernel, 79

processor affinity, 77

project activities, 255

project management, 249

project planning, 250

proprietary software, 55

public domain, 62

Q

QsNet, 211

R

RAID, 308

rdesktop, 303

RDMA, 196

Red Hat, 90

remote desktop protocol (RDP), 165

replacing Microsoft Exchange, 139

return on investment, 314

Richard Stallman, 24

risk management, 274

risk mitigation, 251

ROI, 231, 237, 241, 314

rollout preparation, 251

rollout tactics, 265

royalty-free patents, 74

RRD Tool, 324

rsync, 324

S

Samba, 129

SAN, 307

scalable coherent interconnect (SCI), 211

scaling techniques, 217

SCO Group, 49

security updates, 281

Sendmail, 144

server-based computing, 166

service level agreements, 122

service-oriented architecture, 189

Slackware, 25

SMP, 76, 210, 215

SMT, 79, 215

SMTP, 138

Snort, 324

SOA Projects, 190

software compliance strategy, 68

SpamAssassin, 145

SQLite, 134

Squid, 129

Steven Weber, 33

storage networks, 307

Struts, 129

Sun Community Source License, 62

Sun Microsystems, 23, 29, 33, 34, 41

SUSE, 90

Sybase Adaptive Server Enterprise, 133

T

TCO, 231, 232, 315

testing, 275

TFTP, 320

thin clients, 168

TOE, 311

Tomcat, 129

TOP500, 9, 197

total cost of ownership, 315

training, 259

translation lookaside buffer, 83

Turbolinux, 90

U

Ubuntu, 91

UnitedLinux, 86

up2date, 279

user mode Linux (UML), 184

utility computing, 178, 180

V

value-driven information technology, 111, 113

vertical scaling, 209

viral licensing, 51

virtual machine, 165, 181

virtual private servers, 184

virtual processors, 79

VirtualCenter, 304

virtualization, 83

virtualization techniques, 183

VMware, 184, 304

VNC, 167

W

Webmin, 324

Win4Lin Terminal Server, 304

Wine, 304

workload rebalancing, 206

X

X Window System, 151

X11 License, 62

X64, 107

Xen, 84, 186

XFS, 81

Y

Yellow Dog, 92

YUM, 279